UNCERTAIN PLACES

"Mitch Horowitz is at his best when he throws new light on the hidden subtext of accepted dogma. From 'anarchic magick' to 'reclaiming the damned,' *Uncertain Places* stands as a sweeping reinterpretation of major themes at the sharp edge of American imagination."

JACQUES VALLÉE, COAUTHOR OF
TRINITY: THE BEST-KEPT SECRET

"This book is nothing less than a masterpiece. It introduces, informs, inspires, and ignites critical thinking in a way that is unique to Horowitz's creative mind. He is a constant source of infectious curiosity and open-mindedness; no esoteric stone, small or big, is left unturned in his pursuit of new perspectives and connections. His mind and work are those of a restless rebel who provokes the stagnant and causally dull with sparks and nuggets of great wisdom. In many ways, Horowitz is the perfect mix of Manly P. Hall, Joseph Campbell, and Prometheus, eloquently carrying the torch of mythic and spiritual illumination into the twenty-first century."

CARL ABRAHAMSSON, AUTHOR OF *SOURCE MAGIC, OCCULTURE,*
AND *ANTON LAVEY AND THE CHURCH OF SATAN*

"In *Uncertain Places,* Mitch Horowitz achieves the impossible. He provides a crystal-clear look at topics that are drenched in the murkiest of ambiguities yet continue to fascinate every living soul. Horowitz aims a brilliantly lucid lens toward the great unwashed domain of the occult, and he magically manages to bring into view shocking truths about a realm that has always been hiding in plain sight."

DEAN RADIN, PH.D., CHIEF SCIENTIST AT THE
INSTITUTE OF NOETIC SCIENCES AND AUTHOR OF *REAL MAGIC*

"I admire Mitch Horowitz enormously. He has struggled virtually single-handedly to get the American intelligentsia to give occult and esoteric currents the serious attention they deserve. This collection exemplifies the intelligence, sincerity, and integrity Mitch has always brought to his inquiry. He has fearlessly faced some of the most awkward subjects in his field and cast his own unique light on them. Fascinating and erudite."

RICHARD SMOLEY, AUTHOR OF *A THEOLOGY OF LOVE:
REIMAGINING CHRISTIANITY THROUGH A COURSE IN MIRACLES*

"What a welcome guide in these uncertain times! Mitch Horowitz continues his program for bringing esoteric ideas out of the closet and into the public forum. Here he reveals the New Age for what it really is: the exoteric face of the Hermetic philosophy. Once we realize that the human mind is the extension of the divine creative power, the rest follows, like a flood sweeping away the debris of religions and anti-religions alike. To paraphrase: Mind is the ultimate arbiter of reality. All self-expression is sacred. The only evil is to prevent other beings from reaching their highest potential. We are all gods in the making, but more than gods, being forged in the crucible of the world. Even those familiar with this line of thought will relish the parade of characters, charlatans, and sages that emerge from *Uncertain Places*."

JOSCELYN GODWIN, AUTHOR OF
THE GREATER AND LESSER WORLDS OF ROBERT FLUDD

"Who are we? What are we? Have we ever really been entirely human? Whether or not we have or have not, if we want to make any advancement in this respect, we will have to delve into certain quagmires such as the occult and the paranormal to discover ourselves. This work is dangerous, but Mitch Horowitz has the courage to undertake it. As a bonus, his writing is very amusing."

PETER LAMBORN WILSON, AUTHOR OF *PEACOCK ANGEL*

"Here is a learned yet accessible book about the shaping power of will and intention, about the reality of an extraphysical world (or worlds), about just how wrong and stupid the debunkers and conspiracy theorists have been, and about religious belief as dissociation—the still unknown mirror in which we will someday come to recognize ourselves. Here are the 'uncertain places' that many of us have not yet gone but will."

JEFFREY J. KRIPAL, AUTHOR OF *THE SUPERHUMANITIES:
HISTORICAL PRECEDENTS, MORAL OBJECTIONS, NEW REALITIES*

"To make the density of countless esoteric teachings and life-changing mind metaphysics accessible to nearly anyone is a gift Mitch Horowitz is currently in the practice of leaving us all with."

JESSE DRAXLER, AMERICAN VISUAL ARTIST
AND AUTHOR OF *MISOPHONIA*

UNCERTAIN PLACES

Essays On Occult and Outsider Experiences

MITCH HOROWITZ

Inner Traditions

Rochester, Vermont

Inner Traditions
One Park Street
Rochester, Vermont 05767
www.InnerTraditions.com

Text stock is SFI certified

Cataloging-in-Publication Data for this title is available from the Library of Congress

ISBN 978-1-64411-592-3 (print)
ISBN 978-1-64411-593-0 (ebook)

Printed and bound in the United States by Lake Book Manufacturing, Inc. The text stock is SFI certified. The Sustainable Forestry Initiative® program promotes sustainable forest management.

10 9 8 7 6 5 4 3 2 1

Text design and layout by Virginia Scott Bowman
This book was typeset in Garamond Premier Pro and Gill Sans with WTC Benito and Pepperoncino used as the display typefaces

To send correspondence to the author of this book, mail a first-class letter to the author c/o Inner Traditions • Bear & Company, One Park Street, Rochester, VT 05767, and we will forward the communication, or contact the author directly at www.mitchhorowitz.com.

▲

To Jacqueline

The Indiculus supertitionum et paganairum (*Index of Superstitions and Pagan Practices*) *is a remarkable document from early medieval Germany (around 740). The list must represent things that were still occurring in Central Europe at the time the Index was published. The list reads: . . .*

> 17. *On the heathen observations of the hearth-fire, or ignition of these things*
> 18. *On uncertain places, which they hold sacred*

STEPHEN E. FLOWERS, PH.D.,
LORDS OF THE LEFT-HAND PATH

CONTENTS

PART V
Damned History

REINTRODUCTION

POWER AND UNCERTAINTY

To write on metaphysical themes is to live in a state of constant uncertainty. Or at least it ought to be that way. The simple fact is: we do not know the foundations of reality and when or whether anomalous experiences are "real" or subjective; whether repetition equals validity (the gold standard of social science, which conceals its own shortcomings behind methodology "corrections," which render its clinical literature largely irrelevant in generational cycles); and, finally, how to weigh individual testimony. We possess statistical evidence as good as any for the anomalous transfer of information, or ESP, in laboratory settings—but that fact raises more questions than it answers and is rejected by a modernist intelligentsia that regards countervailing evidence to materialism as the catechist does heresy.

Indeed, metaphysics and modernist thought have never fully gotten along. The authors I most admired in my late teens and early twenties, and whose tutelage I sought and occasionally found, were political thinkers Irving Howe (1920–1993) and Michael Harrington (1928–1989). Both were democratic socialists and literary critics who wrote with rigor, scrupulousness, and critical sympathy about radical politics. If they thought at all about esoteric spirituality, to which I later dedicated myself, they probably would have considered it trifling, more or less agreeing with Frankfurt School philosopher Theodor W. Adorno that "Occultism is the metaphysic of dunces."*

---

*Adorno's reference appears in his essay "Theses Against Occultism," written in 1947 and published in 1951 in his *Minima Moralia*.

Regardless, by my early thirties my passions for intellectual experiment shifted away from politics and toward the occult. I would like to believe that I took my literary heroes' critical style, if not their approbation, with me. The factors that drove my shift were both personal and philosophical. My outlook had always included the spiritual, by which I mean the extra-physical. Yet I came to feel that much of modern intellectual culture excluded or neglected spirituality as a legitimate field of inquiry—I considered that a blind spot.

The defining principle of modernist philosophy is that life, in all its expressions, results from unseen but detectable antecedents. In politics this might mean economic clashes and inevitable cycles of revolution (Marx); in biology, evolution and natural selection (Darwin); in psychology, childhood trauma and sexual repression (Freud); in physics, time-space relativity (Einstein); in human performance, self-image (James); in health and illness, germs and microbes (Pasteur); and so forth across myriad fields. I believe that the modernist approach must also encompass the spiritual—or, in my sounding, the occult. *Occult* comes from the Latin *occultus,* meaning hidden or secret; it is how Renaissance thinkers referred to mystical philosophies and religions of the pre-Christian world, including those of Egypt, Persia, Greece, and Rome, which were rediscovered in the West beginning in the mid-to-late fifteenth century.

In current terms, the occult is a freeform spiritual philosophy that draws upon or remakes ancient traditions but exists outside of any single doctrine, liturgy, or congregation. (You can substitute other terms for what I am describing; I use occult for its historical integrity.) Occultism's philosophical gambit is that there exist unseen dimensions whose forces can be felt on and through us. Whatever you make of that prospect, the existence of nonlocal intelligence and metaphysical influence are not innately opposed to modernist thought. Such concepts clash only with the modernist sub-philosophy of materialism, or the belief that matter creates itself.

Yet materialism, which has dominated our intellectual culture since the Victorian age (and accounts for statements such as Adorno's), covers fewer and fewer bases of life in the twenty-first century. The natural sciences are increasingly defined by quantum data, interdimensional formulas, and fields like neuroplasticity, which uses brain scans to demonstrate the capacity of thought to alter neural matter. The findings of neuroplasticity, uncontroversial by themselves but seismic in implication, are summarized by one of the field's pioneers, UCLA research psychiatrist Jeffrey M. Schwartz, who wrote in 2002 in *The Mind and the Brain*: "I propose that the time has come for science to confront the serious implications of the fact that directed, willed mental activity can clearly and systematically alter brain function; that the exertion of willful effort generates a *physical force.* . . . " More than a generation earlier, magician and artist Aleister Crowley described magick (he used the early modern spelling to distinguish it from stagecraft) as "the Science and Art of causing Change to occur in conformity with Will." Those two statements differ only in degree.

UFOs are not directly related to the occult. But it is worth noting that recent to this writing UFOs have gone mainstream to the extent that no serious person questions the existence of some kind of engineered phenomena captured on Navy cockpit videos—not natural occurrences, delusions, or "mistakes." Moreover, evidence is mounting for primeval or microbial life, either past or present, on Mars and Venus. In late 2020, water was detected on the sunlit surface of the moon. Our ordinary reference points of life are in greater flux today than any time since Darwinism upended what it meant to be human in the Victorian era.

▲

We like to ennoble ourselves with the notion that every bend in our path is precipitated by some internal epiphany; but we get led by outer terrain as much as or more than private determination. Preceding my shift in focus, I got fired from a conservative political press. They wanted a progressive editor to expand their list and it was supposed to be my "dream job." (Advice: if you are seeking a career in conservative publishing do not advocate for a book opposing the death penalty by Jesse Jackson.) I started over as an editor at what was then a backwater New Age publisher. The turn of events seemed random if fleetingly painful. But was there some portent in it?

Rather than view my new job as a springboard to a more respectable position, as many friends encouraged, I instead embraced the self-developmental philosophies I encountered. I grew intrigued with the prospect, alluded to earlier, that the mind possesses causative qualities, a claim often associated with "positive thinking" and variants of practical or therapeutic spirituality. Through the study of related ideas, both ancient and modern, spiritual and psychological, as well as my personal experiments, I came to regard many concepts of practical metaphysics as tantalizing, defensible, and powerful. I came to believe, and still do, that the popular literature of mind power, or New Thought, conceals rejected stones. As a field, New Thought has done a better job of popularizing than refining itself. The philosophy has not grown much since the death in 1910 of philosopher William James, who took deep interest in "the religion of healthy-mindedness." There is, for example, no compelling theology of suffering within New Thought, which is unacceptable in a generation confronting pandemics, end-of-life issues, and management of chronic disease. I felt this intellectual climate could be improved.

In the Talmudic book *Pirkei Avos,* or *Ethics of the Fathers,* a student asks a teacher: "What is the best way to live?" The teacher responds: "Find a place where there are no men, go there, and there strive to be a man." That became my guiding principle within the corner of the spiritual culture I occupied. When I experienced feelings of exile, I took succor from John Milton's Dread Emperor: "Here we may reign secure, and in my choice." I would develop and not flee from the uncertain place where I found myself.

My interests and personal dedication expanded to the work of philosopher G.I. Gurdjieff; my publishing list grew to include an unusual range of authors, living and dead, from filmmaker David Lynch to esoteric scholar Manly P. Hall to philosopher Jacob Needleman to the intellectual eminence of esoterica (and a personal source of inspiration) Richard Smoley. I strove, above all, to foster a climate where outsider spiritual thinkers could write seriously and be taken seriously. (Did I succeed? Author Whitley Strieber told me:

"You're the only editor I've ever had who I didn't suspect hung up the phone and started laughing about the UFO nut." So there.)

All of this activity served a greater and, for me, culminating purpose. That was rediscovering myself as a writer. Writing careers are made by the right marriage of author to subject. For me, that moment arrived when I realized the need to document and defend the lives and careers of the founding lights of modern occultism. If you do not write your own history, it gets written for you, often by people who misunderstand or are unconcerned with the values and driving factors behind your work. This is among the reasons why I disclose myself as a "believing historian"—a designation that actually describes many historians of religion, who often emerge from the congregations they write about. Most historians fear that declarations of belief invite perceptions of bias or limited critical perspective; for good thinkers, however, familiarity with, and even participation in, a thought system can produce deeper and subtler shades of critique. This approach resulted in my first book, *Occult America,* in 2009, and much else that followed. The essays collected in *Uncertain Places* are part of that effort.

I am proud of these pieces, one of which, "The War on Witches," appears here for the first time. I include bibliographical information and a backstory for each piece in a short introduction (or reintroduction) preceding it. My wish to share this body of work stems from several factors: 1) These pieces tell the truth. There are no stretches, feints, or convenient rearranging of facts for dramatic purposes. 2) These writings frame occult and mystical figures, ideas, and applications in a way that I think captures their workability, greatness, and weaknesses. And, finally, 3) these essays reflect the fuller reckoning, intellectually and intimately, that I determined to bring to my encounter with the metaphysical when it began more than twenty years ago.

Whatever satisfaction I feel with this book is tempered by an attendant somberness: it is difficult to present a selection of one's work without experiencing the turning of a personal page. What that turning represents, I am not yet sure. But I felt a transition begin to stir within me in the closing days of the first summer of Covid. At that time, I masked up and entered a used bookstore in the Catskills town of Kingston, New York. For the first time, I did not know what section to look in. I wandered, of course, to the occult aisle, filled with golden oldies and names that I love, from Neville Goddard to Carlos Castaneda. Yet I felt oddly unmoved. Where, I wondered, if you will allow me some excess, is the hammer of the gods? This question arose from a conviction that I reached in recent years and to which I allude at various points in this book: *the spiritual search is the search for power.* It is the reach for expansion. It is not about losing oneself in the numinous whole but finding oneself as a creator. This is true however much we prevaricate over or reject the term "power" for its seeming brutality.

Let me be clear: I invoke *power* to indicate humanity's wish to construct, strive, make, and grow. Even as we face inevitable physical decline, we cultivate agencies, some personal and some related to greater laws and forces, that allow us to enact our will. I believe in pursuing my search with reciprocity, the principle at the back of most ethics. Power without reciprocity is force. It is unrenewable. I recognize human wholeness and lawful consequence. I once considered it necessary for seekers to select a classical religious or ethical system to function as a guardrail in their search. I no longer feel that way. Next to reciprocity, my other key principle is nonviolence, which I mean not exactly in the physical sense but rather doing nothing to denigrate or dehumanize another person or community, or to deprive another of the search for self-potential that I claim for myself. Finally, I am the sole object of my experiments. No one else's life or safety is under my purview other than if I am called to its defense.

▲

In the preceding passage, I framed the ethics of the spiritual search as it exists for me. Let me expand on the purpose of the search—on what power is *for.* As alluded, I see generativity as the essential human need. That is at the heart of all our endeavors. We are driven to produce and establish. If one takes seriously the scriptural principle that the Creator fashioned the individual in Its own image, then it stands to reason that our imperative to create follows from that act. As the Hermetic dictum puts it: "As above, so below"* The urge toward generativity is innate but differs in kind for every individual. The exercise or frustration of that impulse determines, more than any single factor, the happiness or despair that mark our lives. I believe that a great deal of what is diagnosed as neurosis is the frustration of personal power. Turn back the pages of your life and see if you disagree.

But wait!, critics say—you are confusing the temporal with the eternal, power with grace, dominion with truth. I believe strongly that each person must verify for him or herself ideas about the nature of interior life and its relation to one's surroundings. Our most readily repeated spiritual principles are often *"copies of past decisions,"* to use the phrase and emphasis of philosopher Paul Feyerabend.† Be very scrutinizing before accepting what someone else identifies as the means by which your sense of selfhood will be satisfied.

If I am right that our existence consists of both physical and extra-physical qualities, it follows that spirituality is a valid path by which to pursue the type of power I am describing. Then again, I may be wrong about the reality of the spiritual or extra-physical. If so, however, the consequences may not be so bad. Psychological dimensions of belief are incredibly powerful. Believing in the possibility of an outcome, as William James noted, may be the vital ingredient for that outcome to occur at all. Both doubt and belief represent a leap; we all live by *something* not wholly verifiable.

---

*I often refer back to this principle. The phrase appears in the late-ancient Greek-Egyptian manuscript called *The Emerald Tablet*. For generations, *The Emerald Tablet* was considered a work of pseudo-Hermeticism created in the medieval era. In the early twentieth century, however, scholars located Arabic versions of *The Emerald Tablet* that date to at least the 700s or 800s AD. This suggests a still-earlier source because much of the original Hermetic literature was preserved in both Greek and Arabic. One of the first English translations of *The Emerald Tablet* came from Isaac Newton (1642–1727): "'Tis true without lying, certain and most true. That which is below is like that which is above."
†*Science in a Free Society* (Verso Books, 1978, 1982).

I am not hedging, however. I do believe in the reality and validity of the ideas explored in this book. Whether these ideas will fulfill your needs or mine is an open question, requiring participation and effort. In that vein, I hope that *Uncertain Places* expands your sense of possibility, as well as elucidates the roots from which our modern spiritual concepts arise—and to which they may yet extend.

▲

The urgency of the questions I address in this book—what is ethical power? is extra-physicality real? can spiritual forces be harnessed?—have led me through discursive terrain. In 2021, culture critic Zack Kruse wrote in his insightful study, *Mysterious Travelers:* "Horowitz . . . comfortably blends an interest in the Church of Satan, Madame Blavatsky, New Thought, and Objectivism as part of this work."* Indeed, an unseen and deeply personal inner tissue connects apparently diffuse territories for nearly every seeker; I am sure you have felt this in your own search. Hence, all the thought-stations I have visited or dwelt in have served my pursuit of these core questions.

If I have succeeded in these essays, it is not in convincing you of my point of view: agreement or disagreement is the lowest form of engagement with an idea. Rather, it is in framing spiritual issues in ways that encourage your own experiment, query, and unimpeded search.

Everything in life eventually gets taken away from us, from our physicality to our certainties. Since I take seriously the principle of extra-physicality, I assume that *something* survives death. But I do not know. The one thing that is provably eternal is a question. May this collection deepen yours.

---

*In 2015, I wrote in an essay, "New Thought: Selfish or Socialist?" at HarvBishop.com: "Seen in a certain light, the mystical teacher Neville Goddard—the New Thought figure whom I most admire—was a kind of *spiritualized objectivist*. Or perhaps I could say that Ayn Rand, the founder of philosophical objectivism, was a secularized Neville. Neville and Rand each believed, with uncompromising conviction, that the individual creates his or her own objective reality and circumstances. Rand saw this as a matter of personal will; Neville saw it as a matter of imagination. But both held, more or less, the same principle." I have areas of agreement with and dissent from that perspective, as will be explored.

PART I

Strange Fire

And Nadab and Abihu, the sons of Aaron, took either of them his censer, and put fire therein, and put incense thereon, and offered strange fire before the Lord, which he commanded them not.

LEVITICUS 10:1

1

RECLAIMING THE DAMNED

Toward a New Understanding of Bigfoot,
Flying Saucers, Leprechauns,
and Other Inconvenient Realities

This essay began as a lecture I delivered in Fall 2019 at the Philosophical Research Society in Los Angeles. I later adapted and expanded it into an article in the March-April 2020 issue of New Dawn Magazine. *My title is in tribute to the paranormalist writer Charles Fort whose 1919 work,* The Book of the Damned, *I discuss within. This piece ventures a sweeping theory behind generations of reported anomalies. When it appeared,* Reclaiming the Damned *heralded the arrival of the UFO thesis into the mainstream and considered what may follow from that.*

Several years ago a critic wrote about me, "Horowitz is an okay historian, but the guy believes in leprechauns for *chrissakes.*" That is true—I plead guilty. In this paper, I will try to explain why my critic is right.

Although I am not a cryptozoologist, I am a great admirer of the paranormal investigator Charles Fort (1874–1932), after whose work this essay is named. People would not necessarily call me a Fortean, though. I do not study anomalies. But my critic was referencing a series of events that I once related, which happened to me about twenty years ago in the Central American nation of Belize.

For anyone who does not know Belize, it is a very beautiful, English-speaking country that borders Guatemala and Mexico on the Caribbean. Belize is filled with lush rainforests, and snaking rivers and hills—including vast hills in the highlands, which are the subject of folklore and mysteries.

I was staying in the hill country, at an eco-jungle lodge founded by a very enterprising couple and their kids from Maryland. They carved the whole place themselves out of the jungle interior. The area attracted a fair amount of ecotourism. Staying at a lodge next door was the actress and model Brooke Shields (who was very nice).

Now, a cabdriver was taking us to this jungle lodge from the airport in Belize City. It was a long drive of about two-and-a-half hours. The final leg ascended a very rocky, unpaved road up a mountain. It was difficult to navigate in a standard car because the rocks and roots and undulating landscape caused the car to hit bottom from time to time, and the terrain could damage the chassis.

As we drove up the hill, the driver started saying, "I really don't like going up into these hills. As soon as I drop you off, I am going to turn around and speed off and get out of here." It seemed odd to speed away on such treacherous landscape. "What's the rush?" I asked.

"Well," he said, "there are little men who live in these hills. They're called *aluxes*. They've lived here for centuries. If you see one of them while you're walking around in the forest, you'll get so frightened that you won't be able to speak. Your voice will get caught in your throat. I really don't like coming up here."

Sure enough, he dropped us off, turned around, and sped away. I thought, "Well, that's kind of strange."

We checked into the lodge, and the next day went canoeing down a river that ran below the ridge on which the lodge was perched. I started telling one of my traveling companions that I was a little pissed off at this cab driver, because I thought he was playing "scare the tourist." I assumed he was trying to have a little fun at our expense.

As I was talking about this, drifting along this deadly quiet river, a big boulder came crashing down in front of us, having been rolled or fallen from somewhere along the ravine we were canoeing through.

I got nervous and thought, "All right, I need to watch what I say." Because there is a folk tradition that if you talk about these creatures, they come around. This is why some people in Ireland today will not refer to "little folk" or leprechauns—they use euphemisms like "the other crowd." This opens an interesting point: you find traditions of these little creatures all throughout the world. This folklore exists in Central America, in Ireland, in Polynesia, in West Africa. Virtually every continent has these legends, going back centuries, which include the detail that if you start talking about these little beings, sometimes called wood sprites or fairies or brownies, you invite them into your life, and they can cause mischief.

Many traditional-minded people in Ireland today believe so strongly in the existence of "the other crowd" that in 1999, a major highway under construction in County Clare was rerouted to avoid running past a "fairy bush"—the domain, so it is said, of these little beings. The fear was that if you run a highway through a fairy bush you will incur their wrath and they will cause accidents. A folklorist and historian named Eddie Lenihan, with whom I have worked and greatly respect, helped prompt the change.

WHO GOES THERE?

Perhaps I am sympathetic to these events because I do not want to live in a world where no mysteries linger. I do not want to live in a world where you hear a twig snapping in the woods and don't wonder, *"Who goes there?"* I do not want to live in a digital, fluorescent-lit environment in which we feel that we know everything that is out there.

Call it sentiment, but I think that most of us feel intuitively, and sometimes through personal experience or study, that the belief that *nothing at all* is lurking in dark corners does not cover all the bases of life.

There exists so much testimony and so many stories of people having unusual experiences with things that are not supposed to be there, whether little men or Bigfoot or something lurking in the water. We are all attached to these stories to some degree. Obviously, the concept of Bigfoot, or some kind of mysterious simian, not only runs through much of our folklore, but wields a great hold on people's attention today.

The question is, *why?* We face so many crises and problems in the world: war, climate change, disease, political and cultural tensions. Why would we be interested today in the persistence of mysterious winged beasts or Bigfoot or yeti or fairies? For what reason?

I think part of the reason is not only that some of these things may be empirically real—when considering the paranormal, I do not remove empiricism from the table prima facie, a point to which I will return—but also that our fascination with mysterious beasts and natural wonders speaks to how we feel, and have reason to feel, about the existence of an unseen dimension of life. Something beyond our workaday, five-sensory existence.

What I am describing goes beyond a wish to believe in the mythical or escapism. Rather, it touches upon our understanding of a world that does not fully disclose itself, but that we experience intuitively, insightfully, and even cognitively in terms of phenomena that may be causatively related to our minds—as well as to unseen dimensions, the reality of which we are unable to fully decipher but of which we may catch glimpses from time to time

This is also true of so-called UFO or extraterrestrial sightings. I think that we are actually living through a moment, in the here and now, where we are experiencing a cultural breakthrough of understanding about the existence of unknown forces and expressions of life.

This can be seen, in particular, with regard to the UFO thesis. In September 2019, the Guggenheim Museum in New York City hosted a remarkable, and I would say unprecedented, panel on UFOs and extraterrestrials. This was notable in itself because the Guggenheim is not considered a fount of occult passions. This is the first time I can recall any major cultural institution in the city hosting a panel like this and earnestly exploring this question.

The panel was the work of a very innovative curator, Troy Therrien, who oversees the Guggenheim's architectural collection. It featured writer and scholar Gordon White, a wonderful occult intellect, and philosopher and historian Diana Pasulka. It was a fascinating program before a packed house. The path was blazed for this kind of event, I think, because the Guggenheim was coming off a tremendous success, both critically and publicly, with its exhibition of the Theosophy-inspired paintings of Hilma af Klint. The occult and UFOs are, of course, different topics, but both branch off from the family tree of the paranormal.

Afterward, the curator asked me: "At what point do you think it is going to become intellectually embarrassing within our culture not to take seriously the question of UFOs?" I told him that I do not refer casually to paradigm shifts. I often deflect questions from mainstream journalists about supposed occult revivals because I think such framings are usually a way of trying to find a news hook. I do not speak casually about these kinds of cultural shifts. With that in mind, I replied, "I actually think, in all honesty, that we have just now, at this very time, entered the point culturally where it is no longer sustainable or even intellectually serious to wave off the notion of UFOs."

This shift arose in part from an event in spring 2019. A few months before this panel, the Pentagon and the Navy released cockpit footage and recordings of pilots witnessing UFOs, including vehicles moving at unbelievable speeds, behaving in ways that airborne vehicles are not supposed to behave, leaving the pilots asking: "*Wow, what is that?*" This is not the first time such footage has appeared. But this material was so plain, so clear, and so persuasive that it moved even holdouts in the gatekeeping culture to acknowledge its significance.

The footage appeared in a prominent and widely read piece in the

New York Times, co-written by the excellent researcher Leslie Kean.* I consider it one of the most significant news stories of the year, because it finally moved the dial on the debate. The question of what UFOs are remains unsettled, of course—but that the testimony and records of such phenomena raise profoundly valid questions is now denied by no serious person.

I date the before-and-after of this shift to a pair of columns that appeared in the same newspaper by the opinion writer Ross Douthat. This writer considers himself a no-nonsense, old-school conservative, of which we have few remaining in the United States. On December 23, 2017, Douthat published a column headlined "Flying Saucers and Other Fairy Tales." As you can gather, the column denigrated interest in UFOs as a persistent and silly trope. Oddly enough, as a device for dismissing the delusions of UFO acolytes, Douthat used the work of my friend Jacques Vallée. Jacques is known for co-designing the prototype of collective interaction on the internet, but he is also one of the most trenchantly intelligent UFO researchers of our time, as well as a brilliant social observer and writer. His published diaries, *Forbidden Science,* revive a style of serial-memoir writing that has not been seen since the early-to-mid twentieth century.

The columnist cited Jacques as saying that there is mechanical unlikelihood of vehicles from outer space being able to reach our terrestrial confines. But what Douthat omitted in Jacques's work, and what is most distinguishing in his theorizing about UFOs, is that he long ago posited that there are so many apparent mechanical impossibilities involving UFOs that, following the principle of Occam's Razor, it is plainer and broader to theorize that some of these sightings may be extra-dimensional. I will say more about that and define what is meant by "extra-dimensional." Oddly, the columnist entirely omitted that key facet of Jacques's outlook.

---

*"'Wow, What Is That?' Navy Pilots Report Unexplained Flying Objects" by Helene Cooper, Ralph Blumenthal and Leslie Kean, May 26, 2019.

Flash forward to August of 2019, now a month before the Guggenheim panel. The same columnist changed course and wrote a piece,* although not related specifically to UFOs, in which he noted the persuasive (if unsettled) nature of some of the UFO data that had recently been released—without noting that less than two years earlier he dismissed the validity of considering such data. I tweeted my thanks that he had seen fit to reverse his rejectionism. To my surprise, the *New York Times* opinion section retweeted me—another institution not known for its occult passions. I began to realize, typified by this little turn of events, that we have reached a turning point where it is intellectually untenable to dismiss the UFO question. I would challenge any materialist scientist or philosopher to push back against that statement.

Considering how far we have come, I was reminded of attending a conference ten years earlier at the Esalen Institute. It was an invited gathering of writers and scholars who had a longstanding interest in the esoteric. Michael Murphy, Esalen's cofounder, was speaking one evening, and he said, regarding UFOs, "I want to know what this stuff is. I want time and energy and resources dedicated to the study of this stuff, so we can begin to get our arms around what it actually is." Someone else in attendance (Jacques was there, too) said, "The truth is that large swaths of the American public are never really going to believe in the UFO thesis unless they see something on radar. We're a materialist culture; we've got to see something on radar."

A decade on, we do have things on radar, publicly. This is not controversial. We have video, we have cockpit recordings, we have radar images. We have had variants of these things before, but today we have it on the homepage of CNN, on the front page of the *Washington Post,* the *Wall Street Journal,* and the *New York Times.* We have it in such a way that it can be discussed at a panel at the Guggenheim Museum. This empirical evidence is plain. There is no way in our time, right now,

---

*"Jeffrey Epstein and When to Take Conspiracies Seriously," October 31, 2019.

to maintain intellectual seriousness while dismissing the UFO thesis as fantasies about "little green men."

I am speaking only of the most elementary data that we possess. I am leaving aside everything that is disputatious or controversial. No one questions the validity of this data—only its implications. That marks a dramatic change. I urge you to watch very carefully for how this plays out in our society over the next eighteen months or so, because I also believe that the political predicament we find ourselves in, and the impeachment process in the United States and the 2020 election, will unleash tremendous amounts of energy.

Let me be clear: what is going on in our culture is fearsome. We cannot sustain climate-change denialism anymore. Environmental disasters are playing out all over the world. I do not mean to suggest that there is a wonderful new era opening to us. The stakes are high and daunting. At the same time, whenever there is a sense of fluctuation, when there is a sense of chaos, it can unleash tremendous energy, an energy that we do not really understand. I am speaking in metaphor and I want to speak more concretely.

Until 2007, there was a parapsychology lab at Princeton University, the Princeton Engineering Anomalies Research lab or PEAR. This was a serious parapsychology lab in existence for about thirty years. When PEAR was operating it conducted a series of experiments with machines known as random number generators. We use random number generators every day—they produce an infinitely variable pattern of numbers, which we commonly use to set online passwords.

Parapsychologists sometimes use random number generators to test for ESP or psychokinesis (PK). Researchers might place a subject in proximity to a random number generator to see if he or she proves capable of disrupting the randomness—of creating a signal in the noise, so to speak. Perhaps I jump to a conclusion by using the term "create." But there is congruity between the individual's efforts to interrupt randomness and the appearance of a pattern that should not be there.

One of the things the Princeton lab did, going back many years, was to place random number generators at various locations around the world. They found—and there have been journal articles about this and I am simplifying it somewhat—that during the events of 9/11, immediately preceding the events and immediately following, the random number generators started displaying patterns.*

An interruption appeared in these completely randomized and chaotic displays of numbers. Suddenly numbers would repeat. There was a traceable pattern at certain moments. Researchers were left with an enormous question, which begs further research and further understanding: why, at a moment of what could be loosely described as global trauma, did this network of random number generators demonstrate a pattern, an interruption in the noise?

This raises the tantalizing prospect of mental causation—of whether we, through the agency of thought, are able to impact and produce outcomes. This is not a paper on mental causation, but there are many different scientific fields, including neuroplasticity, quantum mechanics, placebo studies, and psychical research, that have suggested causation relating to thought or perception. One way of empirically discussing the manifestation of energies is to note that during that period of global trauma, we saw some apparently unified impact of thought, which was exercising probable PK influence on this network of random number generators.

UNCERTAIN PLACES

We are going through a period of trauma today. There is good reason to feel anxiety over climate change. There is tremendous friction, politically, in our country and elsewhere. There is anxiety about the immediate future, a great deal of political dispute, and a high pitch of emotions.† What does

---

*For a summary of the Global Consciousness Project, see: "Terrorist Disaster, September 11, 2001"; "Formal Results: Testing the GCP Hypothesis;" and "Global Consciousness Project Brief Overview" at noosphere.princeton.edu.
†This was written before the Covid pandemic and the events of January 6, 2021.

this mean practically for you as an individual? I cannot respond meaningfully to that. I can say only that it falls to you to be very watchful for some kind of energetic spike. I certainly do not think it is accidental that epic works of art and new ideas and directions and designs for living emerge from periods of crisis. It is interesting to me that during this time of friction and division, we have turned a corner regarding our understanding of UFO phenomena. It is possible that we may turn a similar corner regarding psychical research.

I should note that we have lost at least a generation of progress in ESP research in the United States. This is because polemical skeptics have been very successful. They have pushed most psychical and ESP-related research off college campuses. The closing of the Princeton lab is one instance. Labs have closed previously at Duke University. This research has invited a huge amount of controversy at Cornell University. It is next-to-impossible for any young person to find a program in parapsychological studies at an accredited mainstream college or university here in the United States. This was not always true.

Even though psychical research is very inexpensive relative to most scientific or psychological research, the critics, for now, have prevailed. They got what they wanted. They closed down the debate, closed down the study, and pushed many of these labs off of campuses. The scholarly labs that do exist, like the Institute of Noetic Sciences (IONS) in northern California, where my friend Dean Radin is chief scientist, must do all of their fundraising privately. If you have written grant proposals, you know the energies and resources that consumes.

So, it is difficult. But researchers have soldiered on. It is possible that, just as we have seen an opening in UFO studies, we are going to see a reversal in this situation. Watch for that.

Likewise, I think that we are seeing signs of a third-wave occult revival. The first wave occurred in the late-nineteenth century, when figures like Madame H. P. Blavatsky, and some earlier occultists, including Eliphas Levi and various American Spiritualists, generated a wave of interest in phenomenally based communication. The second wave arrived with the Woodstock generation, when psychedelia, Zen, yoga, and all kinds of channeled and New Age therapeutic religious systems exploded. It is possible that right now, at this moment, we are seeing a third wave of occult religious movements. We are seeing this most prominently with regard to Wicca and witchcraft. Recent to this writing, an article appeared in the *New York Times* on October 24, 2019, "When Did Everybody Become a Witch?" It was timely, not just one of those contrived pieces that get written around Halloween, and it cited and quoted the output of a wide range of authors, mostly women, who are writing in the space of witchcraft and Wicca. (As I was writing these words I heard from a fact-checker at the *Atlantic,* which is preparing its own article on the topic*—I have no illusions about how that is going to turn out, but even cynicism is a sign of interest.) The literary output of the witchcraft community has been extraordinary, and it is not slowing.

With the opening in the study of UFOs, the flowering of all this literature and participation in Wicca and witchcraft, and the possibility of new openings in psychical research, we are seeing the results of what I describe as new energies being unleashed at pivotal and sometimes unnerving moments in history. If you are an artist, if you are a creative, this is a very interesting moment to pay attention to.

A friend was consoling me over Trump's victory in 2016, and he said, "Don't feel so bad. Fascism is a great time for art." His gallows humor had a certain point. Hopefully, we will not go that far, but his dark humor captured something that I have been driving at.

So, how does all this relate to the topic of natural wonders and mysterious beasts? I think we may also be approaching a new way of understanding Bigfoot sightings, UFOs, and persistent reports of anomalous beasts, things that go bump in the night, and twigs snapping, so to speak.

It is possible that all of this testimony could point to something of

---

*"Why Witchcraft Is on the Rise" by Bianca Bosker, March 2020.

a non-materialist or extra-physical quality. People in many reaches of our society are obsessed with the existence of Bigfoot. It is the subject of many mostly awful cable TV pseudo-documentaries; it fuels an enormous stream of books, articles, debates, and controversies. Scientists complain that no one has been able to produce viable DNA evidence of Bigfoot. One might argue that point, but that is the broadly held critique.

If one concedes the point, however, it could open a more radical and supple thesis. Several scientists, including Richard Feynman, have observed that you cannot get out of a problem by employing the same thinking that got you into it. I have found that is a universal principle. It is a good principle in writing, for example. If you write a sentence or paragraph, and are wrestling with it, and clarity keeps eluding you, there is probably something wrong with the foundation. It is best to toss out the line or paragraph and start fresh. If something proves chronically difficult—this is true in relationships, too—there is probably a flaw in the foundation itself.

The same may hold true for the question of mysterious beasts and natural wonders. Maybe the reason we do not find more physical or DNA evidence is that, while these persistently reported phenomena are real and are actually occurring, they do not necessarily conform to our five-sensory material lives.

This returns us to the observation that Jacques Vallée made about UFOs probably being some kind of interdimensional manifestation, which enter our awareness intermittently and then vanish. There may exist an infinitude, or superposition, of events occurring all the time and everywhere that we are capable of measuring or experiencing only intermittently (such as in the cases of documentary imagery), fractionally, or at periods of extreme sensitivity, in the same way that ESP or PK may manifest at highly receptive moments. This ties into the question of psychical energies being unleashed during instances of trauma or crisis or intensity.

SUPER EVENTS

Consider it this way: within the particle lab, more than eighty years of quantum experiments demonstrate that subatomic particles occupy a state of superposition, or a wave state. As such, they appear everywhere at once. They exist in a state of infinite possibility. We know this because subatomic particles display interference patterns, which demonstrate that they are nonlocalized. They exist in a state of potential until an observer takes a measurement. When an observer decides to take a measurement, the particle collapses from a wave state to a localized state. Without that measurement, the particle will not occupy a definite, locatable place.

This is not controversial. No quantum physicist would challenge eighty years of this data. What is controversial are the implications of the data, and the willingness of our culture to follow those implications. In the 1930s, physicist Erwin Schrödinger devised a thought experiment known as Schrödinger's Cat, by which he intended to force his colleagues to acknowledge the impossible possibilities observed in the particle lab. Schrödinger challenged them to acknowledge the evident absurdity of what was being documented—of a surreal reality in which everything exists everywhere at once, in a state of infinitude.

One variant of the Schrödinger's Cat experiment could be put this way: you take a house cat and place around its neck a collar with what Schrödinger called a "diabolical device." Upon contact with a single atom this device releases a fatal poison. You take the collared cat and place it in one of a pair of boxes. You then direct a single atom at the two boxes. After, you go to check the boxes to see the outcome. What would you find?

All commonly observed reality dictates that if the atom went into the empty box, the cat would be alive. If the atom went into the box that held the cat and tripped the poison device, the cat would be dead. Simple, right? But Schrödinger said: no, that is not reality at all. You would have to allow for the existence of a *dead/alive* cat. Because at one time, when that atom was in a wave state, it appeared in both boxes at once. It became localized in a single box only when you went to check.

Hence, reality demands that you would have a dead/alive cat. It is impossible, it makes no sense, and yet it is absolutely required if we are to accept the data from quantum physics.

In the 1950s, physicist Hugh Everett III extrapolated further from the Schrödinger's Cat experiment. Everett contended that the timing of your decision to look or not look in the boxes would create a past, present, and future for that cat. If you were to wait eight hours, say, until you checked the boxes, you would not only have a dead/alive cat, but the alive cat, having been stuck in the box for eight hours, would be hungry. You would actually have created a past narrative and present for that animal. Your decision to look, not look, wait, or not check it all would create an arc of life for this animal.

That could be the actual nature of reality: all outcomes exist in infinite potential and become localized or actualized only when they reach our perspective. This may be a matter of measurement, focus, or awareness—accident or choice.

Leaving aside the question of free will (another issue entirely), what I have described raises the possibility that these persistent, extraordinary events—sightings of everything from serpents in the water to mysterious winged beasts to otherworldly beings to gnomes to Bigfoot—may be the result of perspective, and of these things intermittently localizing in our reality.

A related possibility comes from what is called string theory. String theorists try to explain the strange behavior of subatomic objects, as well as why such objects affect one another at distances, and why, as Isaac Newton observed, even macro objects at vast removes mirror each other's motions. String theory holds that all particles and all matter are not separate entities, but rather are part of vast, undulating networks of strings. When an object at one point in space affects another object, we are not seeing two distinct entities, but a unified string of objects. What's more, different dimensions and universes exist along these strings, so we may not always see the thing causing an effect. In string theory, all material and events are of one whole. We catch only hints of this through exquisitely fine measurement.

When speaking of measurement, we naturally think of laboratory instruments. But what are our senses if not instruments of measurement through which we navigate reality? On the psychological scale, it may be that at moments of profound sensitivity, or at moments in which we are emotionally primed in a certain way—maybe through trauma, euphoria, or a sense of crisis—we catch glimpses of things that are real, but do not usually register with the senses or mechanics through which we experience daily life. Anomalous entities exist, but they exist at other points on a vibrating, cosmic string, or what we might call another dimension. That is one theory. Another, not necessarily at odds with string theory, is that these anomalies occupy a state of superposition that you select into your locality—not manifest but *select,* which is my preferred term—through perspective.

Hence, these strange events or entities may be real, but they are perceived only occasionally, and we give them names like Bigfoot or fairies or UFOs. These potentialities exist all around us, but we do not possess the instrumentation to measure such things. Our way of viewing the world is coarse and limited—even illusory. For example, we organize our lives by linear time. Linear time feels very real. It is overwhelmingly persuasive. But linearity itself is an illusion. It is a necessary illusion, which we use to organize life, but it is not real.

We know that time slows down at or near light speed. The aging process slows when a being is moving near light speed. We likewise know that time slows or bends in environments of extreme gravity, like black holes. These things are no longer theoretical; they have been measured, they are real, they are actual. Yet they make no sense to us. As we go through daily life and our commutes and so on, it makes no impact on us that time can actually slow.

Even knowing this, being able to understand this, being able to talk about this, does not necessarily impact our everyday experience of linearity. Because linearity is probably a very necessary illusion for five-sensory beings. But it is a device, not ultimate reality. Ultimate reality is stranger than we are given to believe.

WHY DON'T WE SEE REALITY?

Why don't we pick up more on this material? Why does life seem so orderly to us? There is just one of me here, there is just one of you there, there is one chair that you are sitting on. There is not an infinitude of chairs. It feels so practical, so actual. It is difficult to imagine that any of this quantum or string phenomena can be real in more than an abstract way or on the subatomic scale. Philosopher William James, in his Gifford lectures in 1902, made an observation that speaks to this. When a mystic sees something, James said, it is as if he is viewing it through a microscope. The mystic sees more and more of what is really going on because of his extreme sensitivity.

If I look at a drop of water, all I see is a common drop. It is translucent; it feels like what I call "wet." But if I look at that same drop through a microscope, all kinds of things are revealed. There are single-cell organisms, there are bacteria, there are molecules moving around. The molecules are made up of atoms and other particles that are similarly moving around. All kinds of things are occurring that I do not normally see.

James made the contention that the mystic is always viewing things as though through a microscope. But when you pan the camera back, so to speak, you experience less and less of what is really happening. Without crediting James, quantum physicists today call this phenomenon "information leakage." They respond to the apparent disparity between the particle world and our macro world by saying what James said, which is that when you are measuring things with extremely fine and well-tuned instruments, you are seeing more and more of what is really going on. But when your capacity for measurement coarsens, you lose data and see less and less of what is occurring.

Just as linear time is a device, just as particles exist in a wave state or state of superposition, it is possible that we live amidst an infinitude of extraordinary events, which we perceive only in fragments or at fleeting moments. Maybe these are moments of great awareness; maybe these are moments in which our ordinary thought patterns, for whatever reason, get interrupted; maybe these are moments that are available to some individuals with a gift for what we call ESP, or sensitivity, or intuition. It could be that at such times, the individual is capable of seeing what is really happening. Yet such individuals get smeared with terms like psychosis, fraud, imagination, fantasy, or confirmation bias. Materialists over-rely on the term "confirmation bias" to ignore testimony. Consistent testimony from varying sources forms a record and should be considered. Materialists fail to realize that confirmation bias, or prejudicial thought, is their own problem, too.

If my contention is correct—which is to say, you get what you are looking for—we are all in the same boat. So, let us sit down together in an interdisciplinary way, and have a conversation and try to determine the topography. We must try to understand more of what is going on. We will not get there if we dismiss or underfund or ban the so-called borderline sciences. Think of the possibilities that open to us if scholarly research into psi or extra-cognition really becomes available. Imagine if places like the Princeton Engineering Anomalies Research lab did not have to close because it was time for the founders to retire, and nobody else had the energy to maintain the level of fundraising or fight the battles necessary to keep the lab alive.

We have money for everything in this society. There is no shortage of resources. And yet we always seem to cry poverty when it comes to dispensing resources in a more democratic way or allotting modest sums to keep alive research into the nature of reality itself. The reason I appreciate today's best paranormal investigators, and why I appreciate historical figures like Charles Fort, is because they poke holes in the straight story. They drive us to ask questions that might otherwise never get considered.

A DAMNABLE BORE

Fort himself was a fascinating character. Newspapers used to call him "the Mad Genius of The Bronx."* Fort was born in Albany, New York, in 1874, and lived and worked for much of his life in New York City's northern borough. Like occult scholar Manly P. Hall, Fort did a great deal of his research at the New York Public Library (where I now sit in a research room writing these words). He produced his first of four books in the year 1919. It was called *The Book of the Damned.* By "damned" Fort meant facts that did not fit in: outsider facts, theories, and ideas; facts that were considered unfit for consumption, and so were pushed to the margins.

Fort would gather news reports of things happening around the world that were not supposed to be happening, like mysterious airships in an age before we had the term flying saucers; frogs falling from the sky; strange beasts; spontaneous combustion; teleportation (a term he is thought to have coined)—all sorts of things that did not fit the straight story.

Some people thought that Fort was a genius, that he was modernity's greatest critic of science, because he understood that science in the early twentieth century had formed its own orthodoxy, its own canon, to the point of excluding things that did not fit in.

The novelist Theodore Dreiser was a great admirer of Fort. In 1921, Dreiser wrote in a letter to critic H. L. Mencken, "To me no one in the world has suggested the underlying depths and mysteries and possibilities as has Fort. To me he is simply stupendous."† H. G. Wells, on the other hand, referred to Fort in a 1931 letter to Dreiser as "one of the most damnable bores who ever cut scraps from out-of-the-way newspapers."‡ There was a binary attitude about Charles Fort. But I have

---

*From a recollection by journalist H. Allen Smith in his memoir *Low Man on a Totem Pole* (Blakiston, 1941).

†*Dreiser-Mencken Letters: The Correspondence of Theodore Dreiser & H.L. Mencken, 1907-1945,* Volume 2 edited by Thomas P. Riggio (University of Pennsylvania Press, 1986)

‡*Letters of Theodore Dreiser,* Volume 2 edited by Robert H. Elias (University of Pennsylvania Press, 1959).

always loved the man, and I think his work has retained a legion of fans and readers precisely because he was capable of poking holes in the straight story.

BEASTLY TRAITS

There is another dimension to the presence of mysterious or allegorical beasts. Some of the beasts that appear in parable and mythology, like the sphinx or griffin or centaur, summon us to traits that are actual or potential parts of our personas, of our abilities as human beings—traits we are divorced from, which get pushed off to the margins of our understanding. We can speak of these qualities only in terms of metaphor because they are not accepted, they are not understood, and they are not integrated into the human story. As Charles Fort would say, they are "damned."

Obadiah Harris, the past president of Manly P. Hall's Philosophical Research Society (PRS) in Los Angeles, shared a wonderful story with me a few years before his death in 2019. We held a very moving memorial service for Obadiah at PRS, which you can find online. Obadiah said that when Manly used to ready himself in his office each Sunday morning, before delivering his weekly talk in the campus auditorium, he would pause before his altar and rub a wonderful little Egyptian statuette of a cat. It was a black onyx model of Bastet, one of the Egyptian cat gods. He would rub this little cat for wisdom, because a cat has the ability to see in the dark. Many people felt that Manly displayed a preternatural ability of speaking extremely fluidly and at great length without notes. I am not suggesting a connection, but I did like the story. And this little cat really existed—I held it in my hands—but it has unfortunately disappeared from Manly's office. The current PRS president, Greg Salyer, and I are searching for it. We would like to re-select this little cat into existence.

We often ascribe powers to animals that exist within ourselves, but that we do not feel capable of summoning. So, we mythologize them. In that vein, I want to share the story of two episodes I experienced recently in Egypt in connection with mythical or allegorical animals.

In February 2019, I was traveling in Egypt with my friend Ronni Thomas. Ronni is a brilliant film director, and we are making a documentary about the 1908 occult book *The Kybalion*. I once regarded *The Kybalion* as a kind of early twentieth-century novelty of occult literature. Several years ago, however, I came to realize that I was wrong. I was underestimating the nature and the greatness of that short book. It is a beautiful and very relevant distillation of some of the spiritual psychology found in the Greek-Egyptian Hermetic writings, which appeared during the final stages of Egyptian antiquity.

For the film, we decided to go back to the source, as much as we were able. Ronni made the courageous decision that we should do some filming in Egypt. Off we went to Egypt in the month of February. I can disclose this now that I am safely back home, but we had no license to film, because it is enormously expensive. We had a decent budget, but a license was out of reach. So we had to surreptitiously film in Egypt, which is no small risk: if you are caught without the proper licenses, you could get arrested or thrown in jail. We were very aware of this, but we felt that even without the proper licensure, which we simply could not afford within the confines of our budget, we just had to do this.

We were able to get some extraordinary footage. When the film is released, you will be surprised at how much footage we were able to gather illegally, but very lovingly, in Mother Egypt.* We were also granted some remarkable access and opportunities. I had two opportunities that I want to share, both involving exposure to allegorical beasts.

Subterranean chambers exist in the Valley of Kings that are off the path of most people who visit Egypt. However, these chambers are accessible if you are willing to pay the right people. My wish is that commerce alone would not be what allows people to gain entry to these places, but sometimes you must deal with the world as it is. So, we were

---

*The film released in January 2022. To our surprise, it premiered as the #3 top documentary on iTunes. *The Kybalion* appears on all major digital platforms.

willing, as much as we were able, to pay off the right people to enter some places that are normally off-limits.

After paying, we were able to enter a chamber very, very deep in the Valley of Kings. Within this chamber is a large bas-relief of a bull. In Ancient Egyptian symbolism, a bull represents strength, virility, and personal power. It is an enormously potent image within the pantheon of Egyptian deities and allegories. The guide who took me into this chamber gestured to me that it was permissible to touch and lay hands on this enormous bas-relief. The carvings in the chamber were incredibly well preserved. One of the astounding things that we do not always realize when we look at Egyptian monuments is that they were originally colorized. They were not only three-dimensional, they were not only covered in beautiful precious stones and finishing material, but they were majestically and very vividly colorized. Over time, the most widely seen or weathered monuments have lost this color.

But we were within a very dry, temperate, cool underground chamber, and these images and bas-reliefs had been preserved going back thousands of years. I was a little uncomfortable when the guide invited me to lay hands on the bull—I have tremendous respect for antiquities, and I would never want to do anything that would detract from the power and the beauty of these monuments. I am very aware that if tourists and travelers were traipsing through the place all day and laying hands on the object, it would get damaged or degraded. And yet I felt that I was being given an invitation.

The philosopher Jacob Needleman once said to me, "What do you do when someone offers you a gift?" Brilliant student that I was, I just stared at him blankly. He said, "You accept it!" So, I made the decision to accept this gift. I can only report in all candor what happened. As I laid hands on this bull, I experienced—call it what you will—a tremendous rush of lightning and electricity shooting through my body and felt a sense of inner light within me. The only phrasing I can use to describe the sensation is the feeling of a flash of lightning passing through me. It was an extraordinary and tactile experience.

Of course, one could say, "Look, you're a suggestible guy; you're an excitable person." I do not know, nor would the person saying that know, just what occurred. I can only report that it was, for me, a palpable experience. Here I stood before a magnificent allegorical beast carved in a bas-relief going back more than 3,000 years, still fully colorized and vivid, and the symbol of virility and strength and power, and I was invited to lay my hands on it. I felt lightning pass through me. It was one of the most remarkable experiences of my life.

We had another experience when we were at the Temple of Karnak in Luxor. Our guide was aware that Ronni and I had occult interests. There is a colloquialism in Egypt for people like us—they call us "meditators." Terms like occult and New Age do not translate very well. But once they say, "Oh, you're meditators," then they know what you want to see. Our guide for this leg of the trip was an extraordinary woman who was multilingual despite having never traveled outside the country. She had learned English, French, and Korean on her own through BBC language courses. She brought us to a small temple to the cat goddess Sekhmet, which was tucked away on a side path in the vast complex. This small temple was closed and padlocked. A soldier toting an automatic rifle and a robed guide guarded it. The only way to gain entry was by paying a bribe. Again, you sometimes must deal with the world as you find it. And, of course, people are entitled to earn a living.

The soldier and guide looked at us as if to ask, "Who are these mangy characters?" We very nicely said hello and greeted them with as much money as possible, and then everybody was all smiles. We were invited to enter the chamber to Sekhmet, a goddess with the head of a cat and the body of a woman. I cannot begin to tell you how completely dark it was inside this chamber. The chamber is thousands of years old, and there was not so much as a streak of light, with no cracks or fissures in the wall.

We were guided to kneel at the feet of Sekhmet and were invited to kiss her feet and lay our hands upon her body and recite a prayer. We performed this short ceremony in pitch blackness. This, too, was an experience of absolute transcendence. There seemed to be a complete dissolution between us as separate beings and the goddess before whom we kneeled. I think we both experienced a sense of dissolving, almost a lightness of body that felt akin to an out-of-body experience. We felt a complete disassociation crouched in the darkness before this goddess, almost a sense of transcendent oneness with the being before us. Everything briefly entered a state of nonphysicality. It was remarkable.

I am not someone who goes around collecting experiences, but this left us, two seekers going into places that were off the permissible path, with perhaps some feeling for what our primeval ancestors might have felt in the presence of these extraordinary beings. The episode reaffirmed my belief, which I have explored elsewhere, that we have neglected some of the wisdom of our primeval ancestors, who identified with and personified certain energies in deific form, and who gave these energies names—whether Set, or Sekhmet, or Bastet, or Minerva, or Zeus, or Jupiter, or Athena.

They identified these energies, maybe as projections of their own intellect, or maybe as nonlocalized intellect, and deified them. They also petitioned them. When people come to me in need, when they are feeling at a dead end in life or things are not going the way that they wish, my suggestion, as an ethical and spiritual experiment, is to identify a god or goddess from the ancient pantheon. Whether this deity is from Egypt, Persia, the Hellenic world, or elsewhere, I suggest choosing one with whom you resonate, one that is meaningful to you, and one whose characteristics or traits seem to capture something that you need in life. After doing so, I see no reason why you cannot enter a prayerful state and make a petition to this deity and see what occurs. You may find exactly the help that you need. My contention is that the old gods may be lonely. They hunger for human attention and veneration.

People from all over the world used to travel great distances to honor and petition these gods. That is no longer so. It could be that these personified energies or intelligences yearn for human contact. If you make the personal decision to attempt a relationship with one of these deities, and to make a petition, you could be surprised.

I speak to you from deepest personal experience. I would never offer something as a suggestion that I have not tried and experimented with myself. I have had some of the deepest, most meaningful spiritual experiences of my life by following the path that I just described. You certainly do not need to tell anybody what you are doing; you do not need to tell your shrink or your boyfriend or your spouse. It is yours. It is your private experiment. It is something I have found bountifully fruitful and significant. We displace, onto certain ideals of allegorical beasts and deities and beings, traits that perhaps exist within us and that we are capable of selecting or having a relationship with.

RECLAIMING THE DAMNED

I have written elsewhere of how the snake or the serpent represented wisdom in cultures all over the world. This was true in Egyptian culture, Hebraic culture, Mayan culture, and Celtic culture. Every culture around the world, spanning enormous stretches of time, distance, language, and custom, identified the snake as a symbol of illumination, possibility, provocation, and awareness.

I think that we, in the Western world, have made a tremendous misreading of Genesis 3, seeing the snake who conversed with Eve as a figure of evil or maleficence. Rather, it was the snake who gave Eve permission to eat from the so-called Tree of Knowledge of Good and Evil, which the Creator had placed in the midst of the garden, even though the garden dwellers—who were supposedly beloved and cared for—were prohibited from eating from it and gaining awareness, and were warned they would die if they tasted its fruit. The snake told Eve, "You've been deceived. You will surely not die if you eat the fruit from this tree." She took the challenge and did not die from eating the fruit, which she shared with Adam. Their eyes were opened, and they gained the capacity for measurement and creativity; they gained the capacity to argue with the Creator, and they were expunged from the garden of Paradise.

Their offspring, Cain and Abel—so the parable goes—were caught up in a tragic act of fratricide. But it is very possible that the price of creativity, the price of awareness, the price of perspective, is friction.

Haven't we seen this play out across our culture? Witch burnings were commonplace in Europe for centuries, and they still occur in parts of the world today. People who are clearly capable of functioning in the world are called lunatics or flying saucer nuts when they have extraordinary experiences. Plato famously theorized that if we were all captured in a cave, chained and capable of witnessing reality only as shadows cast on a wall, and someone was somehow able to leave the cave and later return to tell the other captives about the splendor that existed in the outside world, what would the others do? They would kill the individual.

Isn't that the story of the snake in the garden, essentially playing out over and over again? Every time a capable, mature, intelligent person speaks of an extraordinary experience, he or she is told, "Don't talk about seeing a UFO. You're going to lose your rank and your reputation within the Air Force. Don't try to experiment with ESP, everybody's going to think you're a nut, and you're going to lose your departmental funding. Don't question the standard dating of the Great Sphinx or of the pyramids, because if you start questioning the standard timeline people in your department are going to get hostile toward you, and you'll be branded a nut."

So, what do we do? We disassociate from these abilities and experiences and code them into parable, story, myth, and archetype. It is a way of distancing ourselves from abilities and possibilities that exist within the human experience, ones that are easier and less risky for us to understand and talk about when classified as mythology, as anomalies, as wonders, as little green men, as strange encounters. People who testify to these things in an actual way are treated, in effect, like Adam and Eve—expelled from the garden of paradise, or seen differently, expelled from the garden of conformity. Yet this state of affairs is being shaken up at this very moment.

As I mentioned earlier, I do not speak casually about paradigm shifts. Every generation seems to think it exists on some kind of precipice. Some generations did indeed exist on a precipice. The World War I generation existed on a precipice. I do not think one should speak about this casually. But I do believe that we are facing possibilities and questions in our generation, at this very moment, that may upend our idea of what it means to be human as much as the theories of Darwin upended the popular understanding of human nature in the Victorian age.

I think we are poised on this precipice, where we are looking out at the world—at testimony of wondrous beasts, strange beings, and anomalous events—and are coming to realize that we are not necessarily looking at things that are fantasies or chimeras. We are actually looking into a mirror. And what we are looking at is gazing back at us. Because these are the traits of our own personas with which we are becoming reacquainted. Our personas are interdimensional, unmoored by linearity, and symbiotic with a larger cosmic reality than we have previously understood.

2

CHOOSE YOUR OWN REALITY

I believe that some of us who work with experimental spirituality, mind metaphysics, and parapsychology must attempt to theorize the mechanics and delivery systems behind what is experienced and observed. Every generation owes this effort to the search of the next, which will have its own ideas and critiques. This essay is my attempt to describe "what happens" in the process of thought causation, or what is popularly called positive thinking and manifestation. A shorter version appeared at Medium *on December 9, 2019.*

Why should positive thinking, "manifestation," or the "Law of Attraction" work at all? Before you cry "confirmation bias!" (materialism's equivalent of "lock her up!"), take a deep breath.

I use this essay to provide a theory of mind causation. It may be wrong, it may be grossly incomplete, but I feel that we need to at least try to theorize from the intersection of testimony, science, and mysticism. It is necessary, I believe, for our generation of seekers to do more than tell the same stories over and over. We must experiment, we must experience, we must have results—and we must attempt to come up with reasons why mind causation just might work.

I will start by quoting something that mystic Neville Goddard (1905–1972) said in a series of lectures in Los Angeles in 1948:

"Scientists will one day explain why there is a serial universe. But in practice, how you use this serial universe to change the future is more important."

It was a striking observation—Neville is, I believe, the most penetrating voice to emerge from the New Thought tradition—because it was not until years later that quantum physicists began to talk about the many-worlds theory. Physicist Hugh Everett III devised the concept in 1957. He was trying to make sense of some of the extraordinary findings that had been occurring for about three decades in quantum particle physics. For example, scientists are able to demonstrate, through various interference patterns, that a subatomic particle occupies a wave state or state of superposition—that is, an infinite number of places—until someone takes a measurement: it is only when the measurement is taken that the particle collapses, so to speak, from a wave state into a localized state. At that point it occupies a definite, identifiable, measurable place. Before the measurement is taken, the localized particle exists only in potential.

Now, I have just about squeezed all of quantum physics into a couple of sentences. I think it is an accurate description, but obviously I am taking huge complexities and reducing them to the dimensions of a marble. But I believe I am faithfully stating what has been observed in the last eighty-plus years of particle experiments. And we are seeing that on the subatomic scale, matter does not behave as we are conditioned to expect.

Our understanding of matter in our macro world generally comes from measuring things through our five senses and experiencing them as singularities. There is one table. It is solid and definable. It is not occupying an infinite number of spaces. But contemporary quantum physicists have theorized that we may not normally see or experience superposition phenomena because of what is sometimes called *information leakage*. This means that we gain or lose data based on the fineness of our measurement. When you are measuring things with exquisitely well-tuned instruments, like a microscope, you are seeing more and more of what is going on—and that is actual reality. But when you pan the camera back, so to speak, your measurements coarsen, and you are seeing less and less of what is actually happening.

To all ordinary appearances, a table is solid. The floor beneath your feet is solid. Where you are sitting is solid. But measuring through atomic-scale microscopes, we realize that if you go deeper and deeper, you have space within these objects. Particles make up the atom, and still greater space appears. We do not experience that; we experience solidity. But no one questions that there is space between the particles that compose an atom. Furthermore, we possess decades of data demonstrating that when subatomic particles are directed at a target system, such as a double slit, they appear in infinite places at once until a measurement is made; only then does locality appear. But we fail to see this unless we are measuring things with comparative exactitude. Hence, what I am describing seems unreal based on lived experience—but it is actual.

In any event, my supposition is this: if particles appear in an infinite number of places at once until a measurement is taken; and if, as we know from studying the behavior and mechanics of subatomic particles, there exists an infinitude of possibilities; and if we know, as we have for many years, that time is relative, then it is possible to reason—and it is almost necessary to reason—that linearity itself, by which we organize our lives, is an illusion. Linearity is a useful and necessary device for five-sensory beings to get through life, but it does not stand up objectively. Linearity is a concept, a subjective interpretation of what is really going on. It is not reflected in Einstein's theory of relativity, which demonstrates that time slows down when we begin to approach the speed of light. Nor is it reflected in quantum mechanics, where particles appear in an infinitude of places and do not obey any orderly modality. Linearity is not replicating itself when a measurement taken of a particle serves to localize the appearance or existence of the object.

· If we pursue this line of thought further—and this is where the many-worlds theory comes into play—the very decision to take a measurement (or not take a measurement) not only localizes a particle, but creates a past, present, and future for that particle. The decision of an observer to take a measurement creates a multidimensional reality for the particle. This is implied in the famous thought-experiment called Schrödinger's Cat.

As noted earlier, the twentieth-century physicist Erwin Schrödinger was frustrated with the evident absurdity of quantum theory, which showed objects simultaneously appearing in more than one place at a time. Such an outlook, he felt, violated all commonly observed physical laws. In 1935, Schrödinger sought to highlight this predicament through a purposely absurdist thought experiment, which he intended to force quantum physicists to follow their data to its ultimate degree.

Schrödinger reasoned that quantum data dictates that a sentient being, such as a cat, can be simultaneously alive and dead. Let us revisit a variant of the Schrödinger's Cat experiment: a cat is placed into one of a pair of boxes. Along with the cat is a collar fitted with a device which, if exposed to an atom, releases a deadly poison. An observer then fires an atom at the boxes. The observer subsequently uses some form of measurement to check on which box the atom is in: the empty one, or the one with the cat and the poisoning device. When the observer goes to check, the wave function of the atom (the state in which it exists in both boxes) collapses into a particle function (the state in which it is localized to one box). Once the observer takes his measurement, convention says that the cat will be discovered to be dead or alive. But Schrödinger reasoned that quantum physics describes an outcome in which the cat is *both* dead and alive. This is because the atom, in its wave function, was, at one time, in either box, and either outcome is real.

Of course, all lived experience tells us that if the atom went into the empty box, the cat is alive; and if it went into the box with the cat and the poisoning device, the cat is dead. But Schrödinger, aiming to highlight the frustrations of quantum theory, argued that if the observations of quantum-mechanics experiments are right, you would have to allow for each outcome.

To take it even further, a cohort of quantum physicists in the 1950s theorized that if an observer waited some significant length of time—say, eight hours—before checking on the dead-alive cat, he would discover one cat that was dead for eight hours and another that was alive for eight hours (and now hungry). In this line of reasoning, conscious observation effectively manifested the localized atom, the dead cat, and the living cat—and *also manifested the past,* or in other words, created a history for both a dead cat and a living one. Both outcomes are true.

So, whatever a particle is doing, the very fact that a sentient observer has chosen to take a measurement at that time, place, moment, and juncture creates a whole past, present, and future—an entire infinitude of outcomes. A divergent set of outcomes would exist if that measurement were never taken. A divergent set of outcomes would also exist if that measurement were taken one second later, or five minutes later, or tomorrow. And what is tomorrow? When particles exist in superposition until somebody takes a measurement, there is no such thing as tomorrow, other than subjectively.

Consider too: the cat, from its perspective, is local; the observer, from its perspective, is local—but both, in fact, are in a wave state or superposition. We can speak of them as concrete, singular beings only from their personal perspective. From the quantum perspective, they are infinite. Expanding on this idea, research physician Robert Lanza, adjunct professor at Wake Forest University School of Medicine, argued that death itself is ultimately a mental phenomenon: we "die" only insofar as the mind perceives demise.

And, as alluded, what are our five senses but a technology by which we measure things? What are our five senses but a biological technology, not necessarily different in intake from a camera, photometer, digital recorder, or microscope? So, it is possible that within reality—within this extra-linear, superpositioned infinitude of possibilities in which we are taking measurements—we experience things based upon our perspective. This is why I use the term select rather than manifest.

Neville Goddard's instinct was correct in this sense. He taught that you can take a measurement by employing the visualizing forces of your own imagination. You are taking a measurement within the infinitude of possible outcomes. The measurement localizes or actualizes the thing itself. Hence, his formula: an assumption, if persisted in, hardens into fact. But the assumption must be persuasive; it must be convincing. That is why emotions and feeling states must come into play. And Neville observed that the hypnagogic state—a state of drowsy relaxation—helps facilitate that process.

You can use several different techniques in connection with Neville's ideas, and, as he did, I challenge you to try them and see what happens. You are entitled to results. I believe that every therapeutic and ethical and spiritual philosophy should result in some concrete change and improvement in your life or conduct; if it does not, then such an idea should have no hold on you. I feel similarly strongly that the ability to describe a concrete outcome in your life is vitally important. That, too, was always part of Neville's teaching. Testimony is both a critical source of ideas and an invitation to others.

One way of using Neville's approach to mental creativity is to enter an inner state of theatrical or childlike make-believe. Not childish but child*like:* a state of internal wonder and pretending. Children are so good at this. We get embarrassed about this quality as we age, but Neville talked about walking the streets of Manhattan imagining that he was in the tree-lined lanes of Barbados, boarding a ship to some desired destination, or in a location where he wanted to be.

He would say: "Unfoldment will come. You will see." He always argued that an assumption, although false, if persisted in, eventually hardens into fact. He would further advise, "Assume the state of the wish fulfilled. Live from the end. Live from the state of your wish fulfilled." Remember, Neville reminded listeners, you are not in a state of *wanting;* you are in a state of *having received.* Your aim is simply to occupy the emotional and mental state that you would experience after having received.

One simple way to use Neville's method is to freely enter this state of make-believe, as you used to when you were a child. Of course, you must also continue to go about your adult life in this world of Caesar and currency and commerce, and fulfill your obligations and do the things you need to do. You cooperate with the world. You must abide by the world. You must do the things that the world requires. But the secret engine behind what is really going on is what you are imagining. Within are the hidden currents of emotionalized thought, which are the actual engine of what is occurring.

How long will it take you to see your desired changes in outer life? How long will it take for outer life to conform to your internal focus, your living from the end of your ideal? This question of time intervals has recently become very hot for me personally, because with all the stresses that life throws at us, it is not easy to adopt a feeling state and stick with it for weeks. It is very difficult, in part because the world we live in does everything possible to disrupt our inner quietude.

Neville noted later in his life that there could be a substantial time interval between your visioning, your mental imaging, and the appearance of the wished-for thing. He would point out that the gestation period of a human life is nine months. The gestation period of a horse is eleven months. The gestation period of a lamb is five months. The gestation period of a chick is twenty-one days. There is almost always going to be some time interval. You must persist. If you want to find yourself in Paris, and you wake up every day and you are still far away from Paris, you are naturally going to feel disappointed or dejected. But if you really stick with it, I venture that you will see that your assumptions eventually concretize into reality, and the correspondences will be uncanny.

I have had such experiences in my own life; but I have personally observed that in some cases, there have been extended time intervals. This has been true regarding my career as a writer, speaker, and narrator. The philosopher Goethe made an interesting observation. We have all heard the expression, "Be careful what you wish for; you just might get it." It actually has its roots in Goethe. Taking a leaf from Goethe's play *Faust,* Ralph Waldo Emerson noted this dynamic in his 1860 essay "Fate," which led to the popular adage. Emerson wrote:

> And the moral is that what we seek we shall find; what we flee from flees from us; as Goethe said, "what we wish for in youth, comes in heaps on us in old age," too often cursed with the granting of our prayer: and hence the high caution, that, since we are sure of having what we wish, we must beware to ask only for high things.

We are being warned to act with perspective: what we wish for when we are young will come upon us in waves when we are old. Many people would object to that claim, saying that they have all kinds of unfulfilled wishes. But unlocking the truth of this observation requires peeling back the layers of your mind and probing formative images and fantasies from when you were very young. What was the earliest dream you can remember when you first came into conscious memory, maybe at age three or four? I mean a literal nighttime dream. What were your fantasies when you were very young? I do believe that children—certainly this was true of me—have very intense fantasy lives even at age four or five. What were your earliest fantasies?

I believe that Goethe's observation relates to Neville's remarks about the perceived passage of time and the gestation between thought and actualization. If you take Goethe's counsel, you might be surprised to discover an extraordinary symmetry between things that you are living out in your life today, and things that you harbored and thought about when you were very young. These can be positive, negative, or anywhere in between.

Neville recommended that you avoid thinking in terms of, "It will happen this way or that way" or, "I'll do something to make it happen." His attitude was that the event will unfold in its own lovely, harmonious, perfect way. Your job is not to draw the map. Your job is to live from the destination.

I believe that Neville is going to be remembered, and is being looked upon today, as having created the most elegant mystical analog to quantum physics. He was thinking and talking about these ideas long before the popularization of quantum physics. He had a remarkable instinct in the 1940s, which has been tantalizingly, if indirectly, reiterated by people studying quantum theory—people who have never heard the name of Neville. Yet it would not surprise me if, within a generation or so, some physics students begin to read him as a philosophical adjunct to their work. That may sound unlikely, but remember that many of the current generation of physicists were inspired by *Star Trek* and *Zen and the Art of Motorcycle Maintenance,* and I believe there is greater openness today to questions of awareness and mind causation.

▲

We all live by philosophies, unspoken or not. Even if we say we do not have an ideology, we obviously have assumptions by which we navigate life. When I look back upon people like Neville, and Zen teacher Alan Watts (1915–1973), I realize that their greatness is that they lived by the inner light of their ideas. That is a rare trait in our world today. We are a world of talkers. People are sarcastic or cruel over Twitter, and they think they are taking some great moral stand. Is it brave for someone who lives at a great distance and does not even use his real name to call people out online? That is no victory. It is make-believe morality.

When we look back on certain figures in the political, cultural, artistic, and spiritual spheres, those we remember are the ones who lived by the inner light of their ideas, who put themselves on the line, for success or failure, based upon an idea.

My wish for every one of you reading these words is that you provide that same example. And I really must say the following, and I mean this in my heart: if you sincerely attempt what I am describing, I believe that you will find greatness, because, if nothing else, you will be making the effort to live by the inner light of an idea.

3

"MY WILL BE DONE"

One evening at a book release party in 2019, a publisher approached me with the idea of writing a book on Satanism. The term itself is laden with misperception. I assess the Satanic and its historicity from an esoteric, ethical, and highly individualized perspective. (How else to approach the Great Rebel?) I was surprised by the invitation. In the end, however, my inviter was anticipating more of a social/political provocation, including a titular apologia for Donald Trump. Um, no. But I always say: no honest effort is ever wasted. What follows is a slightly adapted version of the essay that opened my rejected proposal. It captures my outlook without compromise—and also, I hope, with uncertainty. It appeared under the title "The Optimism of Satan" on July 11, 2019, as part of a series I wrote for Medium, *"Radical Spirits."*

A friend of mine once had the opportunity to ask the Dalai Lama a single question.

"Who was your greatest teacher?" he asked.

The exiled leader replied, "Mao Zedong."

I once felt provoked in my own sphere by a similarly unlikely teacher: Donald Trump.

Years ago, Trump the Developer rhetorically asked an interviewer: "What good is something if you can't put your name on it?" His comment is indelibly stamped on my memory, though I confess I cannot find a source for it. Did I imagine it? The sentiment, while coarse and easily rebutted, came to haunt me.

Did Trump, the showy conman obsessed with naming rights, capture a nagging truth of human nature—a side none of us can deny or push away, other than by an act of self-regarding hypocrisy? And did I, hopefully in a more integral way, share a kernel of his outlook? Was the voice even his—or something within me?

Soon after hearing Trump's remark, I received what struck me as a bit of ridiculous advice from the editor of an academic spiritual journal. I told him in candor that I wanted to find greater exposure for my byline. "You don't have to put your name on everything you write," he replied. Such a principle could ring true only in the world of abstraction.

Trump's statement about self-exaltation, however ugly, captured half a truth. The whole truth is that our lives, as vessels for various influences—some physical, some perhaps beyond—are bound up with the world and circumstances in which we find ourselves; and within that world we must, at the stake of personal happiness, create, expand, and aspire. Whatever higher influences we feel or great thoughts we think, or are experienced by us through the influence of others, are like heat dissipated in the vacuum of space unless those thoughts are directed into a structure or receptacle. Our purpose is to be generative. Questions of attachment and non-attachment, identification and non-identification, are incidental to that larger fact.

I came to feel strongly about this several years ago when I found that my spiritual search, a path of radical ecumenism with a dedication to esoteric interests, was failing to satisfy me. I began to suspect that I was not acknowledging what I was really looking for, either in spirituality—by which I mean a search for the extra-physical—or therapy. I came face-to-face with an instinct that few people acknowledge and would deny if they heard it spoken. But they should linger on it. Because what I discovered captures what I believe is a basic if discomforting human truth: the ethical or spiritual search, not as idealized but as actually lived, is the search for power. That is, for the ability to possess personal agency. We pray, "Thy will be done." We mean, "My will be done"—hoping that the two comport. This is why, at least in my observations after thirty years as a publisher, seeker, and historian of alternative spirituality, many seekers in both traditional and alternative faiths are ill at ease, fitful in their progress, and apt to slide from faith to faith, or to harbor multiple, sometimes conflicting, practices at once. (One sometimes hears references to the "Left-Hand Path"—a term rooted in Vedic tradition which is often conflated with "black magic," a designation I reject. I define the Left-Hand Path as governed by "My will be done" versus "Thy will be done.")

Power is supposed to be the craving of the corrupt. Is it? The novelist Isaac Bashevis Singer, surveying the modern occult scene, wrote in 1967: "We are all black magicians in our dreams, in our fantasies, perversions, and phobias."* And to this I would add: in pursuit of our highest ideals. As Singer detected, we are not very different from the classical magician when we strive, morally and materially, to carry out our plans in the world—to ensure the betterment of ourselves and our loved ones; to heal sickness; to create, sustain, and, above all, to generate things that bear our markings, ideals, and likenesses. All of this is the expenditure of power, the striving to actualize our drives and images.

I do not view the search for individual power, including through supernatural means (a topic I will clarify and expand on), as necessarily maleficent. Historically and psychologically, it is a fundamental human trait to evaluate, adopt, or avoid an idea based upon whether it builds or depletes our sense of personal agency. "A living thing," Nietzsche wrote in *Beyond Good and Evil,* "seeks above all to *discharge* its strength— life itself is *will to power* . . . "† The difficulty is in making our choices wisely, and ethically.

I know how far I am extending my chin by quoting Nietzsche. I

Book Week, April 9, 1967.
†Walter Kaufmann and R.J. Hollingdale translation, 1968.

sound like a dorm-room libertine. A critic once accused me of harboring an adolescent wish to power. To that charge, I accede—but with a catch. I do believe in universal reciprocity, an indelible oneness of existence, and I operate from a ground rule of nonviolence. By that, I do not mean abstention from self-defense but rather an unwillingness to violate the sanctity of another's search, to knowingly do anything that would deprive another of his or her own pursuit of highest potential. And since the political question is never far away, I will note that my policy preferences run to a mildly redistributive social-democratic state with single-payer healthcare, labor unions, and consumer protections with teeth.

As alluded, sensitive people often deny or overlook their power-seeking impulse, associating it with the tragic fate of Faust or Lady Macbeth. It can be argued, however, that all of our neuroses and feelings of chronic despair, aside from those with identifiably biological causes, grow from the frustrated expression of personal power. We may spend a lifetime (and countless therapy sessions) ascribing our problems to other, more secondary phenomena—without realizing that, as naturally as a bird is drawn to the dips and flows of air currents, we are in the perpetual act of trying to forge, create, and sustain, much like the ancient alchemist or wizard.

The ultimate frustration of life is that, while we seem to be granted godlike powers—giving birth, creating beauty, spanning space and time, devising machines of incredible might—we are bound to physical forms that quickly decay. "Ye are gods," wrote the psalmist, adding "but yet shall die as princes." Immortality and the reversal of bodily decline is the one magic no one has ever mastered. The wish to surpass the boundaries of our physicality is behind some of our most haunting myths and parables, from the Trojan prince Tithonus, to whom the gods granted immortality but trapped in a shell of misery and decay for failing to request eternal youth, to the doomed scientist Victor Frankenstein, who sought the ultimate alchemy of creating life, only to bring destruction on everyone around him.

We live in a sphere of limitations. But we cannot desist from pushing against its limits. It is our heritage.

Many of us grew up learning the story of humanity's fall from grace in the biblical parable of the garden of paradise, where the serpent—long associated with the Great Adversary (a guest who will soon be arriving)—seduces Eve, and then she Adam, into eating forbidden fruit from the Tree of Knowledge of Good and Evil. But take a fresh reading, or a first reading, of the sparsely detailed chapter three of Genesis. When revisiting this familiar story in virtually any translation, you will see not only that the serpent's argument is based in truth—the couple does not perish for eating the apple, and their eyes are, in fact, opened to good and evil (indeed, some scholars contend that the garden's two trees, the Tree of Knowledge of Good and Evil and the Tree of Life, are the same)—but also that Eve, contrary to a shibboleth about feminine nature, does not seduce Adam, who requires little coaxing. The serpent even suggests, as augmented in other texts, that Yahweh displays cruel hypocrisy by forbidding intellectual illumination, even as its availability sits in the garden's midst.

We are taught, too, that the denouement of Eve's misstep was her son Cain slaying his brother Abel. But Cain's tragic act of fratricide may reflect, in discomforting realism, the unavoidable consequence of creativity: friction. Competing ideologies and the wish to measure and evaluate may be the inevitable cost of awareness. But without the rebel, the malcontent, the usurper—the snake in the garden—how could humanity claim sentience?

Lord Byron used his 1821 drama, *Cain,* one of the poet's most alluring and under-appreciated works, to take the marked brother's side. He also introduced the most jarring literary re-conception of Lucifer next to Milton's. Byron's antihero, who befriends the rebellious Cain, is persuasive and penetrating in his denial that he was the serpent in the garden, yet he points out that the serpent greeted Eve as a sexual and political emancipator—an outlook embraced by many proto-feminists and political radicals of that century and the next. Byron's dark lord is a fiery optimist on the side of the malcontents: "I know the thoughts / Of dust, and feel for it, and with you."

I began to question whether the forces of creation with which I most identified—whether parabolic or metaphysical—were these same forces of Promethean defiance. Forces of aspiration who rallied to the cry of the demon Moloch in *Paradise Lost:* "Hard liberty before the easy yoke."

Now, one could ask: why think of any of this other than in material terms? Why not put away my *Bhagavad Gita* in favor of *Atlas Shrugged?* Because, as noted, I believe that truth is not contained within flesh and bone alone. I think we participate in an existence that exceeds the five senses. And I believe that our ancient ancestors were correct in deifying certain energies and understanding oneself in relation to them; they gave them names like Thoth, Hermes, Minerva, and Set. Hence, I began to take a long and considered look at such an energy, to which I have been alluding but have not yet named: Satan. This term has its own complicated past, it has gotten me cast out of a garden or two myself, but I employ it both to acknowledge its colloquial primacy and as a bow to bluntness.

There exists a rich and underappreciated counter narrative of humanity's encounter with what is called "Satanic" in Western life particularly, but not only, in the literature of the Romantics. This countercurrent of spiritual, political, and cultural history—and present—has been insufficiently understood, historically confused, and blurred by entertainment, conspiracy theorists, sensationalism, and fraud, such as the Satanic Panic of the 1980s.

I only wish that the Satanic Panic could be considered part of the past. With the fantasies of QAnon, we are a whisker away from a return to that awful irrationality. I wrote the following in 2020 in a new introduction to *The Temple and the Lodge,* Michael Baigent and Richard Leigh's history of the Knights Templar:

> The destruction of the Templars in the early 1300s serves as a reminder that powerful institutions often project their flaws onto weaker ones, which allows the powerful to persecute the vulnerable for the former's faults or selfish interests.

The Templars played a major role in the Crusades, both financially and martially. But when those conflicts ended in the late-thirteenth century, the Knights' purpose as a combat and financial order was unclear. The French monarchy and the Vatican regarded the Templars as a potential rival. In a push to reassert control over banking and military mechanisms, the papacy decimated the knights with accusations of heresy, leading to forced confessions, jailing, and, in many cases, torture and death.

For generations, this kind of religiously sanctioned persecution was directed against many of Europe's outsiders, in particular Jews, accused witches, Romani, and gnostics. The more lurid accusations against the Templars included infanticide, sexual perversions, ritual abuse, and the worshiping of a disembodied head called Baphomet (probably a mangling of the name Mohammad but later associated with the sabbatic goat and, sometimes, the figure of Satan). This catalogue of accusations got recycled over time, most recently in the "Satanic abuse" scandals that swept the U.S. and England in the 1980s.

During the Satanic Panic, everyday people—some with occult ties and tastes but most with none—got smeared by religionists, local authorities, and self-styled experts with trumped up charges of ritual and child abuse, in many cases leading to shattered lives and sometimes criminal prosecution. As in earlier eras, it is worth noting the surrounding social circumstances: traditional institutions, including the Catholic Church and the Boy Scouts of America, were denying and underreporting cases of child abuse within their ranks, while defenseless librarians who practiced Wicca had to fear for life and livelihood.

One of the historical lessons of the Templars is: whenever a wave of accusation is directed against a marginalized group, look for antecedents within dominant institutions, whose ills often get displaced onto more vulnerable segments of society. This is tragically playing out today in violence against accused witches in economically strained parts of the world. As I write these words during the 2020 pandemic, the need for vigilance is all too clear.

My wish, then, is to encourage a second look where we are not supposed to be looking—that is, to take a more unadorned, elucidating, and even hopeful perspective on the Satanic. Milton has Satan say: "The mind is its own place, and in it self/ Can make a Heav'n of Hell, a Hell of Heav'n." Again, Satan is an optimist. Me too. No cards under the table: my journey—and perhaps yours—includes constructively wondering whether my search for a personal, spiritual, and ethical philosophy (as alluded earlier, I have one—and it is vital to me) lies east of Eden, or within what is popularly but incompletely called the "dark side." That is what I have been describing.

Darkness is not a void; it is a womb. And in the territory of truth and consensual experiment, there exist no boundaries of exploration.

4

IS YOUR MIND A
TECHNOLOGY FOR UTOPIA?

This article began as a talk I delivered at Hauser & Wirth Gallery in New York City on February 21, 2018. I especially liked the evening, organized by Morbid Anatomy, because its program included speakers from both occult and Christian perspectives. And why not? Real seekers are not divided by affiliation. This piece appeared in a slightly different form in Fall 2020 in volume 10 of The Fenris Wolf, *an artistic and occult journal edited by Carl Abrahamsson.*

We are faced today with unprecedented possibilities for how to participate in life. This includes virtual relationships, virtual sex, and the changing of one's physicality in ways that our ancestors could not have imagined. These things can be extraordinary, and I think they can be tonic to the human spirit.

Not all of us fit into conventional, biological intimate relations. Traditional relationships and gender identities are not suited to every life; hence, if someone replicates a biological relationship, whether sexual or social, in a digital, virtual reality, or robotic medium, that individual might discover alternative methods of relating that prove extraordinarily helpful and life-enriching.

Anton LaVey, writer, artist, and founder of the Church of Satan, was foresightful about the possibilities of creating "total environments," his term for self-made settings of life. Before his death in 1997, Anton was among a handful of social critics who foresaw and understood the potentials of virtual reality.

There is, of course, a negative side to all this world-making, which is that rather than playing the instrument of technology, the instrument plays us. That is the grotesque reversal of digital utopia. We see this when we discover our privacy invaded in ever-more pernicious ways. Like many of you reading these words, I have made the discomforting discovery that digital ads and promoted posts often hawk products that relate to the last thing I had been emailing or texting about. I once posted a picture on Twitter of some hoodoo candles I was cleaning out of my kitchen when it was being remodeled, and I started getting bot ads for estimates on cabinets and countertops. An innocent reveal of a more insidious problem.

Amid all of the technological possibilities and challenges facing us, however, one domain of life remains exquisitely private: the mental realm. We must not neglect a sense of the limitlessness we possess within. I believe that our mental lives hold the capacity to reshape our reality at least as much as technology, and I call for a renewed sense of revolutionary possibility in exploring the causative properties of thought.

Earlier generations thrilled over the prospect that a mental act could out-picture in concretized experience. They called it New Thought, among other names, none of them very appealing, such as the power of positive thinking, mental science, and the Law of Attraction. Our generation calls it The Secret. I contend that whatever these mind-power movements may lack in scholarship and aesthetics, they conceal in worthy and practical ideas, which deserve personal experimentation.

Rather than accept any preconceived opinion about such material, often echoed within your peer group or comfort media—which epitomize the insights of "a little learning"—I urge you to take a fresh look, or a first look, at ideas about the formative agencies of the mind. You will find something unexpected.

EXTRA-PHYSICAL TECHNOLOGY?

The question of whether the mind possesses the capacity to make things happen beyond cognitive and motor function involves searching for an extra-physical technology. That search found its most popular expression in America beginning with the New England mental healing movement of the mid-to-late nineteenth century. Yankee seekers from various walks of life wondered whether directed thought, visualization, affirmations, meditations, and prayer could function as a kind of science of mind, capable of producing repeatable and reliable results.

Of course, the ideas and movements to which I am referring are not supposed to be taken seriously by serious people. Rather, a historian is, almost by rote, supposed to speak and write sardonically about such things, lending them only enough notice to say that such notions typify the withering of the American intellect, and sap the individual of his capacity for critical thought, stoicism, political action, and engagement with the grit of daily life. I am aware of that critique, and I sometimes debate those who proffer it.

Although I share critics' concerns that our national psyche is suffering from coarseness and an alarming lack of depth, I break with the contention that the end user of positive-mind metaphysics is fickle, delusional, or unrewarded in his efforts. That conclusion is largely unexamined. In actuality, there exists an undervalued and often unknown counter-record in our culture, in the form of decades of personal testimony, which captures something of the practical experience of many people who attempt these methods. The testimony of seekers is one of the only ways of actually studying the impact of metaphysics on conduct.

About twenty years ago, I personally became very interested in New Thought philosophy, particularly questions of whether, and to what degree, the mind possesses causative abilities, and whether, and under what circumstances, a person's directed thoughts, visualizations, affirmations, and prayer can alter or augment his experience. To be clear, I reject the notion that life is subject to one mental "super law" or Law of Attraction. We live under many laws and forces.* But mind causation may be one, and I am determined to explore the question as a historian and seeker; I consider myself a "believing historian," and personal experience is part of my approach.

Perceived correlations in daily life between thoughts and events could, of course, be attributed to what social scientists call confirmation bias, wherein you get what you are looking for (or put differently, organize data and perceptions in ways that conform to expectation). Yet the record of testimony has not only grown and expanded, but, in certain cases, has proven testable in an ever-thickening stream of studies in cognition, placebo response, neuroplasticity, and psychical research, even if we do not understand the mechanism at work. In this short space, I will not get into the more contentious area of quantum theory, as I have in my books *One Simple Idea* and *The Miracle Club;* but suffice to say the ideas emerging from eighty years of quantum experiments about the manner in which observation impacts what appears and where on a subatomic scale have placed us before questions about human nature that are as revolutionary as when the Victorians first encountered Darwin.

STUDYING THE STRANGE

In recent years, I have been influenced by the spiritual teacher Jiddu Krishnamurti (1895–1986). He emerged from the Vedic tradition but was an unclassifiable voice. In his 1964 book, *Think On These Things,* Krishnamurti observed that the greatest impediment to self-development and independent thought is the wish for respectability. Nothing does more to stunt personal experiment, he wrote, than the certainty that you must follow the compass point of accepted inquiry. Once you grow fixated on

---

*Today I would put it, "We experience many laws and forces." It is possible that consciousness or awareness is the ultimate arbiter of reality, a theme explored elsewhere. But the *experience* of multiple laws, including physical limitation, is indelible to our existence.

that compass point, nearly everything that you read, hear, and encounter gets evaluated on whether it moves you closer to or further from its direction. This makes independent inquiry extremely difficult for many academics and journalists. Now, this doesn't mean that you should not have high standards and ground rules, or that you abandon discretion. Not at all. But it must mean that you do not determine or prejudice your inquiries based on how they will reward your reputation.

As a chronicler of metaphysical experience, I decided several years ago to ask myself: What if I were to turn back the layers on the modern effort to arrive at a utopia of the mind? And what if, in turning back these layers, I were to study the experiences of both seekers and critics, holding neither innately above the other, nor accepting the materialist preconceptions in which I was educated? That is to say, I would not accept as a foundation the various opinion-making literature that has often dismissed occult history. Rather, I would leave myself to ask simply, and in an informed manner: How do I know what is here? How do I know what I am going to find? I have my own unavoidable prejudices and preferences, of course, but this was my effort.

Now, I noted that Americans began experimenting with mind-power ideas in the mid-nineteenth century. This was the dawn of the positive thinking movement. But the concept of mind causation, in the broadest sense, has been around for a long time, and has been expressed in diffuse ways. In *Paradise Lost,* John Milton has Satan say: "The mind is its own place, and in it self/ Can make a Heav'n of Hell, a Hell of Heav'n." But it was not until the mid-to-late nineteenth century that experimenters sought to methodically test this idea. Although the language of New Thought pioneers was often mystical, many of their inquiries persist today in the fields of placebo studies and neuroplasticity, among others. This is one manner in which occult and mainstream history interweave.

I want to explore this intersection here, and what it may hold for us as contemporary people, by examining three threads of history. If properly understood, these threads might give us a little bit of a different sense of who we are, and some of the possibilities available to us. Indeed, these historical examples may induce a few readers to attempt personal experiments of their own, about which I will say more before I conclude.

MIND PIONEERS

Our first thread appears in the years immediately preceding the French Revolution, when there appeared in Paris a Swiss-Viennese lawyer and self-styled healer named Franz Anton Mesmer. Following his arrival in 1778, Mesmer became a sensation in royal courts and salons. The occult healer claimed that an invisible, etheric fluid animated all of life. He called it animal magnetism. Mesmer theorized that by placing a subject into a trance, he could manipulate the subject's animal magnetism and cure him of physical and emotional disorders.

Mesmer was popular among aristocrats who were blissfully unaware that their days were limited. In an overlooked facet of history, however, the occult healer was also popular among revolutionaries and social reformers. Some French radicals reasoned that if Mesmer's theories were correct, and an invisible etheric fluid animated us, it followed that we share in a common life and are innately equal regardless of rank or birth. Early abolitionists were similarly moved by this ideal. If, say, a nobleman and slave in the West Indies, where France maintained sugar plantations, demonstrated equal capacity to enter a trance, and each displayed the same physical susceptibility to Mesmeric methods, it stood to reason that all beings are intrinsically alike and deserving of equal rights.

What Mesmer actually discovered was not an etheric fluid, but rather, as his best students later grasped, an instinct for the subliminal or subconscious mind. That was his pioneering insight. Mesmer indirectly grasped the existence of the unconscious about a century before psychologists such as Frederic Myers, William James, and Sigmund Freud.

Yet France's medical establishment was suspicious of Mesmer. They derided him as a sorcerer, even as he saw himself in league with scientific and political progress. Taking a cue from social reformers, Mesmer began coupling his theories with revolutionary democratic ideals. He was encouraged in this by his student, the Marquis de Lafayette, the French hero of America's War of Independence. With Lafayette's help, Mesmer wrote to the war hero's close friend, George Washington, seeking permission to open teaching institutes in the revolutionary society. In a letter of June 16, 1784, stored in the Washington Papers of the Library of Congress, Mesmer told the president: "It appeared to us that the man who merited most of his fellow men should be interested in the fate of every revolution which had for its object the good of humanity."

King Louis XVI was alarmed by the growth of an occult and revolutionary subculture in France. (Protesting too much, the monarch also chafed at rumors of sexual liberties taken while patients were under trances.) Louis wanted to put an end to Mesmerism. He began by appointing a royal commission to investigate Mesmer's claims. The royal commission convened in 1784 with Benjamin Franklin as its chair. Franklin was then America's ambassador to France and a respected scientist.

In trials, the commission's investigators found that Mesmeric treatments could induce patients to convulsions and other bodily effects, from coughing blood to temporarily losing the power of speech to sensations of heat or cold, and, in a few instances, reports of comfort or cure. The panelists also noted that many patients, when blindfolded, could be induced to convulsions if they merely *thought* they were being subjected to Mesmeric methods. Hence, the Franklin commission concluded in August 1784 that Mesmer's cures were all in the mind. In its report, the committee wrote that it had proved "that the imagination alone produces all the effects . . . & when the imagination does not act, there are no more effects."

But the Franklin committee left dangling its most tantalizing observation: If the subjects' physical manifestations were in the "imagination alone," why should any effects occur at all? And what is this thing called imagination? If thoughts or imagination can produce physical phenomena, doesn't that, in itself, place us before a deepened question? On this, the committee was silent.

Today, we love talking about the prospect of conscious machines and the tipping point at which a computer develops awareness. But we are really no closer than the Franklin committee to defining consciousness, even as we seek to replicate it. I know of no definition that covers all the bases. We cannot even settle on whether consciousness is an extra-physical phenomenon or something restricted to gray matter, no more than the bodily equivalent of bubbles produced in a carbonated liquid. Most materialists would agree with the latter depiction; materialist philosopher Daniel Dennett, echoing the comic strip *Dilbert,* describes human beings as simply "moist robots."* Contrary to such views, researchers in particle mechanics, neuroplasticity, placebo reactions, and psychical research repeatedly find suggestions that intelligence, observation, and perspective affect and alter matter, both biologically and on the subatomic scale. These fields place us in front of our inability to understand consciousness and imagination, even as some engineers insist we can create it.

MIND AS MASTER?

Our second historical thread takes us away from conscious machines and revolutions to Europe in the early twentieth century. By this time, Mesmerism had traveled a jagged and winding path. Many of Mesmer's students fled France or were imprisoned or killed in the Reign of Terror following the Revolution. The master himself retired to Switzerland, where he died in 1815. In decades following Mesmer's death, his trances and theories actually grew more popular in the United States than Europe.

---

*"Philosophy That Stirs the Waters," by Jennifer Schuessler, *New York Times,* April 29, 2013.

American mystics, Spiritualists, and positive thinkers eagerly pursued questions of mind healing, and embraced Mesmer's methods.

By the late nineteenth century, the French themselves displayed new affinity for Mesmerism or hypnotism, the preferred term coined in the early 1840s by Scottish physician James Braid. Leaving behind concepts of animal magnetism and cosmic laws, hypnotists saw their treatment as a method of suggestion-based psychotherapy. The method gained popularity through the influence of France's so-called Nancy School, which promoted hypnotism as a practical form of suggestion, relaxation, and psychotherapy. From this milieu emerged one of the most unusual and influential figures from the hypnotherapeutic field: Emile Coué, a druggist and amateur hypnotist from the northwestern town of Troyes. While working at a pharmacy counter in the early twentieth century, Coué undertook informal experiments with his customers: he discovered that when he spoke in praise of a medication, his clients reported more efficacious results than those who had been told nothing.

These episodes moved Coué toward his signature achievement. The druggist believed that through the power of self-suggestion, or autosuggestion as he termed it, any individual, with nearly any problem, could self-induce the same kinds of positive results he observed in Troyes. In pursuit of a general method, Coué devised a self-affirming mantra: "Day by day, in every way, I am getting better and better." Although most people have not heard of Coué today, many still know his formula. He made his phrase famous through lecture tours of Europe and the United States in the early 1920s.

To critics, Coué reflected everything that was fickle and unsound about the Jazz Age. How, they wondered, could anyone believe that this singsong little mantra—"Day by day, in every way, I am getting better and better"—could solve anything? In a facet of Coué's career that is often overlooked, however, he demonstrated considerable insight, later validated by sleep researchers and neuroscientists, in how he prescribed using his mantra.

Coué said that you must recite the "day by day" mantra just as you are drifting off to sleep at night when you are hovering within that very relaxed state between wakefulness and sleep. Today, sleep researchers call these moments hypnagogia. It is an intriguing state of mind during which you possess sensory awareness, but your perceptions of reality bend and morph, like images from a Salvador Dalí painting. During hypnagogia, your mind is extremely supple and suggestible. Coué understood this by observation, and he deemed it the period to gently whisper to yourself twenty times: "Day by day, in every way, I am getting better and better." He did not want you to rouse yourself from your near-sleep state by counting, so he further recommended that you knot a small string twenty times and use this device like rosary beads to mark off your repetitions. He also said to repeat the same operation just at the moment when you awake in the morning, which is sometimes called hypnopompia. It is similar to the nighttime state insofar as you occupy a consciousness shadow-world and possess just enough awareness to direct your mental workings.

Coué said this routine could reprogram your mind. Was he right? Well, there is one easy way to find out: why not try it? Are you afraid of a little hands-on philosophy? He intended his mantra to serve all purposes and circumstances. But you can also craft your own simple mantra that reflects a specific desire. However, you might want to start with Coué's original to get comfortable with the practice.

The Beatles tried Coué's method and apparently liked it. References to him appear in some of their songs. In 1967, Paul McCartney used Coué's mantra in the chorus of *Getting Better:* "It's getting better all the time . . . " and the lyrics paid tribute to the healer: "You gave me the word, I finally heard/ I'm doing the best that I can." John Lennon recited Coué's formula in his 1980 *Beautiful Boy (Darling Boy)*: "Before you go to sleep, say a little prayer: Every day, in every way, it's getting better and better."

COUÉ REDUX

We now come to our third and final historical thread: placebo researchers at Harvard Medical School recently validated one of Coué's core insights. In January 2014, clinicians from Harvard's program in placebo studies published a paper reporting that migraine sufferers responded better to medication when given "positive information" about a drug.* This was the same observation Coué had made in the early 1900s. Harvard's study was considered a landmark, because it suggested that the placebo response is operative all the time. It was the first study to use suggestion, in this case information about a drug's efficacy, in connection with an active drug rather than an inert substance, and thus found that personal expectation impacts how, and to what extent, we experience a drug's effects. Although the Harvard paper echoed Coué's original insight, it made no mention of him.

I wondered whether the researchers had Coué in mind when they designed the study. I asked one of the principals, who did not respond. So I contacted the director of Harvard Medical School's program in placebo studies, Ted Kaptchuk, a remarkable and inquisitive clinician who also worked on the study. "Of course I know about Coué," Kaptchuk told me. "'I'm getting better day by day . . . ' " He agreed that the migraine study could coalesce with Coué's observations, though the researchers were not thinking of him when they designed it.

It seems clear that Coué's instincts were in the right direction. And I believe that some people have experienced genuine help through his ideas. So, once more, I invite you to disregard expectation and to self-experiment with Coué's method. We all possess the private agency of personal experiment; indeed, it may be the area in life in which we are most free. Yet we often get so wrapped up in the possibilities of digital

---

*"Altered Placebo and Drug Labeling Changes the Outcome of Episodic Migraine Attacks" by Slavenka Kam-Hansen, et al., *Science Translational Medicine*, 8 Jan 2014, Vol 6, Issue 218.

culture and the excitement of social media that we neglect the technology of thought, through which we may be able to significantly reform some aspect of ourselves or our surrounding world.

How tantalizing it is that everyone possesses the capacity to engage in the inner experiments of mental utopianism. These little attempts at revolution are your birthright: exquisitely voluntary and always available. No power source required.

PART II

Magickal Operations

What is a Magical Operation? It may be defined as any event in Nature which is brought to pass by Will. We must not exclude potato-growing or banking from our definition.

ALEISTER CROWLEY, *MAGICK, BOOK 4*

5

ANARCHIC MAGICK

Religious orthodoxy is never planned for. It enters and calcifies whenever someone determines that a spiritual outlook, practice, or approach that has worked for him must necessarily work for another—and, ultimately, deviation is considered fruitless, confused, and violative of settled truths. This process has played out in almost all institutional religions. And not in those alone. It is remarkable how easily orthodoxy settles into the alternative spiritual culture, which is supposed to exemplify its opposite. This article, which appeared on January 17, 2020, at Medium, *is a call to be freehanded (but not frivolous) in your practice.*

The greatest danger to magickal practice is orthodoxy. Orthodoxy can assert itself in surprising ways and at unexpected moments. This is a cri de coeur against orthodoxy. I call my personal system anarchic magick. And if you like my approach, I invite you to honor it by throwing away my term and using your own.

Here is the rub: our alternative spiritual culture is rife with systems, many of which I honor and practice. They go under names like sex magick, ceremonial magick, chaos magick, New Thought, spell work of varying sorts, and so on. All are focused on the same goal: tapping the powers of psychical causation, locating a medium between oneself and creative forces.

If you take a spiritual approach to life, as I do, you share my conviction that we participate in some process of mental and emotional selection (a term I prefer to manifestation). I have written elsewhere about the process of how metaphysical and magical systems may work. Those I mention above have aesthetic and sometimes intellectual differences, as well as different lineages—but all are geared toward tapping and directing one's causative spiritual power. By spiritual I mean extra-physical.

My problem with all these approaches, including the least structured of them, chaos magick, is that each assumes a set of psychological and even liturgical boundaries. This can needlessly limit and box in the individual. Consider, as an example, sigil magick, the central practice of chaos. In essence, this practice asks the individual to distill his or her desire into an abstract symbol; with the symbol as a decoy for your desire, you focus on the sigil and "charge it" in a moment of ecstasy, usually through sexual climax; then you purposefully forget all about it.

The principle is that by transferring your wish onto the sigil, you have eluded the rational apparatus of the mind. You are no longer "in desire," which is a feeling of *want,* not *fulfillment.* You allow the sigil itself, through climax, to enter into the subconscious, where it is joined to the transcendent channels of causative intelligence. Some people offer different explanations; but I think this is a fair representation of what is theorized to occur in sigil magick.

I know many gifted and capable people who report extraordinary results with this method. But, as much as I respect and admire the practice (I have a sigil tattooed on the back of my neck), I have not, as of this writing, personally experienced success with my use of it. I have wondered why. It is probably because I, and maybe you, experience difficulty with one of the key facets of sigil magick, which is *purposeful forgetting.* Virtually every guidebook and every practitioner counsels not to dwell on your desire, not to remain in a state of hope or wanting. Rather, you must transfer your desire onto your sigil and, through the process of concentrated climax, effectively satisfy your desire. This assumption is at the heart of most ritual magick.*

If you are like me, however, the imperative of *bypassing* may prove a chronic barrier. Personally, *I think eagerly and continually about my wishes.* I cannot "forget" or transfer them. It is not in my emotional or intellectual nature. Magickal partners have scolded me about this quality—but it persists. I *think,* just as the bird rides air currents, the shark hunts, or the cat roams nocturnal. It is not a barrier to be negotiated around, as New Age or Eastern orthodoxy often goes. It is my nature.

Here enters anarchic magick. I do not believe there is any sole way to approach New Thought, magick, ritual, affirmation, prayer, or spell work. Call it whatever you will; all of these methods involve externalizing and concretizing your wishes, arousing and employing the causative or selective agencies of the psyche.

Many occult writers and practitioners insist that the royal road to psychical causation necessarily involves working around, not through, the rational mind. I question that. Based on personal result and observation, I believe that we can employ these psychical energies through *consciously aware* means. Our lives are innately physical and extra-physical; five-sensory and extra-sensory; linear and infinite; material and transcendent. You are not bound by any sole method or approach in exploring and exercising the *wholeness* of your nature.

I am not taking issue with any system. A system is valuable based on its results, and on the conduct it produces. That is all. I am taking issue with any dictate about what is required to obtain the result.

Anarchic magick allows you to be you. If you are hyper-intellectual, and hence prone to dwell on your aim, or if you are emotive, or movement-oriented, prone to ponder or roam—mentally, physically, or otherwise—let no one tell you that quality is a barrier or requires

---

*I deepened my personal practice of sigil magick in 2021, experimenting with "charging" a sigil while also pursuing related methods of visualization and affirmation. I write further about sigil magick in *The Miracle Habits.*

compensation or a workaround. Why would that be so? Has that been proven in the laboratory of experience? Not for me. You can devise your own approaches, like the 10-Day Miracle Challenge, to cite one example, which encourages using all means to consciously dwell upon rather than evade your desire. Or you can utilize the practice of "sex transmutation," which involves purposely redirecting your thoughts away from physical satisfaction when aroused and toward some concrete aim.*

The point is to question and overturn every assumption in favor of whatever spiritual method provides you with functionality, variety, self-direction, and result. Anarchic magick is purposeful heterodoxy.

▲

I do poorly with timed rituals and spells. I never fully know when I will be prepared to bring passion and a sense of internal morale (call it faith) to the wish at hand. Mind and emotion united prove a powerful combination. Hence, you must remain open and ready to practice, the same way a sculptor, painter, writer, or noise artist must have his or her tools at hand for when momentum bursts into action. Spontaneous practice can be very powerful. I find it much more efficacious than stratified and orderly spells or rituals. In a previous piece on anarchic magick,† I made this observation:

> On a winter afternoon about ten years ago, I climbed to the top of a stone tower on the banks of the Charles River in Weston, Massachusetts. The Victorian-era oddity was built in 1899 to commemorate a Viking settlement that some believe Norse explorer Leif Erikson founded on the banks of the Charles around 1,000 CE.
>
> Named Norumbega Tower, after the legendary settlement, the thirty-eight-foot column had iron bars on its windows and

---

*I explore both of the aforementioned practices in, respectively, *The Miracle Habits* and *The Power of Sex Transmutation.*
†"Why the Best Spiritual Practice Is the One You Invent Yourself," *Medium,* February 13, 2018.

doors to keep out snoopers, ghost hunters, and beer-drinking high schoolers. All I knew was that I wanted to go inside. I slithered my six-foot-two-inch frame through a loose grill, discovered some graffiti left by devil-worshipping metalheads (Satan love them), and climbed a dank stone stairway to the top.

At that time in my life, I had one great desire burning in my heart: to become a writer. I had already been active in this direction, but I was not young—I was past forty. I swore from the top of that tower that I would establish myself as a known writer. I asked all the forces available to me on that frigid winter day, seen and unseen, physical and extra-physical, to come to my aid.

Something swelled up within me at that moment: I felt in sync physically, intellectually, and emotionally, and at one with my surroundings; my wish felt clear, strong, and assured, as though lifted by some unseen current. It was a totalizing experience, which went beyond the ordinary. In the years immediately ahead, I did become known as a writer—I was published by Random House and other presses, won a PEN literary award, and received bylines in places including the *New York Times,* the *Wall Street Journal, Politico,* and the *Washington Post*—publications not typically drawn to the kinds of occult topics I pursue.

My act that winter day was entirely spontaneous and spur of the moment. I did not plan or prepare for it, and I was not reciting any ceremonies, spells, or rituals from a book.

Recent to this writing, I had a similar experience in the lobby of a magnificently restored neo-futuristic hotel in New York City. I experienced a moment of utter conviction and self-unity, similar to the one I just described, about the people and settings I wish to dwell among. Something went forth from me. I am awaiting (and will report back on) the results.

▲

In anarchic magick, the world is your temple—quite literally. I believe deeply in petitionary prayer, of a radical sort. I think we have overlooked great wisdom and possibilities by neglecting the petitionary outlook of our primeval ancestors. Our ancient ancestors personified energies as deities, giving them names like Set, Minerva, Jupiter, or Kali, and sought relations with these deific beings. I consider such an approach deeply valid and intimate. (In fact, I believe the old gods are lonely and hungry for our attention—note this as a special opportunity.) I offer this exchange from a 2017 interview with the journal *Secret Transmissions:*

Q: Mythology is intimately intertwined with magic, whether it's Norse, Greek, Egyptian, Celtic or other. But let's say that you don't feel compelled to join a group ruled by a specific pantheon but are nevertheless deeply moved and inspired by these deities and want to make them a part of your spiritual life; how might that be achieved?

A: Well, to share a personal story, many years ago on Canal Street near Manhattan's Chinatown, I discovered an old office building that had a beautiful profile relief of Mercury above its entrance. Apropos of what I was saying earlier, I harbor questions about the lingering energies of the old gods.

I made a practice, for many weeks, of taking the subway to that slightly out-of-the-way place every morning before work and praying to that image of Mercury. I used to stand on the sidewalk in plain sight and pray in front of a very nice and indulgent Latin American woman who sold newspapers from on top of a milk crate in front of that building.

I don't know whether she thought I was crazy—there is a greater tolerance and embrace of occult religious methods in Latin America, so I might not have seemed very odd to her. In any case, I venerate the personage and principle of Mercury, and this was a means of expressing that, as well as petitioning favor. I felt some satisfaction, though no sense of conclusion, from this act.

I strongly believe that no one has to join anything or seek valida-
tion from anyone when conducting an experiment. Traditions arise
from experiment. I heartily encourage individual experimentation
backed up by some kind of education and immersion in the history
and practices of what you're attempting.

These are private acts to be conducted based on one's determined
sense of need, aesthetic, disclosure, and passion. Your practice of worship is exquisitely personal. You can experience worship, which I define
as self-expansion ("as above, so below"), in any setting, including a
movie. My friend Michael Muhammed Knight, a brilliant scholar of
Islam, began his conversion at age fifteen after seeing Spike Lee's
Malcolm X. "Can a film be sacred scripture?" Mike wondered. I say,
emphatically, yes. I find a similar experience apropos of the character
Abel, played by Oscar Isaac in the 2014 crime drama *A Most Violent
Year.* Abel embodies the kind of self-sufficiency and hard-won ethics
that I venerate. The movie takes me to an elevated state and opens me
to a wish. A podcaster told me that she saw qualities in artist Courtney
Love that she felt drawn to emulate, even to worship in the sense of
expanding oneself. Traditionalists be damned—I say that all this represents a legitimate spiritual act.

Most traditionalists (I use the term colloquially, not to describe the
thought movement called Traditionalism) do not know what spirituality
is. They know a system, usually one that makes them feel protected from
perceived dangers, such as irrationality or irreligiosity, and call it truth.

If I have any ancestor, it is Emerson, who wrote in his 1841 essay
"Self-Reliance":

I remember an answer which when quite young I was prompted to
make to a valued adviser, who was wont to importune me with the
dear old doctrines of the church. On my saying, What have I to do
with the sacredness of traditions, if I live wholly from within? my
friend suggested,—"But these impulses may be from below, not from

above." I replied, "They do not seem to me to be such; but if I am the Devil's child, I will live then from the Devil."

If I have an adversary, it is an English professor who wrote me several years ago to complain about the paucity of analytic notes that appeared in a small collection of Emerson's essays I had once published. He protested that it is "impossible" (he used that word) to read Emerson without analytic notes. I cannot imagine anything less Emersonian, less validating of the search. But even my Moriarty's dogmatism facilitates my search. We need polarities. To exist is to be in polarity.

In 1790, William Blake wrote in *The Marriage of Heaven and Hell*: "Opposition is true Friendship." Only through being tested, opposed, and thrown onto our hidden reserves do we get anywhere. That is what drove me to anarchic magick. Years of study within more formalized orders and systems (both alternative and traditional—I had an Orthodox bar mitzvah and later spent much time within esoteric communities) forged my conviction that every principle must be challenged, tested, and measured. Including the old saw that a teacher once used on me: "There are no shortcuts." I do not know that. Neither did he.

I noted earlier that we all have a sense of our personal nature—and such a nature should not be mislabeled as a barrier or attachment. Who is to judge what should be considered personality versus essence, inner versus outer, material versus spiritual, higher versus lower, and so on? I am not throwing out ethics or principle. Not at all. I have written widely about the necessity of soundness and purpose in how we treat others. But I am persuaded by years of experience that life, despite whatever terms we use to demarcate it, is all one thing. I can no more criticize my neighbor for the drive to attain than he can criticize my drive to express. (And I honor attainment, as well.)

▲

Now, I have often said that to throw away the rulebook you must have first mastered the rulebook. This principle appears in the process of many artists, writers, and thinkers. It has been part of my own approach. I have argued that the astrologer should know something about astronomy. The Kabbalist should possess a working grasp of Hebrew. The Tarot reader should know the authentic history of the cards (even if it challenges one's sense of romance). The witch or Wiccan should be versed, to the extent possible, in the ancient nature religions. Focus creates power and true choice.

And yet, as I was remarking to a brilliant podcaster this morning, I am loathe to create a new tollgate to experience. Efficacy is in result. Hence, anarchic magick requires only satisfactory outcome on the part of the user. I believe in an ethic of cosmic reciprocity, but that, too, is a truth that the user must forge for him or herself.

Maybe it is a little inflated, but I am touched by the declaration of anarchist revolutionary Mikhail Bakunin (1814–1876): "I cleave to no system, I am a true seeker."* I take that as the informal motto of anarchic magick.

The highest honor you can give my ideas is absorbing what is useful and throwing out the rest, including terminology. Whether I like it or not. Now go and experiment.

Michael Bakunin by E.H. Carr (Vintage, 1961).

6 (66)

GOD OF THE OUTSIDERS

"What if you are praying to the wrong God?" Of everything I have asked or written, nothing has engendered greater blowback than those words. Yet for some people this question has proven a wonderful catalyst. At the end of the day, I serve that portion of readers who pursue experimental spirituality—and meaningful risks. This article is adapted from a lecture that I delivered in New York City on March 6, 2018. It was an important talk for me, as it represented my first public presentation and revisioning of Satanism as a spiritual, ethical, and intellectual path.

"Thou hast conquered, O pale Galilean;
the world has grown grey from thy breath"

ALGERNON CHARLES SWINBURNE,
HYMN TO PROSERPINE, 1866

I am grateful to my hosts tonight because, I can assure you, there are places and venues that did not want to sponsor a presentation of this nature. Some people urged me to change or soften the theme. But actually, I want to be blunt about what we are exploring—which is historical, spiritual, and philosophical Satanism as a personal path. I realize how fraught that topic is, and I hope that I am able to get across a more historically and esoterically integral iteration of my theme than what has traditionally become attached to it.

In fairness, I must be clear that when I use the term Satanism, I am not using it as a metaphor for the psychological shadow or for something indirect. I am speaking about a spiritual path centered around the figure historically known as Satan or Lucifer. This figure appears in many myths throughout the Western and Eastern world under different names. But we in the West often use the Hebrew-derived name Satan, *Shaitaan,* or adversary, or the Latin-derived term Lucifer, or lightbringer. I must add that I do not make a distinction between those two entities, Satan and Lucifer. I am aware that some people do, and I have friends in certain magickal and esoteric orders to whom it is important to use the term Lucifer, which they see as a more productive framing. I respect that entirely, but I do not find it a philosophical necessity. I do not think one needs to apologize for using those terms.

But one does need to be clear. I have offered you a definition that is plain: when I use the term Satanism I am talking about veneration of Satan. But *what is Satan?* That is the key rub. That is what causes friction. That is what causes controversy. The question—what is Satan?—is the crux of what we are going to consider. Because it is my contention that our definitions of the Satanic and of the Luciferian in the West are completely insufficient.

There is an esoteric history behind the Satanic, which I think the mainstream culture has failed to appreciate. Very often when people say that Satanism is synonymous with evil or violence or destruction or cruelty or lies, my first question is: where are those premises from? Are you drawing that from entertainment? Lots of movies like *The Exorcist* and others have value, but those things are entertainment. They are not informed by definitions that I would organize my life around as an ethical and creative being.*

---

*In fairness, I noted earlier that cinema can serve a spiritual function, which depends on what it evokes in the individual. But this requires an experience of engagement and search, not passive acceptance.

Another subset of people will say that their definitions come from Scripture. My response is: do your ideas of Satan really come from Scripture? Because references to the Satanic in Scripture are brief, fleeting, and often ambiguous. The most famous such reference is the story of the serpent supposedly seducing Eve in Genesis 3. And this lands us into the fallen state we occupy today. We are told that Eve eats fruit from the Tree of Knowledge of Good and Evil, and gives it to Adam, who in the text did not need any apparent coercing—contrary to myth, Eve did not seduce Adam. Their eyes were opened and God expelled humanity from paradise.

That is one reading of the story. There is never any statement, in fact, that the figure of the serpent is Satan. It was only later on that some of the writers in the Hebrew tradition, and writers in the Christian tradition, often post-Scriptural, began to use the Hebrew term Satan, or adversary, as synonymous with the serpent.

You can comb through Scripture and find just a handful of references to that supposed maleficent force. It appears fleetingly in Isaiah (probably referencing the king of Babylon), fleetingly in Revelation, fleetingly in Genesis, receives a brief mention in Job, and receives brief references in the Gospels. If you were to actually take all the references from Scripture that are conventionally thought of as defining the Satanic, you would come up with maybe a hundred lines, and most of those would be clothed in ambiguity.

For example, Eve is supposed to have eaten from the Tree of Knowledge of Good and Evil. But it is not entirely clear to Bible scholars whether the Tree of Knowledge of Good and Evil and the Tree of Life, both of which are referenced in Genesis, are two distinct things or are one and the same. One of the earliest exponents of the "one tree" theory was German theologian Karl Budde (1850–1935), followed by Bible scholar Claus Westermann (1909–2000), both traditional figures and highly recognized in their field.*

---

*E.g., see *The Eden Narrative* by Tryggve N. D. Mettinger (Penn State University Press, 2007).

Wouldn't it be extraordinary if the Tree of Knowledge of Good and Evil and the Tree of Life were both one thing? What kind of existence were Adam and Eve conscripted to in so-called paradise, what kind of life were they granted, if they had no knowledge of good and evil? In such a state, they did not create. They did not produce. It is also true that they did not have friction. They ate from the tree, they were expelled from Eden, and they begat two sons, Cain and Abel. Differences were introduced into the world. Cain acted out in anger at his brother with whom he had deep fissures. His brother was pious and theological and favored by God. Cain was independent and a loner and a rebel and was unsuited to worship. Cain loved his brother Abel (passions arise from intimacy) yet had deep differences with him, because their mother and father had eaten from this Tree of Knowledge of Good and Evil. Cain did something he regretted for the rest of his life: acting in rage, he slew his brother.

Yet at the same time, if knowledge of good and evil had not been introduced into the world by this adversarial force represented by the serpent, then not only would there have been no differences between Cain and Abel, but in a very distinct sense there would have *been no Cain and Abel* because everything and everyone would have been classified by a certain sameness. What would be the purpose of creation in the absence of distinctions of measurement, of production and counter production, and even of friction, which inevitably arises from choice?

It is possible to approach Genesis 3 from a different perspective. It is not a Jewish book or a Christian book—those are early-modern terms. It is, like all primeval mythical works, a parable of human development. That does not exclude the spiritual or extra-physical, but all great spiritual works are the product of humanity seeking its origin and purpose. If we approach Scripture that way, we can detect through history a slender thread of insight, from antiquity up through our own time, that reads a compellingly different perspective into our foundational Western myth.

Seen from this standpoint, the serpent was the great liberator of

Eve. The serpent was Eve's emancipator. Many proto-feminists in the nineteenth century, and others during the Romantic age, did, in fact—as artists, rebels, and political agitators—view Satan as a kind of philosophical grandfather.* They saw Satan in league with certain readings in Romantic, anarchist, and socialist literature, not as the enemy of humanity, but as the rough liberator of humanity. (You can learn more about this in my multimedia presentation *God of the Outsiders,* which I delivered in 2019 in New York and Los Angeles; both versions appear on YouTube.)

There were Romantic poets, including Lord Byron, Percy Bysshe Shelley, Mary Wollstonecraft Shelley, and, as a kind of precursor to them, William Blake, who identified with the figure of Satan as the actual creator or co-creator of humanity. Not as a biological fact, but as an intellectual fact—as the bringer of the arts, of the sciences, and as the archetypal hero who rejected conformity, who rejected that which was handed down. You can find a fascinating esoteric storyline that runs through parts of Western culture, including within the traditions of gnosticism.

The Romantic poets offered a particularly powerful expression of this esoteric perspective. They understood Satan not as the seducer of Eve but as a truth-bringer. Because if you look at these few lines in Genesis 3 and 4, which have come to form the moral foundation of Western life, you will see that Satan, as the adversarial energy later came to be known, actually told Eve the truth. Satan asked: what kind of God wants to keep you from your intellectual potential, wants to keep you from making the same distinctions that he makes and that his angels make? What kind of God would plant a Tree of Knowledge of Good and Evil, a Tree of Life, the two being synonymous, in the midst of paradise, only to tell you that you cannot eat from it? What kind of

---

*Useful and compelling overviews appear in *Satanic Feminism* by Per Faxneld (Oxford University Press, 2014) and *The Devil's Party: Satanism in Modernity* edited by Per Faxneld and Jesper Aa. Petersen (Oxford University Press, 2012).

paradise prohibits measurement, evaluation, and growth? What kind of God would tell you that if you eat from the tree you will die? None of these things are true, the serpent told Eve. And they did not die. They did gain knowledge of good and evil. The fruit apparently tasted good because, however much this trope has persisted in Western culture, Eve did not seduce Adam into eating the apple.

For millennia, women have been culturally treated as guileful, counter-truthful figures, and subjected to horrific persecution during the witch craze—which persisted in Western and Eastern Europe for centuries—based on this unwarranted ur-myth that Eve seduced Adam. Eve simply offered him the fruit, and he ate it. He then possessed knowledge, and she was no longer just a physical adjunct to him created out of his rib, but was a thinking, dynamic, choice-driven individual. This is why when feminism, anarchism, socialism and other causes formed into a radical body politic in the early-to-mid nineteenth century, there were many reformists, artists, political rebels, and so on, including the Romantics, who selected Satan as a kind of political forefather.

So, when I say that Satanism is the veneration of Satan—and I want to be very direct that I am not trying to hide that—it is vital to understand what definition and perspective I am operating from. Again, we have a definition of Satan from entertainment. And we have definitions from the standard Western storyline. But we also have an esoteric insight, which I have been briefly describing, and which reads a whole different story into the myth of Satan. And myths are, of course, repositories of great truth. People throughout history codified psychological insights, metaphysical insights, and insights into human nature into myths. A myth may not be historically true but it is ultimate truth.

We all know the Greek myth of Icarus, who flew too close to the sun and fell to earth. We all understand that this parable contains a verity of human nature. It warns of hubris. Our greatest truths are couched within myths. So, I do not use the term myth as a synonym for falsehood. A myth is a portrait of truth. This can include spiritual truth. When I say spiritual, I mean extra-physical. The basis of my belief system is that there exists a facet of life that goes beyond the physical. Not everyone who claims the name of Satanist agrees with me. Many of my friends in the Church of Satan, which was founded by Anton LaVey in 1966, and of which I am not a member, consider Satan a metaphor for the highest potential of human will; many would not agree with me that there is an extra-physical aspect to life.

There is another organization founded by a brilliant man named Michael Aquino (1946–2019) who broke off from the Church of Satan in 1975 and started the Temple of Set. Aquino's perspective is more of an occultic Satanism. In general terms, you could say that there exists a materialist Satanism, which views Satan as a kind of allegorical figure, and an occultic Satanism, which views Satan as an actual force that can be appealed to.*

My sympathies are more in the direction of occultic Satanism because I do believe in an extra-physical dimension of life. I am going to say more about that but I must add that I also believe that both those paths do not run perpetually parallel but converge. I think they converge because we are always using terms in the West to describe things that we cannot see, whether psychological or metaphysical, but that seem palpably real to us. Show me the ego. Show me consciousness. Show me awareness. Show me inner. Show me outer. Show me personality. Show me essence. These are all just terms that we attach to experiences and about which we generalize. We reach a cultural consensus and roughly agree on what they mean. I cannot prove to you that some kind of nonphysicality exists. I could probably talk about ESP experiments and other things that point us in that direction. I could probably talk about some things in quantum physics that are very suggestive that the mind or human awareness is a palpable force, which goes beyond the local. But I am not going to be able to demonstrate to you in immediate terms that there is some nonmaterial existence, although that is my conviction.

---

*A more recent, and socially impactful, Satanic organization is The Satanic Temple, which aligns with atheistic or materialist Satanism and has become a powerful defender of First Amendment rights.

I do believe that there is a nonphysical approach to life, which can complement the physical, and that is important to me for the following reason: I am interested in all kinds of metaphysical philosophies. I am interested in New Thought or mind metaphysics. I am interested in a very wide variety of outlooks and all of them are oriented toward heightening the individual's abilities through some kind of appeal to, or awareness of, agencies that exceed motor function and cognition.

I think that we have all faced tremendous frictions and difficulties in life. All of us have things in our past that are cripplingly difficult. We have things within us that we seem unable to find an antecedent for. You can be in therapy all your life and talk and talk, and there are still certain aspects of character that seem to elude analysis. And sometimes the individual just feels broken down. I do believe there is some modicum of unseen help at such moments. That has been my personal experience. That has been the testimony and experience of countless numbers of sensitive people over millennia. We are broken and we are driven to our knees sometimes by psychological, emotional, and physical difficulties. Circumstances batter us. But I do believe that we are not completely bereft of assistance. I do not think we have been entirely set loose on an ocean of circumstance.

I was brought to a particular question about this, and I want to put that same question to you. It is a question for you just to hold. This is not something that you have to disclose or talk about. It is an intimate question—and it is just for you. It is for you to take home and to hold over the next week or whatever period of time is meaningful to you.

I wish for you the same thing that I wish for myself, which is that this question becomes one of the most pivotal and meaningful in your life. I am not exaggerating, because I would never exaggerate to people who have given me their valuable attention for this fixed period. Everything in life could seem to you as a kind of "before and after" pivoting on the axis of this question, which I am going to put to you in just a moment.

As a short preface to what I am about to offer, let me note that

William Blake produced a very beautiful work of epic verse with a portfolio of paintings called *The Marriage of Heaven and Hell,* in 1790. In *The Marriage of Heaven and Hell,* Blake assembled the "Proverbs of Hell." It makes exciting, stimulating reading. One of the maxims that Blake uses is: "One Law for the Lion & Ox is Oppression."

Blake was attempting, among other things, to validate the existence of polarities in our lives. This is what he called "the marriage of heaven and hell." This is what brought me to this inquiry and to the question I was referencing—which I now put to you. I ask you to consider it carefully, regardless of whether it squares fully with your perceptions or your language. Do not get hung up on terms. Just hear the essence of what I am putting to you. It is very simple:

What if you are praying to the wrong God?

What if you are praying to the wrong God? What if there exists an extraordinary wellspring of help for you as an artist, as a person who wants to get things done in the world—which to me is sacred—and you may be able to avail yourself of that help by turning on its head the spiritual maxim, *Thy will be done,* to its Satanic opposite, *My will be done?* And what if there is an extant force, call it Satan, call it Lucifer, call it whatever you please—we live by myths and I use those terms—that can be appealed to on these grounds? The ancients deified or personified energies. I am talking about experimenting with that same approach, about petitioning the radically individualistic energy that we have never been able to fully codify, and that goes under the Abrahamic term Satan.

You do not have to join anything. You do not have to pay anybody. You do not have to declare yourself a member of anything. I am not a member of anything. I do not recruit for anything or anyone. What I am describing belongs to the sanctity of your private life, with rituals, prayers, maxims, affirmations, reading, and exploration that *you* devise. Because I am telling you there *is* a counter-tradition that you can find in the form of very precious threads and fragments, which I think of as an illuminated Satanic tradition. Just threads and fragments, which you can research, look at, and use to your own ends.

And what are your ends? You have things you want to accomplish in life. I believe that is the highest sacred expression that a human being can make. Many of you reading these words are artists. All of us are in relationships. We have financial lives. We have creative lives. We have things that we want to do. What do you want to do?

Eve did not want to sit around all day barefoot in a garden, so to speak; she made a decision. She made a decision and she became an extraordinary individual. In so doing, she is the hero of Genesis. And, yes, there was pain. Something I wish for no one. Friction did enter into the world. That may be the cost of creativity and sentience. Would we be human without it?

Now, some of the people encountering this material may say that if you engage in the experiment I am proposing, you are going to get "possessed." You are going to give yourself over to the dark side. I must tell you that I take people's ethical objections very seriously. I am not a glib person. I care deeply about people's ethical lives. And if somebody confronts me with an ethical argument, I want to hear it. But I have found that the key foil of human nature, the key brokenness within human nature, is the persistent drive to tell other people what to do. When people object to your spiritual or ethical or artistic or individual path, most of the time they do not want to be heard; they want to be heeded. They want you to do what they are telling you to. And that is where most conflicts begin; most people could not care less about truth or ethics, so long as you are doing what they want you to. They do not have an ethical or religious position. They have a demand.

The central tenet of Christianity is to love your neighbor and love your enemy. So, if Satan is the great enemy, what would follow from a Christian perspective? But in reality—and you can see this on social media and elsewhere—people start out arguing from a Christian perspective, and the moment they detect resistance, the moment you answer back or make a counterargument, they grow angry. And I am not picking on Christians at all. It is human nature. It is in me, it is in them, it is in all of us. People rarely walk around with ethical or principled positions. They walk around wanting to tell you what to do. And you do not have to listen to them.

People tell me sometimes that if you read Anton LaVey's *The Satanic Bible,* it will open you to possession. And I must tell you very frankly, and I say this as a friend, I am not the least bit frightened of that. The only thing that scares me is that my search or your search will not produce anything. What I fear is that maybe there is no Bigfoot hiding in the woods, so to speak, and I must contend with that. Maybe the materialists are correct. Maybe there is nothing other than flesh and bone, and the mind is just a localized phenomenon driven by the gray matter of the brain. And when it is gone, we are gone. That scares me. Although not so much that I am willing to cling to my beliefs in a wish for certainty.

In the past several years, the Vatican has more than quadrupled the number of church-certified exorcists in the United States. The number has risen from about twelve to fifty. This has been more widely reported in Great Britain than it has in America.* People in Britain are wondering what is going on in America—why are so many exorcists being certified? Now, I have never witnessed what I consider a demonic possession. I have never personally met anyone who related such a story to me who I felt prepared to hand my trust to. I would never deny that it is a strange world, and there are a lot of strange things going on, of which we have only the foggiest notions. So, I would never present some sort of a rejectionist analysis.

But I will offer the following observation: historically speaking, in the history of religion, in the history of religious literature, and in most of the stories that people tell and pass around, including stories that you happen upon online, those who claim to have experienced or witnessed some sort of demonic possession were not seeking what we call Satan. Usually, they were either very religious people, or they

---

*"Leading U.S. exorcists explain huge increase in demand for the Rite—and priests to carry them out" by Rachel Ray, *Telegraph,* September 26, 2016.

were innocent bystanders, and something tragic and chaotic happened to them. But the tradition that I am talking about involves people actively seeking Satan and the so-called dark side. Yes, the dark side. The womb is dark. The night sky is dark, which allows the human eye to see the cosmos. The dark is nurturing. If you have ever had trouble sleeping, you know full well that ambient light is disruptive. We need the dark.

Those of us who go looking for the dark, looking for the Satanic, looking for the Luciferian, provide very little record of so-called possession; there are very few such individuals in history who describe any sort of possession or negative encounter.

And, yes, there are all kinds of stories that someone's kids started listening to Ozzy Osbourne or Judas Priest and then got possessed, and so on. Ozzy is a Christian. Black Sabbath, a band that I love, is completely and always has been a Christian band lyrically. In any case, I do not believe those stories. I think they are propaganda. I think they are the lowest kind of urban legend or, worse still, they are devices to dislocate family responsibility onto cultural tropes. Ultimately, such stories serve to proscribe the human search, and that to me is evil.

▲

Some people ask: where is the role of ethics within a Satanic or Luciferian outlook? The role of ethics for me is that the only evil, and the ultimate evil, is proscribing or limiting or violating another individual's pursuit of his or her highest potential. Anything that visits a forced limit upon an individual, whether because of their community, where they come from, who they are, how they identify themselves, or just because they are isolated and vulnerable—anything that visits limits on the development of the individual—is to me an act of violence. It could be physical violence, emotional violence, political violence, or what have you. I do not believe in anything that limits the right of the individual to explore his or her highest human potential, provided it does not curb another's parallel right. That, to me, is the ethic of Satanism.

I think there are other ethics that one could speak of, including loyalty. Loyalty is an almost lost virtue in our time. Loyalty is a word that we should be using more. Of course, whenever you invoke loyalty people object and ask: well, do you mean if you work for Hitler, you should be loyal to him? I reject those kinds of framings. Because most of us, most of the time in our day-to-day lives, never confront questions of ultimate evil. Most people want to take every ethical or philosophical discussion to its extreme. But on a daily basis, neither I nor my neighbor encounters ultimate questions of evil. To force the conversation in that direction is to evade its imperative. Loyalty should not be conflated with corruption, but with solidarity toward those who have displayed generative behavior toward you.

The real question is: what level of decency and value and integrity do you demonstrate to your own friends and colleagues? Do you keep your word? If you promise somebody that you are going to help him move, show up to help him move. And show up on time. If you cannot keep your word, you have nothing to offer the world. What's more, if someone is suffering, do not engage in gossip about that person, which I think is the most poisonous thing that we do to ourselves and to others. Individual loyalty is a primal ethic that we have lost sight of. And, yes, if you encounter corruption, there are other ethical questions that enter; but the kinds of corruption that we encounter are usually quite petty. And corruption, to my mind, is often self-generated. It is taking pleasure or entertainment in seeing somebody else humiliated, or seeing somebody in reduced circumstances, or gossiping about somebody. We spend unbelievable amounts of time gossiping. If you have ever gotten together with a friend and spent an hour-and-a-half or two hours gossiping, I will venture that you have had the experience of feeling physically drained afterward, almost like you are suffering a hangover or have eaten too much of something unhealthy. And then you experience a comedown, where you feel sluggish and slow and depressed, and you might even feel a sense of ennui or sadness. Gossip is bad for you. It is disloyal. It is poison. So, I think there are Satanic ethics. Loyalty is one. Keeping your word is one. And the most important is doing nothing that would deny another person his or her reach for their highest potential.

▲

I want to recommend a few things for you to read, if you feel like this journey is one that you want to take. And, again, I do not belong to any organization. I am not recruiting. I am simply encouraging this as your own path of exploration.

Michael Aquino, who is the founder of the Temple of Set, is a brilliant man, a long-time Satanist, and a retired lieutenant colonel in the U.S. Army.* Aquino made a fascinating observation, which I believe holds true for everybody who resonates with these words. He said that when you go down a path like this, you are dedicating yourself to self-development, and it gives you an artistic quality that makes you less likely to want to belong to an organization; so it is very difficult to maintain a Satanic organization because success almost militates against itself. In other words, as soon as people start finding things, they want to leave, or they want to become the leaders. His response to that was: well, bravo—if we need to be a small organization, then we will be a small organization, because the mark of success is that nobody can be contained by it. I say this not only in tribute to Aquino as a great intellect, but to underscore that this path is exquisitely your own.

I do recommend that you read the book of Genesis. Read Genesis 3 and 4 and see what you make of the creation myth of the serpent supposedly seducing Eve. John Milton (1608–1674) took those few lines and made them into his epic *Paradise Lost*. For a long time, Western culture was uneasy with *Paradise Lost*. It was banned in Czarist Russia for generations because the first two or three chapters, which I think

---

*Aquino was living when I delivered this talk. News of his death (which Aquino had apparently intended to keep private—and largely succeeded) began circulating online in 2020. According to San Francisco County records, the Temple of Set founder died at age seventy-five on September 1, 2019.

are the most alluring in the whole book, present Satan as a heroic rebel who is vanquished, who is defeated, but who rouses his troops from a lake of fire in Hell. He arranges them into a grand council, called Pandaemonium or gathering of all demons, and urges them to rise up and set themselves to a new task. He impels them to determine how they are going to create a new world in their vanquished state. And he says famously, "The mind is its own place, and in it self/ it can make a Heav'n of Hell or a Hell of Heav'n." Satan is an optimist.

Also read William Blake's *The Marriage of Heaven and Hell*. It is all of thirty pages. It is very stimulating, very simple reading, probably the most beautifully straightforward thing Blake ever wrote. Read the Proverbs of Hell if you are looking for ethics. If you feel that what I am describing is alluring and inspiring, but you are concerned about the ethical implications of walking away from conventional religious traditions, and you are wondering where the guardrails are, you may find them in *The Marriage of Heaven and Hell*. Blake lays out a brilliant set of ethics that you can read, live, and abide by.

Most especially, and I say this personally, read Lord Byron's play *Cain*. It is extraordinary. It is the Cain and Abel story told from Cain's perspective. Lucifer appears as a very intriguing, powerful character. Lucifer speaks to Cain about how only he, Satan, can understand the situation of the vanquished individual, of the suffering individual, of the person who lives in dust, because he has been there. He challenges a God who preaches love but sentences those who pursue violative behavior to eternal suffering.

Speaking to Cain, Lucifer disputes that he was the serpent, or that the serpent was possessed by a demon.* He says, rather, that it was Eve's independent decision to violate an absurd order against eating from an illumined tree placed in the midst of the garden. Lord Byron elevates Eve's decision; he elevates rebelliousness; his Lucifer speaks to Cain of

---

*The term demon or *daemon* was, in its original use, a Greek title for spirit; it was morally neutral and only later came to denote maleficence.

the sanctity of nonconformity and non-obedience. And yes: Cain kills his brother. As I was saying earlier, the Tree of Knowledge of Good and Evil, in our Western mythical structure, introduced choice, possibility, ideology, and ethics into the world. It also introduced friction. The tree was a polarity. Cain and Abel became bound by this polarity. Cain was the rebel, the nonconformist, the malcontent. Abel was the religionist, the moralist, the follower. He was not completely innocent, because he had a way of life to which he wanted Cain to conform, and Cain had a way of life that said: leave me alone. Friction ensued. Cain, to his everlasting sorrow, committed fratricide.

So, I ask you, and I ask myself, to put yourself in Cain's position. Consider whether there was some other possibility, whether there was some manner of life that Cain could have adopted to defend himself without resorting to violence. It is a question. Maybe they were just caught in an inevitable existential struggle. They had differing points of view and it erupted into violence. It is the human tragedy. But what would be the alternative? If Eve had never eaten from the tree, the alternative would be no humanity to speak of. Humans would hardly even be deserving of the plural case if they were just one consensus-based, averaged-out humanity—which I do not think we could even recognize and would not recognize ourselves within.

We are human and some large number of us, mythically speaking, are descendants of Cain, whether we like it or not. Abel had no bloodline. (Adam and Eve had a third son, Seth.) So, for many of you, your titular parents are Eve and Cain. What would you have done? Is it possible to live a life of self-defense that does not involve violence, that does not involve encroaching on another person?

Another work that I recommend, and which you can find online, is a short book written by Michael Aquino in 1970 called *The Diabolicon*. Aquino, as I mentioned earlier, is the founder of the Temple of Set. In *The Diabolicon*, he retells the myth that appears in the most fleeting lines in the Book of Revelation and a few other places in Scripture, which makes mostly metaphorical allusions to a war in heaven that led to the expulsion of Satan and his legions. The short book re-visions and re-pictures, according to Aquino's insights, the friction between what he would describe as a passive, hypocritical force of conformity—represented by the figure of God and his legions—versus a radical, unbending individualism and wish for growth and development, as represented by Satan and his forces.

It is a very interesting book because Aquino suggests that if you wish to devise some sort of appeal or petition or prayer to the Satanic, you need not do so in a dramatic way or on bended knee. Rather, you speak to the figure represented as Satan as a friend, as a colleague, as an equal—because he wishes for your development and your productivity. Satan did not deceive Eve, but emancipated Eve. Hence, you speak to this figure as an ally.*

▲

I briefly mentioned another organization that is central and important to the things I am exploring: the Church of Satan, founded by Anton LaVey in 1966 (which he declared the Year Zero, the year of Satan). Anton lived in San Francisco and died in 1997. He was a very media-friendly figure, instantly recognizable with his shaved head and goatee. He looked like the figure of Satan as we picture him in the popular mind. Anton was an ingenious man—and he was a tricky man. He told a reporter from the *Wall Street Journal* in 1969 that he had played the figure of Lucifer in the movie *Rosemary's Baby,* and this detail continues to be repeated in the press, up to the present day.† In fact, he invented the story and the reporter accepted it, as it was probably a believable enough claim. One thing I learned as a historian is that you must verify everything.

But it is also probably true that Anton's aesthetic, and his reframing

---

*Aquino expanded on this theme in his 1975 book, *The Book of Coming Forth by Night.*
†"Strange Doings: Americans Show Burst of Interest in Witches, Other Occult Matters" by Stephen J. Sansweet, *Wall Street Journal,* October 23, 1969. The most recent repetition of the claim that I have seen appeared in "Did the Devil kill Jayne Mansfield?" by Helen O'Hara, *Telegraph,* May 9, 2018.

of the Satanic as a religion of self-development, influenced *Rosemary's Baby* novelist Ira Levin and filmmaker Roman Polanski and others who created the movie. So, one could say that Anton told the truth in the form of a myth. His aesthetic, outlook, and intellect probably informed the events, visuals, and storytelling found within it.

I must say a special word of tribute to Anton, and to my friend Carl Abrahamsson, for exposing me to the real value of his work.* Anton was probably the first person in modern life who put forth the idea of the Satanic as an ethical and religious philosophy by which the individual could really live. *The Satanic Bible,* which was published in 1969 and has probably sold well over a million copies, is a paean to individualism, and offers a set of ethics not much different from some of what Blake explores in *The Marriage of Heaven and Hell.* Some feel that Anton's point of view was a bastardization of Ayn Rand and Nietzsche. And perhaps there is truth to that—but I ask: so what? *The Satanic Bible* is very easy to read, and in any case, most philosophy is syncretic. I think the work exposed a whole generation to ideas that it might not have otherwise encountered. I think it made a difference in people's lives.

I strongly believe that truth should be simple, and I do not believe that alluring ideas must be weighted down with excessive verbiage or introductions. I think one of the poor legacies that great lines of literature like Penguin Classics have visited upon our contemporary culture is thickly written, overly long introductions. You cannot imagine why you would want to read Mary Shelley's *Frankenstein* by the time you are done with a sixty-page introduction. Just read the work. She wrote it without an introduction. Is it really necessary to have that kind of introductory statement? I believe strongly in diving right into things.

Anton was very simple in the things that he said and did, for the most part. *The Satanic Bible* is a wonderful popularization of Nietzsche, of individualistic philosophy, and it contains Anton's own shrewd obser-

---

*I write further about Anton LaVey in my introduction to Carl Abrahamsson's *Anton LaVey and the Church of Satan* (Inner Traditions, 2022).

vations on human nature and the role of ritual. Anton is often derided as a showman, a trickster, a media sensationalist—and he was all those things. It is true that he made up his past. A Chicago native, his real name was Howard Stanton Levey. He became Anton Szandor LaVey, and that says a lot: he was a performer, he was an entertainer. He never claimed that he was not a carny; he had a trickster background. But he was also a very insightful figure and a great artist. He would provoke and push and press buttons. If you read his philosophy, you will find that it is a very life-affirming, humanistic philosophy. And although I am aware that he chose the name Church of Satan to be provocative, I deeply appreciate the straightforwardness of it. That is probably what inspires me to use the term Satanism, because I do not want to play games with people and try to disguise what I am conveying.

Satan is supposed to be the lord of lies and the lord of deception. If I were interested in deceiving anybody, I would opt for coy or opaque language. I think Anton had a way about him of combining showmanship with great ingenuousness. For all his self-mythologizing, he really did introduce into Western culture the idea that the Satanic could be a philosophical and ethical path.

Before I conclude, it is important to briefly address the media misrepresentations of Satanism, and the false notion that there is a horrible cabal of child-sacrificing, death-worshiping, cannibalistic Satanists out there somewhere. Throughout Western history and up to the present day this has existed as a complete canard—it is historically a total and utter fantasy, and I give absolutely no quarter to it.

It is important to point out that before Anton founded the Church of Satan in 1966, there really was no cohesive Satanic tradition in Western culture. There were individuals, rebellious figures who made counter-readings and esoteric readings of some of the foundational Western myths. Some of these very individualized, rebellious readings appeared in some of the literature that we have been considering. There were people like the novelist J.K. Huysmans (1848–1907) and others who wrote about black masses and related things that were largely fanciful, although they might have picked them up from self-styled Satanic occultists in turn-of-the-century culture or in some reaches of Romantic culture. But in order for there to be an overt tradition that one can speak of, there must exist a liturgy, a family tree, a foundational literature, a congregation. None of this has been true for Satanism.* Satanism is an anarchistic tradition. It is important to understand that. With regard to elements like a black mass, there is no tradition that you can point to that goes back centuries or millennia, in the same way that you can point to traditions in Buddhism, Islam, Judaism, or Christianity. The practice of Satanism is not a tradition in those terms. It never has been.

For the most part, charges of Satanism (in a negative sense) were directed by the early church fathers against the remaining bastions of pagan power in late antiquity, because the church wanted to define these people—who were on their way to being vanquished—as part of something evil and maleficent, against which military and judicial power could be directed. As the early church became more powerful, and as Christianity became the officially sanctioned religion of the Roman Empire, the fading pagan powers were depicted as demonic (again, this was once a neutral term), as Satanic. They were described in terms that they had never applied to themselves. If the pagan powers had won the struggle of ideas in late antiquity, they would have done the same thing to the church fathers. This is not about good guys and bad guys. This is about human nature. To some extent it is true that the victors get to write history, especially in matters of religion.

The irony for me, as a historian, is that I am always defending pagan antiquity and various occult figures from charges that they are

---

*I should note that one significant magickal order, Germany's *Fraternitas Saturni,* founded in 1926 and operative today, incorporates an element of "Luciferian" philosophy. This is explored in Stephen E. Flower's commendable study, *The Fraternitas Saturni: History, Doctrine, and Rituals of the Magical Order of the Brotherhood of Saturn* (Inner Traditions, fifth edition, 2018).

Satanic—because they never conceived of themselves in that way. And yet I am also describing a counter-tradition, an esoteric tradition of Satanism, that would not make any sense to the persecutors (and does not today) because they misapplied that label.

We misapply labels to people because we want to tell them what to do, or to punish them for disobedience. Hence, for most of Western history, Satanism has been a false charge, directed by victors against vanquished. That was certainly true during the hundreds of years of witch crazes that swept through Europe, where countless numbers of women were accused of being consorts of Satan and were killed. This is still going on. I have a piece in the *New York Times* called "The Persecution of Witches, 21st Century Style."* Thousands of people around the world today, very often children and women, on all continents, are accused of some sort of Satanic witchcraft and subjected to murderous violence. This occurs in West and Central Africa, in Indonesia and Papua New Guinea, in India—and there are instances in London and New York City. People, very often women, are accused of being agents of Satan, of practicing demonic witchcraft, and they are killed or violence is visited upon them in the grisliest way. In the vast majority of cases, there is no spiritual content, no magick, nothing of any mystical nature going on. It is just predators leveling a charge against somebody as a pretext for violence.

That is mostly the history of Satanism in our Western world—not violence being done *by* Satanists but violence being done *to* people accused of being Satanists. There was a media sensation during the 1980s, the so-called Satanic Panic. The storyline went that daycare workers, healthcare workers, preschool teachers, and so on were torturing kids, or sacrificing them, or inducting them into Satanic cults. It was complete falsehood. Not a fragment or thread of truth to it.† I can tell you for a fact that there were people—like many of you reading these

---

*A version of this piece appears in Part V as "The War on Witches."
†E.g., see "It's Time to Revisit the Satanic Panic" by Alan Yuhas, *New York Times,* March 21, 2021, and my "Familiarity Is Not Truth: How We 'Demonize' the Occult and Satanic," *Medium,* October 30, 2021.

words, artistic, sensitive, capable, decent people—who had these accusations leveled against them. And their lives were severely and wrongly damaged. (The Satanic Panic was probably a partial reaction to women entering the workplace en masse and families relying more on daycare employees.)

The overwhelming likelihood is that anybody who is into the Satanic is like the person sitting next to you. Yes, they have a proclivity for wearing black, which I am convinced is a positive sign. And they are of an artistic bent. They are sensitive outsiders, misfits of the best variety. I am sure many people reading these words have had some experience at a very young age of feeling out of step, out of sorts, like a square peg—and that is a wonderful thing. That is what forges individuality.

So, when people talk to you about evil or possession or Satanic abuse scandals or black masses or any of this stuff—where is this information from? What are their premises? Why should their definitions mean anything to you? Most of the time it is a set of hand-me-down ideas from books that they have never read, from articles that they have heard about somewhere, from rumors and stories that have been proffered in the form of gossip over social media or among friends, or from entertainment, which they assume has at its back some factual truth. It is fear. It is propaganda. And, above all, it is just conventional thinking—which is exactly what, from the earliest stages of our culture, the Satanic and the Luciferian have opposed.

Recall that Blake said, "One Law for the Lion & Ox is Oppression." Hence my question: *What if you are praying to the wrong God?* You may feel a terrific yearning for something that has not been satisfied by the circumscribed offerings that we are told represent the only valid spiritual choices in our society. So, I offer this to you as another choice. Something for you to explore entirely on your own.

My deepest wish for everyone reading these words is that you find something. Something extraordinary. And that something builds and asserts your will—that which is creative, that which is productive, that which is Self in you.

7

"DOWN WITH THE BLUE BLOODS"

Mind Metaphysics for Working People

Declaring yourself an adherent of "positive thinking" is a near-guarantee
of being misunderstood. But I believe in defending a principle or path
from being defined solely by its detractors. This essay, "Down With the
Blue Bloods," (a term of Neville Goddard's), draws in part on my 2018
book The Miracle Club. *It is my definition and defense of positive-mind*
metaphysics, with an emphasis on how mind-power philosophy and an
aspirational ethic have figured into my life. Aspirational and motivational
philosophies are often derided by those for whom material security is a
given; for the rest of us, no query is out of bounds.

The conventional rap on positive thinking is that it is for corporate finks (or those who aspire to be), fuels Trump-like reality distortions, and forms a therapeutic miasma that keeps working people in their place. My view is different. My story is different. And I write it from lived experience.

▲

My philosophical hero is Neville Goddard (1905–1972), an English, Barbados-born mystic, who wrote under his first name. He heard the following words in the midst of a personal vision: "Down with the blue bloods!"* To Neville, privilege did not belong to the rich, but to the truly imaginative.

Because of Neville's English background and elegant bearing, many people assumed he was born wealthy. He was not—far from it. Likewise, because of my New York background and surname, many people judged the same of me growing up. A school bus driver upon hearing that I lived in a suburban development with gaudily named streets like Royal Way and Regents Lane said, "Oh, a rich kid, huh?" A truculent writer with whom I worked once (just once) called me "college boy," inferring the same thing.

Here is the truth, of which I rarely speak: my father was a Legal Aid Society attorney in New York City who defended the poorest of the poor. For reasons beyond his control, he lost his job and profession, leaving us to consider applying for food stamps and warming our always-unaffordable home with kerosene heaters. We wore used clothes and scraped together change and coupons to pay grocery bills. There were no Hanukkah, Christmas, or birthday gifts. My sister and I would buy them with our own money, earned from odd jobs, and pretend to friends that they came from our parents. In the words of The Notorious B.I.G., "Birthdays was the worst days."

One night, in desperation, my father stole my mother's engagement ring to pay debts, over which he may have been physically threatened. (He had started carrying pepper spray.) They divorced. My older sister and I got by through after-school jobs, student loans, and the precious availability of health benefits through my mother's labor union, the 1199 hospital workers. Given the economic devastation visited on many American homes, including during the still-unhealed 2008 recession, I do not consider our story exceptional.†

But when someone assumed then, or does today, that the son of a Jewish lawyer is necessarily born on easy street, he is wrong. This brings

---

*The Law and the Promise, 1961.

†These words were written before the Covid lockdown, which disproportionately multiplied the burdens on working people.

me to something else that I rarely mention: I write these words as a millionaire. It is not because I am a hotshot media figure, bestselling author, or dealmaker. For decades in my day job, I published occult and New Age books—not your typical path to wealth. I co-raise two sons in New York City. I have no family cash cow. And yet, to draw again on The Notorious B.I.G.: "Now we sip champagne when we thirsty."

Why is that?

Because Neville, in my estimation, was correct. Wealth, to some extent, comes from within. For our purposes here, let me quote Helen Wilmans. An early-twentieth-century suffragist and New Thoughter (New Thought is the spiritual philosophy behind positive thinking), Wilmans rose from dirt poverty on a Northern California farm in the late 1890s to command a small publishing empire.

"What!" Wilmans wrote in her 1899 book *The Conquest of Poverty*. "Can a person by holding certain thoughts create wealth? Yes, he can. A man by holding certain thoughts—if he knows the Law that relates effect and cause on the mental plane—can actually create wealth by the character of thoughts he entertains." But, she added, such thought *"must be supplemented by courageous action."* Never omit that.

Wilmans's career was a New Thought parable of liberation. While working as a newspaper reporter in Chicago in the early 1880s, she became one of the pioneering female reporters of that era. Everything had gone against her in life. She was fired from jobs, divorced from her farmer husband, left to raise two daughters on her own, and lived one step ahead of eviction from her Chicago boarding house.

More than anything, Wilmans yearned to start her own labor newspaper. She wanted to bring the ideas of mind-power to working people. One day in 1882, she asked her Chicago editor if he would invest in her venture. He dismissed the idea out of hand. In despair, Wilmans ran from the newspaper offices (probably not wanting her male bosses to see her in tears) and wandered the darkening streets of Chicago on a November afternoon.

She thought to herself: *I am completely alone; there is no one on whom I can depend.* But as those words sounded in her head, she was filled with a sense of confidence. It occurred to her that she did not *have* to depend on anyone else—she could depend on the power of her mind. This was the New Thought gospel. She wrote: "I walked those icy streets like a school boy just released from restraint. My years fell from me as completely as if death turned my spirit loose in Paradise."

Like Wilmans, I had never dreamed of wealth or wanted to be surrounded by fancy things. I believe in labor unions, moderately redistributive tax policies, and personal thrift—not gross consumption.

But there is something vitally important to earning a good living, and that fact cannot be hidden or ignored. Nor can this: *your mind is a creative agency, and the thoughts with which you impress it contribute to the actualized events of your existence—including money.*

This statement is absolutely true and should never be neglected. I have tested and verified it within the laboratory of my existence. If you want money, I ask you to wholly embrace it as true. This necessary act of conviction will not, in any case, lead you to rash behavior. *It does not suggest neglecting daily obligations or loosening your hands on the plow of effort.*

AGAINST "NON-ATTACHMENT"

Someone who is thirsty needs water, not a discourse on water. If spirituality is real then it should aid in vital pursuits. Strong people acknowledge what they want, including money, and in so doing they are in service neither to falsehood nor shame.

The same holds true regarding attainment. Spiritually minded people, and all others, should honor their ambitions and pursue them openly and transparently, with due respect to colleagues and competitors. Yet this is frowned upon in many reaches of the contemporary alternative spiritual and New Age cultures. Within these worlds, we often recycle ideas from the Vedic and Buddhist traditions and use them to prop up unexamined ideas about the need for non-attachment, transcendence of the material, and the value of unseen things.

Writers who cannot decipher a word of Sanskrit, Tibetan, or ancient Japanese—the languages that have conveyed these ideas from within the sacred traditions—rely upon a chain of secondary sources, often many times removed from their inception, to echo concepts like non-attachment and non-identification. We are told that the ego-self grasps at illusions and fleeting pleasures, formulating a false sense of identity around desires, ambitions, attachments, and the need for security.

I question whether this interpretation is accurate. In recently working with the Shanghai-based translator of a Chinese publication of my book *One Simple Idea* (of which the Chinese government censored about thirty percent),* I found, to my chagrin and bemusement, that Buddhist concepts I thought I, as a Westerner, had understood, were in my retelling, completely alien to my translator's experience as someone raised within a non-Western religious framework.

Our popularized notions of the Eastern theology of non-attachment are often cherry-picked from religious structures that were, in their originating cultures, highly stratified and hierarchical. Hinduism and Buddhism, moreover, addressed the lives of ancient people for whom distinctions of caste, class, and status were largely predetermined, and who would have regarded cultural mobility almost as unlikely as space travel. There were social as well as spiritual reasons why worldly transcendence beckoned. Shorn of their cultural origins, concepts of non-attachment today sound tidy and persuasive to Westerners who understandably want something more than the race to the top. (Or, just as often, who fear they may not reach the top, and thus desire an alternate set of values.)

But this transplanted outlook is often ill fitting and brings no more lasting satisfaction to the modern Westerner than so-called ego

---

*My censored preface appears restored in Part V as "The Preface the Chinese Government Banned."

gratifications. This kind of ersatz "Easternism" has been with us for several decades, most recently popularized by writers such as Eckhart Tolle and Michael A. Singer. Yet it has not provided Westerners with a satisfying response to materialism, because it often seeks to divert the individual from the very direction in which he may find meaning, which is toward the compass point of achievement.

Some of my spiritual friends and colleagues have told me that I am too outwardly focused. Isn't the true path, they ask, marked by a sense of detachment from the outer? Doesn't awareness come from within? Isn't there, finally, a Higher Self or essence from which we can more authentically live, rather than succumb to the illusory goals of the lower self or ego, which directs us toward career, trinkets, and pleasure? I have been on the spiritual path for many years. I have sought understanding within both mainstream and esoteric movements. My conviction is that the true nature of life is to be *generative.* I believe that in order to be happy, human beings must exercise their fullest range of abilities—including the exertions of outer achievement.

Seekers too often divide, and implicitly condemn and confuse, their efforts by relying on terms like *ego* and *essence,* as though one is good and the other bad (while neither actually exists beyond the conceptual). A teacher of mine once joked: "If we like something in ourselves, then we say it comes from essence; if we dislike it, we say it comes from ego." I contend that these and related concepts, like attachment/non-attachment and identification/non-identification, fail to address the needs, psychology, and experience of the contemporary Western seeker. And, in fact, such concepts do not necessarily reflect the outlook of some of the most dynamic recent thinkers from the Vedic tradition, including the Maharishi Mahesh Yogi (1918–2008) and Jiddu Krishnamurti (1895–1986).

Let me be clear: the inner search and the search for self-expression are matters of extraordinary importance—and extraordinary mystery. I am not a Christian but I believe that the simplest and most resounding truth on the question of the inner life and attainment appears in the dictum of Christ: "Render unto Caesar what is Caesar's and render unto God what is God's." We are products of both worlds: the seen and the unseen. There is no reason to suppose that our efforts or energies are better dedicated to one or the other. Both exist. Both have veritable claims on us.

I do not view non-attachment as a workable goal for those of us raised in the West, and elsewhere, today. Rather, I believe that the ethical pursuit of achievement holds greater depth, and summons more from within our inner natures, than we may realize. "Satisfaction with our lot," Emerson wrote in his journals on July 28, 1826, "is not consistent with the intentions of God & with our nature. It is our nature to aim at change, at improvement, at perfection."

"YES I CAN"

I recently read a book that I recall my mother borrowing from our local library when I was eight or nine years old: *Yes I Can,* the autobiography of entertainer Sammy Davis, Jr., published in 1965, the year of my birth. In the public mind, Davis is remembered as a flashy, somewhat self-parodying Vegas performer—but decades before his tuxedoed stage shows, Davis was an innovative prodigy, raised on the vaudeville circuit, where he was subjected to the brutality, insults, and physical assaults that often characterized Black life under Jim Crow. These threats followed him into the army during World War II, where he used his skills as an entertainer to mitigate some of the racism around him—though indignities and violence always snared him at unexpected moments. When Davis left the military, he made an inner vow that shaped the rest of his life:

> I'd learned a lot in the army and I knew that above all things in the world I had to become so big, so strong, so important, that those people and their hatred could never touch me. My talent was the only thing that made me a little different from everybody else, and

it was all that I could hope would shield me *because* I was different.

I'd weighed it all, over and over again: What have I got? No looks, no money, no education. Just talent. Where do I want to go? I want to be treated well. I want people to like me, and to be decent to me. How do I get there? There's only one way I can do it with what I have to work with. I've got to be a star! I have to be a star like another man has to breathe.

I challenge anyone to question the drive, purpose, and canniness of Davis's words—not to challenge them from a meditation cushion or living room sofa, but from within the onrush of lived experience. Davis was viewing his life from a pinnacle of clarity. Would his worldly attachments and aspirations cause him pain? He was already in pain. At the very least they would relieve certain financial and social burdens—and probably something more. Would his attainment of fame ease his inner anguish? I think he owed it to his existence, as you do to yours, to find out. Whatever your goal may be, you cannot renounce what you have not attained. So to conclude that success, in whatever form, is not meaningful is just conjecture without first verifying it.

Do not be afraid of your aims, or slice and dice them with melancholic pondering. Find them—and act on them. Clarity is critical.

By living as a productive being, in the fullest sense, you honor the nature of your existence and perform acts of generativity toward others. If you are able, you may then determine, from the vantage point of experience and attainment, whether your aim responded to an inner need of profound meaning. I will not tell you what you will find—you may differ from me. I will only tell you that this has been the case for me.

8

SUFFERING AND THE LIMITS OF MAGICK

Originally titled "Positive Thinking in a Time of Coronavirus?," this article appeared at Medium *on April 4, 2020, during the first wave of the pandemic. I was sick and quarantined with Covid in New York City that March and April, during which time I wrote this piece.*

The question of suffering ought to haunt people like me who subscribe to New Thought, the metaphysical philosophy of mind causation. It cannot be dodged or responded to with catechism or rehearsed answers.

This came home to me several years ago while I was researching the life and work of metaphysical writer and positive-thinking pioneer Joseph Murphy (1898–1981). I came upon a cache of handwritten letters that readers had sent to Murphy's publisher, Prentice Hall, following his death in 1981. The letters originated from places ranging from Nigeria to Sweden to England to Canada to the United States.

The minister and writer Murphy attained worldwide readership in 1963 with the publication of *The Power of Your Subconscious Mind,* a book of mind metaphysics that is perched in impact and timing between Norman Vincent Peale's *The Power of Positive Thinking* (1952) and Rhonda Byrne's *The Secret* (2006).

An editorial assistant plaintively replied to many of these readers, "We regret to inform you that Dr. Joseph Murphy is deceased. Prentice Hall was notified of this in January, 1983." The editorial assistant attempted small acts of kindness, like sending one writer a Spanish-language edition of Murphy's 1968 book, *The Cosmic Power Within You*. Most of these readers had burning questions. It saddened me to encounter the needs of seekers who were reaching out to an author no longer alive to reply.

In the midst of our global pandemic—the opening weeks of which I witnessed quarantine with a mild case of coronavirus from my apartment on New York's Lower East Side—I offer one of these letters; it poses the unavoidable question about the persistence of suffering. I also present my response to the writer from across the space of a generation.

1991 (month unknown)
Billdal, Sweden

Dear Mr. Murphy,

First of all I want to thank you so much! I've just read your book: Miracle of Mind Dynamics and I feel that it has given me so much! Every word seems so right to me. I read a few pages every night before I go to sleep. I don't want to read too much at a time, since there are so many things to learn and think about on every page and besides I want something left to read.

Ever since I was young I've felt that God has done a lot of miracles for me, but since I read the book my days are bordered with miracles. I am deeply grateful and I try to show God's love to the people I meet.

There is just one thing I cannot understand and that is, why me? I mean I'm no better, nor worse than anyone else. Why so much love to me? Why are children hurt, tortured and killed. Why do so many have to starve. Are they more evil? They must also be loved by God since they too are his children.

This is so hard for me to understand—and I would so much want an explanation . . .

Lots of love,

_____

▲

Dear _____,

Thank you for your thoughtful and honest note. You pose the most sensitive question in mind metaphysics: *why me?* This question can be asked in the negative or in the positive, as you have.

I am responding to your long-ago letter during the first weeks of the Covid pandemic that has gripped the world and, in particular, my city of New York. I write you quarantined in my apartment on the Lower East Side, nearing week three of my own (thankfully mild) bout with coronavirus.

Joseph Murphy wrote about the impact of accumulated thought—of parents sometimes passing down thoughtforms to a child. He further theorized that the cumulative thoughts of humanity, extending to deep antiquity, can outpicture in our present world and in the physical life of an individual.

I accept neither of those views.

If we surmise that all the thoughts that have ever been can outpicture and cause suffering in the physical life of someone today, we more or less accept the premise of randomness, since vast and unknowable thoughts have occurred for thousands of years. Randomness contradicts the rest of Murphy's system and the purpose of New Thought in general.

If we propose that the thoughts of a parent can be visited upon a child, and can result, apropos of your concerns, in profound physical suffering or illness, I also reject that cause and effect.

I have witnessed circumstances, as I am sure you have, of a child suffering and dying from chronic disease in an atmosphere of love and support. Pointing to a parent (a ghastly proposition), or pointing to a thinker or thinkers in antiquity, seems like an effort to plug a philosophical gap, rather than respond meaningfully to suffering.

Matters get more troublesome when New Thought tries to explain chronic tragedies or catastrophes by appending ideas of karma onto positive thinking philosophy. Past-life sins, in this view, could explain why a person, or millions of people, experience painful lives or violent deaths. Such reasoning appeared in the late 1950s in the work of a widely read metaphysical writer, Gina Cerminara. Cerminara had previously done a great deal to popularize the work of psychic Edgar Cayce in her 1950 book, *Many Mansions*. In a later book, *The World Within,* deemed "one of the best books on reincarnation" by Cayce's son and collaborator Hugh Lynn, Cerminara attempted to bring a karmic perspective to global suffering. "Present-day Negroes," she suggested in 1957, might understand the roots of their racial oppression if they

> can project themselves back into the past and in imagination see themselves to be brutal English slavetraders, arrogant Virginia slaveholders, or conscienceless Alabama auctioneers, smugly assured of their white supremacy—if they can make this imaginative leap, their own present situation may seem far more intelligible and far more bearable.

Her advice continued:

> Present-day Jews who feel that they are the victims of unjust prejudice should reflect that a long racial history of regarding themselves as a "chosen people," and of practicing racial exclusiveness and pride, cannot but lead to a situation where they themselves will be excluded.

Such arguments collapse under any degree of ethical scrutiny.

Spiritual insight arrives through *self-observation*—not justifying the suffering experienced *by another.* To judge others is to work without any self-verification, which is the empirical tool of the spiritual search.

The private person who can maturely and persuasively claim self-responsibility for *his own* suffering, or endure it as an inner obligation, shines a light for others. The person who justifies *someone else's* suffering, such as through collective fault, only casts a stone. Retrofitting current spiritual or ethical conundrums onto the ancient philosophy of karma, a vast and complex thought system, is almost admitting that one's chosen outlook does not work. Yet I believe that New Thought or mind metaphysics *does* work. As a seeker, I believe that thoughts are causative.

So why do we witness mass suffering in a purportedly self-created mental universe? I venture that we live under and experience many laws and forces. Physical decline and mortality alone tell us that. Although I believe, like my intellectual hero Neville Goddard, that mind is the ultimate arbiter of reality, its effects are mitigated by circumstance.

A law, in order to be a law, must be ever operative. The law of gravity is ever operative. But you are going to experience radically different effects from gravity on Earth than on the moon or Jupiter. In the vacuum of space, gravity appears absent. Introduce mass into the cosmic vacuum and gravity is experienced. Gravity is, in a sense, mass attracted to itself. Hence, natural laws are conditioned by circumstance. I see the law of mental causation no differently.

A child who is born into circumstances of war, disease, natural disaster, violence, or poverty faces crushing (and socially reinforced) mitigating factors. Thought is one powerful vehicle among others in the possession of the individual. Thought has, I believe, causative properties, as I have argued widely in books and articles. But we must never harbor the illusion of an equal playing field, geographically, socially, physically, or politically. Until New Thought allows for the experience of multiple laws and forces within our physical framework (a topic well handled in the 1908 book *The Kybalion* and in classical Hermetic literature) the field of mind metaphysics will fail to deal maturely with suffering.

Suffering is inevitable. "As above, so below," goes the Hermetic dictum. That principle does not abrogate the philosophy of mind causation. But it must affect it. New Thought's acolytes, if they are theologically serious, must persuasively respond to suffering. In that vein, I offer you the words of Rabbi Joshua Loth Liebman (1907–1948), one of the few leaders in the positive-mind movement who directly addressed the Holocaust. Two years after the war, the Boston rabbi said:

> Mine has been a rabbinate of trouble—of depression. Hitler's rise, world crisis, global war, the attempted extermination of my people. . . . For those who have lost loved ones during the tragic war, all of the rest of life will be but a half loaf of bread—yet a half loaf eaten in courage and accepted in truth is infinitely better than a moldy whole loaf, green with the decay of self-pity and selfish sorrow which really dishonors the memory of those who lived for our up building and happiness.

We honor life by valuing the sacrifices that others have made for us, and the opportunities we are granted for developing our highest potential.

Philosopher Jacob Needleman once asked me: "What do you do when someone offers you a gift?" After I looked at him blankly, he replied: "You accept it." The continuation of one's life following a tragedy is to accept an irreplaceable gift. We have been given life for a purpose, which is: to be *generative*. Use your life. Go and build.

9

AGAINST TRADITION

A Second Look at Forgiveness

Forgiveness is a topic that ironically engenders polarized opinions. One morning this piece of writing came pouring out of me. It arose from asking myself: what if what we are told about the traditional imperative of forgiveness is not necessarily or universally true? This is not a question we are encouraged to consider. In fact, this piece met with resistance from editors and curators whom I found surprisingly closed to its inquiry. As it happens, the piece received a warm outpouring of response from readers after I posted it at Medium under the title "Forgiveness: A Dissent" on April 28, 2020. Many seemed elated that someone was willing to question the manner in which religionists, therapists, and peers often urge us to forgive as though it is an unqualified necessity. One reader wrote, "I am so relieved to read this argument. I find that forgiveness gets forced on us, and people get upset with me if I say I haven't forgiven, even if they have nothing to do with the situation themselves!"

Virtually every religious tradition, as well as every new religious movement, affirms the necessity of forgiveness. Turning the other cheek and forgiving the transgressor are at the heart of Christianity. This principle is less pronounced but still deep seated in Judaism. Forgiveness resonates, albeit with different rationales, in Vedic traditions. To forgive is at the center of modern spiritual philosophies like the Twelve Steps and *A Course in Miracles*.

Friends whom I consider brilliant have argued to me, with persuasiveness, that without forgiveness history could not march forward: Jews could never forgive Germans, Armenians could never forgive Turks, Japanese could never forgive Americans. My friend Richard Smoley writes with sterling precision in his book *The Deal* that forgiveness is the one escape hatch we are given from our own karma—and that we will soon enough require the same forgiveness we offer another.

I have worked intently with forgiveness for seven years. I have prayed, pondered, assayed, and studied. I reject the moral imperative of forgiveness.

My reason, in the end, is simple: I believe that the moral suasion to forgive often places the individual in an unnatural position and produces inner division that gets diverted into other, often hostile or self-negating behaviors.

That does not mean that forgiveness is unwarranted in given situations. Nor that it has not healed wounds. It means only that I reject forgiveness as a blanket rule, spiritual imperative, or ethical necessity.

Am I arguing for revenge? Not necessarily. Rather, I am arguing that a finer, more realistic, and nobler principle than forgiveness appears in *abiding*. In enduring hurt, suffering, wounding, or trespass with the realism that life is reciprocal, suffering is inevitable—and the vow that another person's trespass is wind at your back for the progress toward what you must be and do in life. Have you been defeated? Consider the words of the temporary victor Lady Macbeth: "'Tis safer to be that which we destroy / Than by destruction dwell in doubtful joy."

As I have noted in *The Miracle Club* and elsewhere, we have amassed sufficient evidence, not only from the testimony of seekers, but from studies in psychical research, relativity, quantum theory, and neuroplasticity, among others, to conclude that materialism—the belief that matter alone reproduces itself—is insufficient to cover all the bases of life. Thoughts impact neural pathways. Anomalous transfer of information, or ESP, is statistically settled.* Time bends based on velocity and gravity. Sentient observation effectively determines the locality of subatomic particles. In short, thought is a force. This is true inasmuch as gravity is a force. We can debate terms, conditions, and consistency, but gravity exists: mass is attracted to itself.

Likewise, we participate in detectable extra-physical and nonlinear modes of existence. Hence, to speak of reciprocity (which I prefer to karma) is more than metaphor. What I visit upon another person I ultimately, or in a more immediate fashion, visit upon myself, due to our common metaphysics.

I believe that a better—by which I mean realer—response to pain is to use it as a goad to development. This, I believe, is what nature intended. William Blake wrote in *The Marriage of Heaven and Hell*: "Opposition is true Friendship." Work with that statement for six months. Opposition not only exposes where I need fortification but spurs me to the creative powers of necessity. Without friction we would remain intellectual and emotional children. I see this as the esoteric meaning behind the expulsion from the Garden: the snake emancipated. With emancipation came suffering. And so the individual became a creative actor rather than an object. Should Adam and Eve *forgive* Yahweh for the inconceivable cruelty of condemning humanity to forever being born in sin for a single ancestral transgression? Does the parabolic "sacrifice" of his son redeem or compound that sentence? Friction is neither to be forgiven nor understood (especially when "understanding" results in ethical paralysis). Friction is our human and spiritual situation.

From time to time the comments sections of my articles abound with religionists telling me how I have *completely* misunderstood this or that; quoting Scripture; telling me how they are going to pray for me;

---

*A meta-analysis of psychical research data appeared in the flagship journal of the American Psychological Association: "The Experimental Evidence for Parapsychological Phenomena: A Review" by Etzel Cardeña, *American Psychologist*, 2018, Vol. 73, No. 5, 663–77. I consider the statistical evidence in detail in my book *Daydream Believer*.

how love will overcome all. Try this experiment. Next time someone presents you with one of those arguments, watch how they behave when they are told "no." That response is their philosophy. Philosophy is conduct. I am not a Christian. But in conduct I am a better Christian than most of my detractors.

Someone messaged me recently: "Hello Mitch, I enjoyed watching some of your lectures. I just want to say: infinite love will overcome evil." I replied: "Since some people consider my ideas 'evil' I am careful with statements about overcoming."

Ralph Waldo Emerson cast all this in a refreshing light in his essay "Self-Reliance." Cultural prejudice and the endless need for snappy digital copy are conscripting Emerson to critical mockery. There is no antidote for that. But such trends indicate why the seeker must eschew commentary for source material. Here, again, is his passage:

> I remember an answer which when quite young I was prompted to make to a valued adviser, who was wont to importune me with the dear old doctrines of the church. On my saying, What have I to do with the sacredness of traditions, if I live wholly from within? my friend suggested,—"But these impulses may be from below, not from above." I replied, "They do not seem to me to be such; but if I am the Devil's child, I will live then from the Devil." No law can be sacred to me but that of my nature.

As alluded, a law, in order to be a law, must be ever operative. I do not see forgiveness as an ethical or spiritual law. I see it as an option only. There exist other options. I have given you one. Now go and study.

10

YOU ARE YOUR MASK

The Spirituality of Personal Style

This is another piece that attracted both umbrage and an outpouring of support. It originally appeared as a chapter in The Magic of Believing Action Plan *(2020) and in a shorter form at* Medium *on May 13, 2020. What follows is a slightly expanded version of both. Many readers seemed relieved to encounter a viewpoint that honored the sacredness of outer style and appearance. As a writer, I wish not just to share practical insights that have contributed to my life and search, but also to question how we as a culture reach a consensus of what is "spiritual"—and whether consensus comports with lived experience.*

In this essay I want to explore the power of style and self-image. In some regards, this is a very unusual study, in terms of our spiritual culture, because I am going to talk about the value of your *outer appearance*—how you dress, your tone of voice, your personal gait and composure, the style you adopt, and the self-image you present.

I say this is unusual, because within much of our spiritual culture we are asked to embrace certain principles as self-evidently true, specifically principles of non-attachment and non-identification. We typically hear that what matters is what we cannot see, and that outer life is ultimately illusion or *samsara,* which the seeker should learn to regard as less and less significant as he advances.

I do not think that general principle gets at the real story of our lives. I do not think it encompasses the nature of our existence. In some respects, the ideal of non-attachment is like a carrot forever dangled in front of the seeker; we feel like we are running toward it without getting any closer. I believe the principle of non-attachment to the outer places an unnatural demand on the seeker.

We must be wary of uncritically importing or cherry-picking concepts that belong to ancient religious traditions, both Eastern and Western. We encounter certain concepts, often in translations of translations of ancient literature, which we are taught to regard as sacrosanct and inerrant. But actually, many religious concepts must be understood and evaluated from the context in which they initially arose.

All religions are the product of human hands. Religions are human attempts to codify and structure our relations with the ineffable. Every religion emerges from its own locality and time period, reflecting civic, legal, and social needs of a particular population. All the great religions offer universally applicable lessons; but all religions also bear traits and markings of the cultures, prejudices, attitudes, and circumstances from which they arose. Hence, I feel strongly that religious precepts must be verified. Otherwise, you are imbibing habit as much as tradition.

Hinduism, or the Vedic faith, is a magnificent, world-changing faith. Likewise is Buddhism, which sprang from it. I drop to my knees before these traditions. At the same time, these faiths, from which we receive many of our modern ideas about non-identification and non-attachment, grew from times and places where individuals were almost certain to die within the social caste they were born into. The human situation was not entirely different within Hebraic and Christian variants of religion in the Mediterranean basin. Sometimes our ancient religions were structured to give solace to people who, within a given cultural and social order, experienced very little prospect of escaping the gravity of caste, rank, class, tribe, or gender.

For many ancient people, and especially so in caste-based societies, the need to find a sense of self-worth was relegated almost exclusively to a scale of extra-physical values, and of de-emphasizing attachment to worldly goods or rank. This weighed upon the shaping of some of the ancient faiths. These same urgencies do not necessarily comport with how we live today. Nor are they, I believe, absolutes of human nature. I believe that the highest role of men and women is to be generative: to be co-creators within our sphere of existence, in matters both visible and unseen.

I believe that *all* self-expression is sacred. Scripture tells us that God created the individual in his own image. This principle is at the heart of the Greek-Egyptian philosophy called Hermeticism: "As above, so below." If one takes that concept seriously, then it stands to reason that we are intended to self-create, at least within the parameters of our sphere and circumstances. Creativity and self-expression are sacred.

I believe that part of our self-expression, part of the fulfillment of our purpose, part of what helps facilitate our potentials in the world, involves self-image, in all respects and not limited to one definition or another.

I likewise believe there exists complete and total interplay between the inner and the outer. At this point in my search, I do not think of separations between inner and outer, higher and lower, essence and personality, attachment and non-attachment, identification and non-identification, spiritual and material. It is all one thing. "As above, so below."

Contrary to much teaching within the alternative spiritual culture, I do not think we are called to downplay, disregard, or de-emphasize the so-called exterior as we pursue a fuller sense of life. I think that is artifice. In actuality, attainment of greater selfhood, including in the overt sense, facilitates your ideals, actions, sense of possibility, and the manner in which you relate to others.

In a slightly out-of-the-way 1932 book called *TNT: It Rocks the Earth,* journalist and businessman Claude M. Bristol insightfully explored the question of how artists, businesspeople, and leaders in world affairs convey a very definite, purposeful, intentional image to their audience, listeners, and constituents.

Bristol used Mahatma Gandhi as an example. He observed that Gandhi, who at that time was fomenting peaceful revolution in what is today the largest democracy in the world, was known for nonviolent political change and universal polity. Bristol said that it is not at all cynical to point out that, in addition to Gandhi's political, diplomatic, and ethical genius, he also cultivated a definite image. His walking stick, sandals, spectacles, cropped hair, and traditional robe came from the so-called lower rungs of the caste system in India. His adoption of that appearance is part of what made him into a colossus on the world stage. Bristol observed that it can be enormously helpful to the striving individual to cultivate a sense of showmanship. He did not mean that in a degraded or cynical way. As a newspaperman, he could be blunt and direct.

For those of us who struggle with issues of self-image, as I once did, it can seem very distant to be told to "believe in yourself," be confident, throw back your shoulders and stick out your chest and go through life with a sense of self-possession. There are, of course, affirmations, self-suggestions, and visualizations that can improve self-image from a mental and emotional perspective. We are going to explore some of that material, which I deeply honor and value. In addition to affirmations, however, there are physical steps that heighten self-image and make you a more persuasive and formidable person in the world.

In certain regards, though not all, appearance is an innate trait. We all have things that we like about our appearance and gait, and other things about which we are insecure. These are complexities that every individual must deal with, and some are culturally conditioned. But even within those parameters, you possess greater freedom and possibilities than you may think for a revolution in outer self-image that speaks to your wishes.

I see life as one whole, just as humanity is one whole. We live within a framework of cosmic reciprocity, or what is sometimes called karma. I believe the same is true of your personhood. We are made to feel that we're in pieces; but the interplay of so-called inner and outer is so intimate and total that I believe we misunderstand human nature when we refer to those things separately.

In that vein, let me ask you a question. Are you dressing as you wish? When you get up in the morning—whether it is a weekday, workday, weekend, or vacation—are you comporting yourself in a way that feels natural? How *exactly* do you want to dress in the world? How do you want to wear your hair? How do you want to wear your makeup? What image, what persona, do you feel most comfortable projecting? Do not get lost in thinking that I am just talking about the outer shell of things. Again, I believe in no difference, finally, between the kernel and the shell. It is one great interplay. You are given the gift, as a co-creator, of crafting your image, and it will reverberate through your entire being.

So, once more, I ask: How do you want to dress in the world? How do you want to comport yourself? What gait do you want to walk with? How do you want to wear your hair? Do you want to wear bodily adornments like jewelry, tattoos, or other things? Even if present circumstances make it impossible for you to dress and compose yourself how you wish, you should still know *what that way is*. Live from that mental picture. The day will come, perhaps sooner than you think, when you will actually be able to act on it. But that day will not arrive unless you really ask yourself the question.

What I am describing does not have to do exclusively with physical presentation. It has to do with other cues and signals, such as tone of voice. When I was very young, I served an internship at a newspaper in upstate New York. I knew a police reporter who was very effective and talented, and capable of cultivating good relations with the cops and finding his way in and out of the folds of different stories. He was a man of slight build, very slender, and rather short. In conventional terms, he might seem to cut a rather slight figure. But when he opened his mouth to speak, out came a beautiful, rich, sonorous voice—a very deep bass voice. It got people to listen. It colored his character. I never knew whether it was natural or affect, but it completely changed his relations with the world.

On many occasions I have observed striking and charismatic people who, if they possessed some lesser degree of personal style, might have been considered rather unremarkable, at least on first impression. But through their ability to cultivate a definite style or look, to create something memorable—the frames of their glasses, how they wear a hat, their manner of dress—the self-image that they cultivated made them magnetic. And it did more than that. It made them feel self-possessed and better able to approach people for what they wanted.

The 2012 science-fiction movie *Prometheus* offers an interesting insight in this regard. One of its characters is an android named David, who turns out to be a rather malevolent figure, but who also has his own point of view on creation and reality. In an arresting scene, David, who has been created by man but seeks to surpass his creators, is shown fashioning his self-image while watching the classic movie *Lawrence of Arabia*. David combs his hair in the style of the character of Lawrence. He speaks with the clipped accent of the figure of Lawrence, reciting his lines as if programing himself. I watched this thinking: don't each of us do this all the time, albeit unconsciously?

We populate our perceptions with images, parables, and ideals that we wish to cultivate within. Of course, we live in a very consumer-driven, often conformist, and media-saturated environment. But what I am describing has been true from time immemorial. Every culture, from the Maya to the Polynesians, from the Hebraic to the Hellenic, had its ideals of beauty and adornment. There is nothing new in the human situation.

If a certain image or idea attracts you, allow yourself to experiment with it. What you discover may be the exact opposite of conformity: you may find that you are engaged in an act of self-selection and self-creation, which, as with the figure of David in *Prometheus,* allows you to surpass the boundaries set around your functioning.

Why not give one day to showing up somewhere comported and dressed in exactly the way you want? See what happens. See what kind of impact or influence this has on you and the people around you. There may be peers who do not like what you have done or who run you down. Maybe those are the very people to get away from. Maybe those relationships have been long overdue for reconsideration. Why should you be in proximity to people who are not responsive to your self-image?

At one time in my life, I started getting tattoos, which I thoroughly enjoy having. A family member said with the best of intentions: "Hey, I'm a little worried about you getting all these tattoos because it might close off media opportunities to you." I responded, without conceit: "I hear what you're saying, but just watch the offers roll in." They did roll in. I share this to underscore that *more doors opened when I gravitated toward an appearance that I found self-expressive.* Rather than fear that an off-center look would limit my possibilities, my instinct ran opposite.

Filmmaker Jacqueline Castel once told me: "Anyone who wants to be a public persona should be able to be reproduced as an action figure—and be immediately recognizable." There is great truth to that. The characters that we venerate—celebrities, sports figures, authors— are easily identified. They bear very recognizable traits. This is true of our archetypes, including in mythology: Mercury holds a caduceus or wand with serpents wrapped around it; Pan holds a lyre or harp; Hercules, a club; Diana, a bow and arrow of the hunt. What are your personal symbols?

As you adopt the clothing or look that makes you comfortable, or brings out traits you wish to cultivate, you will find that your tone and voice grow easier and more commanding; your gait and posture become more relaxed and confident; you catch second looks from people; and your expressiveness grows more natural and persuasive, whether you are an artist, writer, or salesperson. An enticing testimony to this power appears in a memoir by KISS drummer Peter Criss and his cowriter

Larry "Ratso" Sloman, *Makeup to Breakup: My Life In and Out of KISS*. Criss and Sloman recall the transformative effect that stage makeup had on the bandmates when they were creating their look and sound in the early 1970s:

> What's scary is that the more we got into roles and the makeup, the more we actually became our alter egos. Once we ditched the female eye shadow and eyeliner and lipstick and actually created these four characters with full-on theatrical makeup, we transformed into different entities. Gene [Simmons] morphed right into a demon. That little Hasidic boy was nowhere to be found when the Demon took over Gene's brain. He would spit right into our roadies' faces. Just plodding around on those platform shoes, which added to his natural height, he exuded menace. People would literally cringe in fear when he came near . . . Gene once told me that if he could leave his makeup on all the time and never leave that persona, he would do it.

That may sound a bit gruesome, but it greatly heightened Simmons's sense of character and theatricality. Other members of the band had similar, if interpersonally milder, experiences: each came to occupy his character and felt elevated confidence, stage presence, and a sense of personal identity. In varying ways, this can happen to you, whether on or off stage, when you are mindful of the intimate connection between outer appearance and psyche.

Many people you may admire cultivate a self-image. Later in life, Steve Jobs embraced the idea of wearing a daily uniform. He had visited a Japanese factory and was very taken with the crisp, clean, and identifiable uniforms that employees wore. He decided to fashion a uniform for himself. He wanted his selection not only to convey an image of independence but also to be comfortable and convenient, dispensing with fuss. The adoption of a uniform meant one less thing to think about as he started his day. Jobs commissioned a designer to produce several hundred units of an identical black turtleneck. He bought New Balance sneakers and Levi's in commensurate numbers. Jobs wore this ensemble every day for years. It became a personal insignia.

Barack Obama had a similar practice. While in office, he said he always wore a blue-gray suit, not only because it looked presidential, but also because it eliminated superfluous decisions. At one time, Mark Zuckerberg wore t-shirts and hoodies. It made him look like a relaxed Northern California startup dude rather than a tech titan.

You can fashion a uniform, too, so that every day you look your best, you are at ease and relaxed, you project the image you want, and you can dress daily and pack for travel with minimum effort. For me, it is t-shirts, leather boots, black jeans, and leather jackets. It is who I am. It is easy. It is versatile.*

When you make that selection, it will go to the core of your being—not because it is influencing from the outside in, but because it is already part of the core.

Let me conclude with an inner truth of life. Other people are always approaching you for what they do not have. They are always looking to others for what they need, for what they feel is deficient in their lives. You do yourself no favors by seeking to accommodate other people, because they are not coming to you for what they already possess. Rather, they are seeking to compensate their perceived deficits. If you present yourself as an iconic or self-directed persona, you not only become more appealing, but your self-crafted image, as you hone it, eventually reflects who you really are. It is not a mask. It is the shedding of a mask.

---

*I further explore the benefits of minimalist dressing in my book *The Miracle Month*.

11

IS MAGICK NECESSARY?

Discovering Your Innate Power May Be All You Need

As I assembled this book in the fall of 2020, this essay reflected a kind of culmination at that phase of my search. It appeared in the publication Human Parts at Medium on April 17, 2020.

Several years ago, I experienced an epiphany in my search.

I was asked to write a new introduction to the fiftieth anniversary edition of Richard Cavendish's 1967 occult history *The Black Arts.* Cavendish's title has always sat poorly with the "white magic" crowd, the witches, occultists, and spellcasters who want to be "understood," who want to signal the beneficence of their work. One British publisher, in an act of chickenshittery, even changed Cavendish's title to *The Magical Arts.*

I wondered how to address the title issue in my introduction. Cavendish died in October 2016—ten days short of his last Halloween—so he was not around to talk it over. I asked myself: Did the English historian make a mistake with his provocative title? Did he leave the misimpression that ancient alchemists, soothsayers, wizards, and their modern equivalents were up to no good?

Help arrived from Yiddish Nobel laureate and novelist Isaac Bashevis

Singer (1902–1991), who was no stranger to the occult himself. In an appreciative 1967 review of *The Black Arts,* Singer wrote: "We are all black magicians in our dreams, in our fantasies, perversions, and phobias." In essence, we are all after the same thing: power. We hate to admit it. We immediately argue with the suggestion, slander the messenger, and insist that our search is about truth, self-knowledge, and service. Yeah, sure.

Cavendish's title does not require defending. It is honest. I believe him when he wrote: "No one is a black magician in his own eyes, and modern occultists, whatever their beliefs and practices, think of themselves as high-minded white magicians." Yet they are driven, as we all are, by the "titanic attempt to exalt the stature of man . . . this gives it [magic] a certain magnificence."

In that sense, I think the categories of white and black magic are artifice. According to convention, white magic is considered beneficent and black magic selfish. I refuse to think in such categories. I think that is ethically muddled and culturally outdated. All magic, as with all spiritual practice, is a quest to bring empowerment and agency to the human condition.

We say, "Thy will be done"—hoping that the will of a higher power comports with our own. We reprocess the wish for personal power through scriptural verse, genuflection, moral vows, and forgiveness. Underneath it all, we are always saying, "My will be done"—but we conceal that. And we assail whomever uncovers it.

I reject the black/white divide, but I celebrate Cavendish's title for its candor and bravery. Finally, after years of search, I could acknowledge the gryphon in the living room: the ultimate end of the spiritual search is power and expansion of the human situation. With this admission, all kinds of intellectual lights began flickering on for me.

▲

British occultist Aleister Crowley (1875–1947) famously called magick (to which he appended a "k" to distinguish it from stagecraft) "the Science and Art of causing Change to occur in conformity with Will." I can live with that definition. But it raises a question: if we accept, as I do, that the individual experiences extra-physical modes of existence—whether expressed in some form of extrasensory perception (ESP), thought causation, reality selection, or projection of will—is what we call "magick" even necessary?

I believe that all forms of spiritual practice—especially in occult realms, but not limited to them—are efforts toward "causing Change to occur in conformity with Will." What else is petitionary prayer? What else is saint veneration? What else is the prosperity gospel? What else is New Thought? What else is witchcraft, chaos magick, spellcasting, or ceremony of any kind?

The issue is not what road you use, but whether you reach your destination. The only empirical measure of a spiritual, personal, or ethical philosophy is its impact on conduct. If your philosophy renders you stronger, abler, more convivial and reliable, then it would have to be deemed a success. Questions of "delusion" are moot since personal philosophies are goal oriented.

At the same time, I do not engage in spiritual practice to fool myself. I have theorized, in *The Miracle Club* and elsewhere, that a great deal of what we call manifestation, attraction, or even assertion of the will may be a kind of quantum selection in which we localize infinite possibilities through perspective, just as a subatomic particle collapses from a place of superposition (or a wave state) into a place of locality (or a particle state) only when a sentient observer takes a measurement.

We know from Einstein's theory of relativity (and specifically his prediction of time dilation) that linear time itself is an illusion, albeit a necessary one for navigating our general perceptions. Time slows for an object moving at or near light speed or within an intense gravitational field, specifically a black hole. Hence, we do not function within fixed time.

Likewise, if we are fleetingly educated in psychical research and are not wed to materialist polemics,* we know from decades of vetted lab data that anomalous transfer of information, or ESP, is also settled fact.

---

*E.g., see "The Man Who Destroyed Skepticism" in Part IV.

Either there exists an extra-physical dimension of mind, or our statistical models are broken in some way that we do not yet understand.

We know from the field of neuroplasticity—and specifically through comparative studies of brain scans—that sustained thoughts alter brain biology. No one challenges this. But its implications upend the underlying premise of materialism, which is that matter produces itself (as opposed to intelligence producing matter). Given all this, there is no question that our innate abilities surpass cognition and motor function. Scholastic philosophers can debate the existence of an intelligent creator, but the jury is in: you possess a metaphysical existence.

▲

I argued earlier that occult, magickal, and spiritual techniques are intended to arouse your extra-physical agencies. That being so, I return to the question: are such techniques necessary at all?

In 2010, Harvard Medical School researchers published an unprecedented "honest placebo" study.* Researchers found that a pill—openly a placebo—brought lasting relief to sufferers of irritable bowel syndrome. Subjects knew they were receiving an inert substance, yet 59 percent reported relief, compared to 35 percent in the control group. What was happening? It seems that patients' belief in the possibility of placebo therapeutics was sufficient to enact the self-healing response, the nature of which is still another question.

So, if belief is present, if effects are measurable, then it would follow that the device itself is ultimately unnecessary. I venture that simply understanding your existence as both a physical and metaphysical being could be sufficient to forgo the formalities of technique.

This applies not only in terms of spellwork and ceremonial magick, but also visualizations, affirmations, image boards, and all kinds of mind-power therapeutics. What I am suggesting extends to

---

*"Placebos without Deception: A Randomized Controlled Trial in Irritable Bowel Syndrome" by Ted J. Kaptchuk, et al., *PLoS ONE,* December 2010, Volume 5, Issue 12.

prayer itself. Is petitionary prayer any different from other methods of arousing mental-emotional energies? "Therefore I say to you, whatever things you ask when you pray, believe that you receive them, and you will have them." (Mark 11:24, NKJV)

▲

I have written about my dedication to anarchic magick, a freestyle occult path that eschews formality. It is a cousin to chaos magick, though it is perhaps even looser in dispensing with devices, such as sigils. Not that I disrespect the use of such devices. I had my first odd success with sigil magick while writing my book *The Miracle Habits* (in which I recount the strange story); I resolved to continue my experiments. But still, charging a sigil is an act of theater that arouses energies inherent within you. Is it necessary?

Next time you wish for something, whatever it may be, remind yourself that you are, in fact, possessed of vaster abilities than cognition, physicality, and ordinary sensory experience. We have amassed too much evidence to doubt this. On that note, I will quote the patron saint of materialism, magician (not with a "k") James Randi, who told a colleague of mine, "I always have an 'out'—I'm right!"* I am not a cynic. I am a seeker. And the evidence I speak of, even the Amazing Randi could not make vanish.

What if we set aside petitionary prayer, spellwork, ceremony, and visualization? What if self-possession and knowledge of your metaphysical existence is, in itself, sufficient to project and actualize your will, at least within the nature of our physical framework?

Try this experiment: Tonight, just as you are drifting to sleep, just as you are entering the supple, drowsy state called hypnagogia, when your rational defenses slacken, think on something you want. Assert its reality. Assert its nowness. See what occurs. Try this on several occasions. Watch carefully for every means of arrival, including

---

*The context appears in "The Man Who Destroyed Skepticism."

through channels mundane or unusual. Neglect nothing. Accept nothing less than clarity. Proof of recovery is in return of function. Be no less concrete.

Of course, asserting your will does not mean ethical indifference. If anything, writing your own book of life requires a more hard-won, road-tested, and self-verified ethical code. I believe in cosmic reciprocity. I believe in human oneness. It is impossible for me to do something to another that I would not be willing to do to myself.

And spare me moralisms about the occult and evil. Evil dwells inside a gray cubicle, decorated perhaps with school drawings of rainbows and class photos, where a customer service rep denies your healthcare claim.

Our spiritual mechanisms may be due for an eclipse by a stronger, greater, and truer realization of self. By this eclipse, you may attain fuller understanding of the Hermetic dictum, "As above, so below."

Try.

PART III

"Up, Up O Ye Gods!"

Up, Up O ye gods! . . . The dawn of a new day of justice invites us.

STOBAEUS, 500 AD

12

THE NEW AGE AND GNOSTICISM

Terms of Commonality

I wrote this paper for the Gnostic America conference at Rice University in March 2018. It was a rare and electrifying gathering of scholarly and academic figures dedicated to the study of esotericism. This piece, in which I draw historical parallels between ancient gnosticism and the modern New Age, appeared in Gnosis: Journal of Gnostic Studies *(vol 4: issue 2, 13 Nov 2019). I have retained the footnotes and bibliography at the end.*

The term "gnosticism" exists today in the eye of the beholder. I repeatedly have to correct the auto-spell function that capitalizes the word, because gnosticism, in my view, can no longer sustain a strict historical and religious meaning. This reflects its innate quality as a heterodox, syncretic, and questioning spirituality.[1]

Indeed, gnosticism is a frustrating term for many scholars today due to the sometimes diffuse manner in which it is simultaneously used to describe practices in early church history and various modern mystical pursuits.[2] For the purposes of this paper, I define gnosticism as a late-ancient religious attitude that regards spiritual traditions, practices, and liturgy as largely combinative, flexible, and open to broad reinterpretation and realignment. Gnosticism is, in a sense, a tradition of anti-tradition and, historically, a collection of loosely encamped seekers and syncretic movements stemming from the early Christian era, and drawing upon Hellenic, Jewish, Persian, and Eastern religious currents.[3]

In that regard, the gnostic thread has much in common with the recent culture of New Age spirituality. New Age is another term that has become largely amorphous but, in my view, can be defined very simply as a radically ecumenical late-twentieth and early twenty-first century culture of therapeutic spirituality.[4] (I continue to capitalize New Age because of its specific meaning and relation to our time.) Some scholars and critics deride the New Age as "cafeteria religion," which, to my mind, does not necessarily signify a disingenuous or unserious quality, but rather suggests New Age's appeal and suitability to the lives of contemporary people facing variegated religious and psychological needs, and for whom a wide array of spiritual and religious options are available. I should note that the term gnosticism, at its scholarly inception in the seventeenth century, was also used pejoratively.[5]

Because of how New Age is often meant to connote a fickle, shallow, and trendy spiritual outlook, one of the oddities of the current New Age movement is that, popular as it is—media expressions range from the blockbuster movie *The Secret* to bestselling books by Deepak Chopra and Wayne Dyer—almost no one wants to be defined by the term. I am in touch with many people who follow various occult, mystical, and psycho-spiritual teachings, whose homes and offices are overrun with crystals, Buddha statues, astrology charts, and motivational posters, but who immediately clarify: "I'm not New Age." For my part, I purposely use the term New Age, and freely describe myself by it, because I do not believe that the term, or any term that is useful and historically pertinent, should be defined solely by its critics, or by those who flee from its connotations.

In this paper, in which I explore three separate episodes of recent alternative spiritual history, I argue that variants of New Age spirituality—which include mystical, psycho-spiritual, and physical methods—are, in many ways, indirect but not wholly unaligned descendants of late-ancient gnostic attitudes and thought. To demonstrate this, I start with an occult and mysteriously titled book from the early twentieth century, *The Kybalion,* for how it illustrates the New Age's proclivity to associate its ideas with the ancient past—not always accurately but not always inaccurately, as I explore. Second, I look at the work of a little-known but increasingly popular mystic, Neville Goddard (1905–1972), in order to consider what his career reveals about the New Age's fascination with charismatic and alluring teachers—and in his case a teacher of greater than usual intellectual depth, who embodied the gnostic and Hermetic ideal of the mind's transformative power. And finally, I explore the life of widely read psychic Edgar Cayce (1877–1945), who probably did more than any other figure of the twentieth century to popularize the key themes of New Age spirituality, particularly mind-body healing, channeling, and clairvoyance, all couched within an ideal of human attainment of gnosis, or higher awareness.

HERMES RESURRECTED?

It is not always easy to find a family tree of connection between ancient and modern religious ideas. This is particularly true of gnostic movements. Due to their anti-traditional nature, lack of canonical literature and liturgy, and general outsider status, gnostic, like occult movements, usually follow very jagged and disjointed ancestries—they change, morph, and vanish (for a time), to reemerge in different ways. Hence, any scholar, historian, or observer who wants to trace the lineage of gnostic or occultic movements from antiquity to the present, especially in the outcropping of the New Age, is on shaky ground.

There are, however, authentic threads of connection, in ideas and thought style, rather than organizations or specific methods, between today's alternative spiritual scene and some of the attitudes and strivings of the late-ancient past. One such connection can be detected between the New Thought movement—popularly associated with the "law of attraction" or the "power of positive thinking"—and Hermeticism, which scholar of religion April D. DeConick has persuasively grouped under the banner of gnosticism.[6] The connection is perhaps on clearest display in an enduringly popular 1908 occult book, *The Kybalion,* which purports to be a commentary by three unnamed seekers on an ancient Hermetic mystery book. Several observers, myself included, once dismissed the short work as a novelty of early twentieth-century occultism; yet today it is the subject of new and serious scrutiny as a modern Hermetic adaptation.

Now, I sometimes suspect that many modern seekers loosely deploy the word Hermetic—a term for late ancient Greek-Egyptian mystical texts attributed to the mythical man-god Hermes Trismegistus, or thrice-greatest Hermes—as a kind of marker, intended to connote a venerable ancestor to modern mysticism, and thus giving contemporary spiritual pursuits the weight of historical gravitas. But, affectations and exaggerations aside, the Hermetic texts or Hermetica, chiefly comprising the seventeen dialogues found in the *Corpus Hermeticum* as well as the work called *Asclepius,* coalesce with some of the key needs and expressions of a twenty-first century person seeking metaphysical insight and clarity.

This is vividly seen in *The Kybalion,* which may be the most widely read occult book of the twentieth century. As a former publisher at a division of Penguin Random House specializing in metaphysical literature, I have personally tracked the book's sales of hundreds of thousands of copies across myriad editions; although still an "underground" book, largely off the mainstream radar, its popularity is rivaled by few other occult works.[7] Pseudonymously published under the provocative byline "Three Initiates" (about which more will be said), *The Kybalion* has also, I think, earned its posterity as something reasonably close to what it claims to be: a "Great Reconciler" of contemporary metaphysical, New Age, and New Thought philosophies, however one judges the efficacy and personal usefulness of those ideas.

Although many of *The Kybalion's* reference points and formulations are plainly modern, the book can be defended as an authentic retention of certain ancient Hermetic ideas. Its author drew upon elements of the Hermetica, the aforementioned late-ancient collection of Greek-Egyptian writings. The various and unnamed authors of the Hermetica, not always agreeing among themselves, codified fragments of immeasurably old oral precepts from Ancient Egypt, which were highly treasured by Egypt's Hellenic ruling and literary class in the centuries following Christ; these writings reemerged, to great sensation, in Latin translation during the Renaissance. It should be immediately noted that some historical scholars dispute the notion that the Hermetic writings possess Ancient Egyptian roots and posit the Hermetica strictly as an expression of late-Greek philosophy with an Egyptian overlay as window dressing. Today's consensus view, however, tends toward the Hermetica as a syncretic work, intermingling Hellenic and authentic Egyptian thought.[8]

Before saying more about the value of *The Kybalion,* and its relation to gnosticism, let me briefly address the question of its authorship. The identity of the "Three Initiates" has long been a source of speculation and drama; this can serve to distract from the book's greater significance. *The Kybalion* was written by New Thought philosopher and publisher William Walker Atkinson (1862–1932), a remarkably energetic Chicago publisher, writer, lawyer, and spiritual seeker, who was one of the most incisive New Thought voices of the twentieth century.

Among the many pieces of evidence, both literary and documentary, that demonstrate Atkinson's authorship, he acknowledged himself as the sole writer in a 1912 entry in *Who's Who In America.* Historical scholars, including Philip Deslippe[9] and Richard Smoley[10] (I also take up the matter in my *Occult America*[11]), have amply demonstrated that there is no reason to argue with him. This prolific figure was the Three Initiates. It should also be noted that in the traditional literature, Hermes Trismegistus addresses himself to three disciples—Tat, Ammon, and Asclepius—which may have been a source of inspiration for Atkinson's byline. Atkinson's title, *The Kybalion,* has no obvious meaning, but may be a Hellenized play on kabbalah.

Atkinson was also the book's original publisher at his Chicago-based Yogi Publication Society. The press published its owner's many influential and not infrequently pseudonymous works, including books under the names of Yogi Ramacharaka and Theron Q. Dumont, as well as Atkinson's self-bylined works. For generations, the writer-publisher's diminutive blue hardcovers were a well-loved mainstay of New Age bookstores and served to influence a wide range of occult and metaphysical seekers.

More important to our purposes than *The Kybalion*'s backstory, is how some of the book's concepts about mind, mass, and thought-creativity demonstrate genuine resonance with the ideas of Hermetic antiquity. This is not a small matter. *The Kybalion* is not merely, or at least not only, modern New Thought clothed in ancient garb; rather, the book connects modern seekers, however tenuously, to concepts that once motivated acolytes from a vastly removed era.

Deslippe and Smoley have admirably tracked some of Atkinson's sources; to their work I would add only that Atkinson was a capable surveyor of Victorian-era and Theosophically based translations of Hermetic literature, which is how the corpus was available to early twentieth-century readers. In particular, he would have encountered the translations of G.R.S. Mead (1863–1933), a scholar of ancient mysticism and one-time secretary to Madame H. P. Blavatsky (1831–1891), a figure whom Atkinson revered. The influence of Blavatsky's 1888 occult opus *The Secret Doctrine* is evident at several points in Atkinson's writings.[12] Mead's three-volume 1906 translation of the Hermetica, *Thrice-Greatest Hermes,* published two years before Atkinson's effort, while turgidly worded in late-Victorian prose, and sometimes almost purposely written as if to assume an antique affect, was then one of the few sources of Hermetic ideas in English. With a skilled and discerning eye, Atkinson identified and distilled insights that corresponded to the sturdiest aspects of New Thought, or what William James had contemporaneously called "the religion of healthy-mindedness,"[13] a field in which Atkinson was deeply steeped. The seeker-writer used his considerable curatorial abilities to produce a marriage of ancient and modern psychological insights.

Atkinson focused primarily on the authentic Hermetic principle that Mind is the Great Creator. According to Hermetic literature, a Supreme Mind or *Nous*, uses as its vehicle a threefold process consisting of: (1) subordinate mind (*demiurgos-nous*); (2) word (*logos*); and (3) spirit (*anthropos*), concepts that echo, albeit distantly, in Atkinson's work.[14] *The Kybalion* is structured around "Seven Hermetic Principles," which follow from the Hermetic concept of "seven rulers" of nature. Man, we are told in book I of the *Corpus Hermeticum*, the body of work translated during the Renaissance, "had in himself all the energy of the rulers, who marveled at him, and each gave him a share of his own nature."[15]

Atkinson is particularly supple in adapting the Hermetic conception of gender, in which the masculine (conscious mind, in Atkinson's terms, and original man in the Hermetica) impregnates the feminine (subconscious mind to Atkinson, and nature in the Hermetica), to create the physical world.

Further still—and this is vital to the book's appeal for its seeking reader—*The Kybalion* ably ventures a theory of mind causality. The book explains why, from the perspective of metaphysical belief, our minds are said to possess formative, creative abilities, and yet, even as we evince powers of causation, we are also subject to limits of physicality, mortality, and daily mechanics. As articulated in Atkinson's chapter "'The All' in All," the individual may wield traits of a higher manifesting Force, but that does not make the individual synonymous with that Force. Man, the book counsels, may accomplish a great deal within given parameters, including transcendence of commonly presumed limitations, influence over the minds of others, and co-creation of certain circumstances; but the book reminds the enthusiast that we bump against physical parameters even as we are granted the capacity, within a given framework, to imitate the Power that set those parameters. In this, *The Kybalion* honors the views of the ancients.

Atkinson offers philosophical definitions of concepts of rhythm, polarity, paradox, compensation, and "Mental Gender." In a sense, the philosophy found in *The Kybalion* is a modern application of Hermeticism, Neo-Platonism, Transcendentalism, and New Thought. The book also attempts, however fitfully, to correspond its ideas to the early twentieth century's nascent insights into quantum mechanics and the "new physics," which gained currency in the decades immediately following its publication. In this sense, the author exaggerates only slightly when he writes: "We do not come expounding a new philosophy, but rather furnishing the outlines of a great world-old teaching which will make clear the teachings of others—which will serve as a Great Reconciler of differing theories, and opposing doctrines."[16]

ASPIRATIONAL SPIRITUALITY

In its scope and ambitions, *The Kybalion* captured the mood and aspirations of the dawning New Age culture, which it also helped shape. The overall spirit of *The Kybalion* can be traced to book XI of the *Corpus Hermeticum*, in which Hermes is told by Supreme Mind that through the uses of imagination he can discover the workings of Higher Creation: "If you do not make yourself equal to God you cannot understand Him. Like is understood by like."[17] This echoes the famous Hermetic dictum, "as above, so below," enunciated in the text called *The Emerald Tablet*.[18] Hermes is told to use his mind to travel to all places, to unite opposites, to know all things, to transcend time and distance: "Become eternity and thus you will understand God. Suppose nothing to be impossible for yourself." Hermeticism teaches that we are granted a Divine birthright of boundless creativity and expansion within the imagination. This teaching is central to the Hermetic philosophy, and its modern re-sounding in *The Kybalion*.

For all that, I must note that Hermeticism is not the religious ancestor to New Thought. The paucity of translations and the rural surroundings of most of America's New Thought pioneers in the mid-to-late nineteenth century placed these ideas off their path. Early

New Thoughters were largely independent investigators who arrived at their insights about the mind's causative abilities chiefly through self-experiment, a topic I explore in my *One Simple Idea: How Positive Thinking Reshaped Modern Life.*

But aspects of Hermeticism do represent a distant historical parallel to New Thought, especially Hermeticism's core idea that a Great Mind of Creation brought all things into being, and that this same creative mental faculty dwells in all men, beings the Higher Mind created not only in its own image but to function in its own likeness. In book I of the *Corpus Hermeticum,* sometimes called the Divine Pymander of Hermes Trismegistus, we hear specifically of the mind's causative abilities: ". . . your mind is god the father; they are not divided from one another for their union is life."[19] As we come to realize our creative capacities, the author of the Pymander reasons, we grow closer in nature and perspective to the Eternal: ". . . he who has understood himself advances toward god."[20] This outlook is at home in nearly every New Thought book of the last century.

Were it somehow possible for contemporary metaphysical seekers to reach back in time and have an exchange with the ancient Hermeticists, something like *The Kybalion* is probably as good an estimation as we can venture of what would appear.

MODERN GNOSTIC: NEVILLE GODDARD

Recent to this writing, I received an ebullient letter from a barbershop owner in Lafayette, Georgia, who loves the work of twentieth-century mystic Neville Goddard. As a historian of the occult, I receive few fan letters from Lafayette—this one made me take special notice.

The metaphysical teacher Neville, who wrote and spoke under his first name, has been growing in popularity since his death, in 1972, and particularly in the past decade or so, when a wide range of New Age writers, including Rhonda Byrne and Wayne Dyer, named him as an influence.[21] A historical profile of Neville that I wrote in 2005 has become one of my most widely read and reprinted pieces.[22] Neville's books are entering multiple editions, and his lectures, preserved digitally from recordings that he freely allowed during his lifetime, receive hits numbering in the hundreds of thousands.

This is an unlikely renaissance for a British-Barbadian metaphysical lecturer who died in near-obscurity, and whose ten books and thousands of lectures center on one theme: *your imagination is God*. This is a radical re-sounding of a Hermetic principle. Everything that you see and experience, Neville wrote, are your emotionalized thoughts and mental images pushed out into the world. The God of the Hebrew and Christian scriptures, he taught, is simply a metaphor of your own creative faculties, and your surrounding world is self-formed in the most literal sense. In his heterodox reading of Scripture, Neville is among the most alluring gnostics of the New Age.

From a modern perspective, Neville promulgated ideas that serious people immediately want to argue with or wave off—but this is where Neville differs from most of the mystical thinkers of the previous century. In his books, pamphlets, and lectures, Neville argued for his radical thesis with extraordinary precision, vividness, and persuasiveness. With his appealing Mid-Atlantic accent, encyclopedic command of Scripture, and gentle yet grand speaking style, Neville could, in the space of a twenty-minute lecture, upend an eager listener's view of life. Humanity, he taught, does not respond to circumstances—rather, it creates them and reacts after the fact without knowing the true origin of events.

Neville's method of mind causation is simplicity itself. It can be reduced to a three-step formula:

1. Form an absolutely clear sense of what you want—be starkly honest with yourself about an accomplishment, possession, or relationship that you desire with all your heart and intellect. "Feeling is the secret," Neville wrote.[23]

2. Enter into a state of restful physical immobility, such as what

you experience just before drifting to sleep at night (this is sometimes called the hypnagogic state)—and you are free to do this step at that time. When the mind and body are blissfully relaxed, your intellect is unusually supple and suggestible.

3. From this state of physical stillness, picture a short, emotionally satisfying scene that implies the fulfillment of your desire, such as someone shaking your hand in congratulations, or feeling the weight and density of an award in your hands or a wedding ring on your finger. Do not witness the scene as if you are passively watching it on a movie screen but feel yourself in it. Run this scene through your mind for as long as it remains vivid and satisfying. You can allow yourself to fall asleep after doing this.

The simple yet bold scale of Neville's methods, and his own charismatic and disarming intellectual and personal style, earned him unusual loyalty among post-war seekers, and a burgeoning new audience in our time.

METAPHYSICAL LINEAGE

Neville was not traditionally educated. The mystic grew up in an era when young people were expected to venture out into the world at an early age. Born in 1905 to an English family in the West Indies, the island-raised teenager, hungry to experience more of life, migrated to New York City in the early 1920s, at age seventeen, to study theater.[24] Neville's ambition for the stage eventually faded as he encountered various mystical and occult philosophies. By the early 1930s, Neville embarked on his new and unforeseen career as a lecturer and writer of mind-power metaphysics. In his lectures, Neville often referred to an enigmatic, turbaned, Black-Jewish man named Abdullah, whom Neville said tutored him in Scripture, number mysticism, Kabbalah, and Hebrew.

Whatever the source of Neville's education—a topic I consider more fully in my book *One Simple Idea*—I want to locate the ancestry of some of his ideas in metaphysical history. I have come across phrasing in his early writing that suggests influences from French mind theorist Emile Coué and American psychical researcher Thomson Jay Hudson, whose 1893 book *The Law of Psychic Phenomena* was influential in the late nineteenth and early twentieth centuries. Hudson attempted to demonstrate that mediumistic phenomena resulted from natural laws of clairvoyance rather than spirits or the supernatural.

Although Neville took his ideas in a bracingly original direction, the basics of his system were New Thought, which rejects materialism as the foundation of life, and sees reality based primarily in spiritual rather than physical laws. Modern positive-mind philosophy is a distinctly American phenomenon, and, as alluded earlier, is a largely homegrown thought school, the roots of which are traceable to the Transcendentalist culture of New England in the mid-nineteenth century, and the mental-healing movement that grew in its wake.

Those are the modern points of reference. But when tracking the history of ideas, one learns (or ought to) that virtually every thought in currency has been encountered and articulated in varying ways at diffuse points of history. And here, concepts about the causative nature of thought return us to Hermeticism. Another of the key ideas in Hermetic philosophy is that through proper preparation, including diet, meditation, and prayer, the individual is permeated by divine forces, and gains higher powers of mind. This approach is also suggested in Neville's three-step method.

Some Hermetic ideas and concepts about the divinity of the mind reentered modern culture through the influence of individual philosophers and artists, including British poet and mystic William Blake (1757–1827). Blake's thought made a direct impact on Neville.[25] Blake believed that our limited perceptions imprison us in a fortress of illusions. But the one True Mind, the great Creative Imagination or God, can permeate us. "If the doors of perception were cleansed," Blake wrote in *The Marriage of Heaven and Hell* (1790), "every thing would appear to man as it is, Infinite." In states of higher sensitivity, the visionary poet reasoned, we can feel the effects of this Great Mind coursing through us.

Neville was also influenced, as noted, by Emile Coué, the self-trained French hypnotherapist famous for his mantra, "Day by day, in every way, I am getting better and better." Coué died in 1926, but shortly before his death he lectured on two tours to the United States. Coué was, for a time, hugely popular in the United States and Europe. It was Coué who first spread the idea of using the drowsy, hypnagogic state for mental reconditioning.[26] Another of Coué's ideas that figured into Neville's thought—you can find the language in Neville's 1945 book *Prayer: The Art of Believing*—is that each of us contains two competing forces: *will* and *imagination*.[27] The will is our self-determinative and decision-making apparatus. The imagination is the mental pictures that govern us, particularly with regard to self-image and emotional judgments we hold about others and ourselves. Coué said that when will and imagination are in conflict, the imagination invariably wins. The emotional state always overcomes the intellect.

As an example, Coué said, place a wooden plank on the floor and ask someone to walk across it. He'll have no problem. But if you raise that same wooden plank twenty feet from the ground, the subject will likely be petrified, even though there is no difference in the physical act. He is capable of crossing the plank; the risk of falling is minimal. But the change in conditions makes him imagine falling; this fosters an emotional state of nervousness (which also makes him more accident-prone). Coué reasoned that we must cultivate new self-images—but we cannot do so through the intellect. We must do so by suggesting new ideas to ourselves while in the subtle hypnagogic state. He called his method autosuggestion. It was essentially self-hypnosis. I find some hint of that in Neville—though his outlook far surpassed it.

The purpose of human existence, Neville taught, is not to recondition your imagination, but be reborn from within your imagination. You experience your imagination—your true self—as physically lodged in your skull, which functions as a kind of womb. Neville, in the culmination of his mystical vision, believed that you must be reborn from within your skull, and that you will have that actual physical experience, maybe in the form of a dream, but nonetheless a vivid, tactile experience of actual rebirth from the base of your skull. You will know in that moment that you are fulfilling your central purpose. This echoes the variegated gnostic view of humanity's capacity to attain self-divinity and higher realization.

Neville described all this vividly.[28] He had the experience himself in New York City in 1959. He told of the tangibly real dream of being reborn from his skull. Minerva was said to be reborn from the skull of Zeus or Jupiter. Christ was crucified at Golgotha, the place of the skull. You and I, Neville said, will be reborn from within our skulls. Later in Neville's career, a speaking agent warned him to stop emphasizing this kind of esoteric material in his talks—he had to return to more familiar themes, like the wealth-building powers of the mind, or he would lose the audience. "Then I'll tell it to the bare walls," Neville replied.[29] Although he drew smaller crowds, Neville continued to speak of this mystical rebirth for the rest of his career, until his death in Los Angeles in 1972.

Neville was not widely known when he died, but his popularity has recently surged. His books have probably sold more copies over the past decade than they did throughout his lifetime. In a modern culture rife with metaphysical voices, Neville's was not only the most radical, but also among the most integral and infectious. This gnostic visionary reimagined the divine as the very nature of the individual.

MESSENGER OF THE NEW AGE: EDGAR CAYCE

In autumn of 1910, the *New York Times* brought the first major national attention to the name of Edgar Cayce, a young man who later became widely regarded as the forefather of holistic medicine and the founding voice of alternative spirituality in the twentieth century.

The Sunday *Times* of October 9, 1910, profiled the Christian mystic and medical clairvoyant in an extensive article and photo spread: *Illiterate Man Becomes a Doctor When Hypnotized.*[30] At the time, Cayce (pronounced "Casey"), then thirty-three, was struggling to make his way as a commercial photographer in his hometown of Hopkinsville, Kentucky, while delivering daily trance-based medical "readings" in which he would diagnose and prescribe natural cures for the illnesses of people he had never met.

Cayce's method was to recline on a sofa or day bed, loosen his tie, belt, cuffs, and shoelaces, and enter a sleep-like trance; then, given only the name and location of a subject, the "sleeping prophet" was said to gain insight into the person's body and psychology. By the time of his death in January 1945, Cayce had amassed a record of more than 14,300 clairvoyant readings for people across the nation, many of the sessions captured by stenographer Gladys Davis.[31]

In the 1920s, Cayce's trance readings expanded beyond medicine (which nonetheless remained at the core of his work) to include "life readings," in which he explored a person's inner conflicts and needs. In these sessions Cayce employed references to astrology, karma, reincarnation, and number symbolism. Other times, he expounded on global prophecies, climate or geological changes, and the lost history of mythical cultures, such as Atlantis and Lemuria. Cayce had no recollection of any of this when he awoke, though as a devout Christian the esotericism of such material made him wince when he read the transcripts.

Contrary to news coverage, Cayce was not illiterate, but neither was he well-educated. Although he taught Sunday school at his Disciples of Christ church—and read through the King James Bible at least once every year—he had never made it past the eighth grade of a rural schoolhouse. While his knowledge of Scripture was encyclopedic, Cayce's reading tastes were otherwise limited. Aside from spending a few on-and-off years in Texas unsuccessfully trying to use his psychical abilities to strike oil—he had hoped to raise money to open a hospital based on his clairvoyant cures—Cayce rarely ventured beyond the Bible Belt environs of his childhood.

Since the tale of Jonah fleeing from the word of God, prophets have been characterized as reluctant, ordinary folk plucked from reasonably satisfying lives to embark on missions that they never originally sought. In this sense, if the impending New Age—the vast culture of Eastern, gnostic, and therapeutic spirituality that exploded on the national scene in the 1960s and 70s—was seeking a founding prophet, Cayce could hardly be viewed as an unusual choice, but, historically, as a perfect one.

THE MESSENGER'S SCRIBE

It was this Edgar Cayce—an everyday man, dedicated Christian, and uneasy mystic—whom New England college student and future biographer Thomas Sugrue encountered in 1927, and later brought serious national attention to in his 1942 biography, *There Is a River.* The book informed how Cayce has been viewed ever since, and the Sugrue-Cayce collaboration hugely impacted the development of alternative spirituality.

When Sugrue met Cayce, the twenty-year-old journalism student said he rolled his eyes at paranormal claims or talk of ESP. (This is typical of the "background story" of twentieth-century seekers: the inquirer begins as a skeptic.) Yet Sugrue had also met a new friend at Washington and Lee University in Lexington, Virginia, who challenged his perceptions: the psychic's eldest son, Hugh Lynn Cayce.

Hugh Lynn had planned to attend Columbia, but his father's clairvoyant readings directed him instead to the old-line Virginia school. Sugrue grew intrigued by his new friend's stories about his father—in particular the elder Cayce's theory that one person's subconscious mind could communicate with another's. The two freshmen enjoyed sparring intellectually and became roommates. While still cautious, Sugrue wanted to meet the agrarian seer.

Edgar and his wife Gertrude, meanwhile, were laying new roots about 250 miles east of Lexington in Virginia Beach, a location the readings had also selected. The psychic spent the remainder of his life in the Atlantic coastal town, delivering twice-daily readings and developing the Association for Research and Enlightenment (A.R.E.), a spiritual learning center that remains active there today.

Accompanying Hugh Lynn home in June 1927, Sugrue received a "life reading" from Cayce. In these psychological readings, Cayce was said to peer into a subject's "past life" incarnations and influences, analyze his character through astrology and other esoteric methods, and view his personal struggles and aptitudes. Cayce correctly identified the young writer's interest in the Middle East, a region where Sugrue later issued news reports on the founding of the modern state of Israel. But it was not until Christmas of that year that Sugrue, upon receiving an intimate and uncannily accurate medical reading, became an all-out convert to Cayce's psychical abilities.

Sugrue went on to fulfill his aim of becoming a journalist, writing from different parts of the world for publications including the *New York Herald Tribune* and the *American Magazine*. But his life remained interwoven with Cayce's. Stricken by debilitating arthritis in the late 1930s, Sugrue sought help through Cayce's medical readings. From 1939 to 1941, the ailing Sugrue lived with the Cayce family in Virginia Beach, writing and convalescing. During these years of close access to Cayce—while struggling with painful joints and limited mobility—Sugrue completed *There Is a River,* the sole biography written of Cayce during his lifetime. When the book appeared in 1942, it brought Cayce national attention that surpassed even the earlier *Times* coverage.

Sugrue was not Cayce's only enthusiast within the world of American letters. *There Is a River* broke through the skeptical wall of New York publishing thanks to a reputable editor, William Sloane, of Holt, Rinehart & Winston, who experienced his own brush with the Cayce readings.

In 1940, Sloane agreed to consider the manuscript for *There Is a River.* He knew the biography was highly sympathetic, a fact that did not endear him to it. Sloane's wariness faded after Cayce's clairvoyant diagnosis helped one of the editor's children. Novelist and screenwriter Nora Ephron recounted the episode in a 1968 *New York Times* article.

"I read it," Sloane told Ephron. "Now there isn't any way to test a manuscript like this. So I did the only thing I could do." He went on:

> A member of my family, one of my children, had been in great and continuing pain. We'd been to all the doctors and dentists in the area and all the tests were negative and the pain was still there. I wrote Cayce, told him my child was in pain and would be at a certain place at such-and-such a time, and enclosed a check for $25. He wrote back that there was an infection in the jaw behind a particular tooth. So I took the child to the dentist and told him to pull the tooth. The dentist refused—he said his professional ethics prevented him from pulling sound teeth. Finally, I told him he would have to pull it. One tooth more or less didn't matter, I said—I couldn't live with the child in such pain. So he pulled the tooth and the infection was there and the pain went away. I was a little shook. I'm the kind of man who believes in X-rays. About this time, a member of my staff who thought I was nuts to get involved with this took even more precautions in writing to Cayce than I did, and he sent her back facts about her own body only she could have known. So I published Sugrue's book.[32]

There exist many other works on Cayce—it would take several paragraphs to appreciate the best of them. But it was Sugrue, an accomplished print journalist who worked and convalesced with Cayce for several years, who fully captured Cayce's personal warmth and earnestness; this made his mystical and gnostic visions palatable to a broad public.

Sugrue's historical Edgar Cayce is the man who grew from being an awkward, soft-voiced adolescent to a national figure who never quite knew how to manage his fame—and less so how to manage money, often foregoing or deferring his usual $20 fee for readings, leaving himself and his family in a perpetual state of financial precariousness. In a typical letter from March 29, 1940, Cayce replied to a blind laborer who asked about paying in installments: "You may take care of the [fee] any way convenient to your self—please know one is not prohibited from having a reading . . . because they haven't money. If this information is of a divine source it can't be sold, if it isn't then it isn't worth any thing."

Sugrue also captured Cayce as a figure of deep Christian faith struggling to come to terms with the occult concepts that ran through his readings beginning in the early 1920s. This material extended to numerology, astrology, auras, crystal gazing, modern prophecies, reincarnation, karma, and the story of mythical civilizations, including Atlantis and prehistoric Egypt. People who sought readings were intrigued and emotionally impacted by this material as much as by Cayce's medical diagnoses. What's more, in readings that dealt with spiritual and esoteric topics—along with the more familiar readings that focused on holistic remedies, massage, meditation, and natural foods—there began to emerge the range of subjects that formed the parameters of New Age spirituality.

GNOSTIC ENCOUNTER

Licking his wounds after his failed oil ventures in the early 1920s, Cayce had resettled his family in Selma, where he planned to resume his career as a commercial photographer. He and Gertrude, who had long suffered her husband's absences and unsteady finances, enrolled their son Hugh Lynn, then sixteen, in Selma High School. The family, now including five-year-old Edgar Evans, settled into a new home and appeared headed for some measure of domestic normalcy. All this was upturned in September 1923, however, when a wealthy printer and Theosophist named Arthur Lammers visited from Dayton, Ohio. Lammers had learned of Cayce during the psychic's oil-prospecting days. He showed up at Cayce's photo studio with an intriguing proposition.

Lammers was both a hard-driving businessman and an avid seeker in ancient religions and the occult. He impressed upon Cayce that the seer could use his psychical powers for more than medical diagnoses.

Lammers wanted Cayce to probe the secrets of the ages: What happens after death? Is there a soul? Why are we alive? Lammers yearned to understand the meaning of the pyramids, astrology, alchemy, the "Etheric World," reincarnation, and the mystery religions of ancient Egypt, Greece, and Rome. He felt certain that Cayce's readings could part the veil shrouding the ageless wisdom.

After years of stalled progress in his personal life, Cayce was enticed by this new sense of mission. Lammers urged Cayce to return with him to Dayton, where he promised to place the Cayce family in a new home and financially care for them. Cayce agreed, and uprooted Gertrude and their younger son, Edgar Evans. Hugh Lynn remained behind with friends in Selma to finish out the school term. Lammers's financial promises later proved elusive, and Cayce's Dayton years, which preceded his move to Virginia Beach, turned into a period of financial despair. Nonetheless, for Cayce, if not his loved ones, Dayton also marked a stage of unprecedented discovery—and a pivotal gnostic encounter.

Cayce and Lammers began their explorations at a downtown hotel on October 11, 1923. In the presence of several onlookers, Lammers arranged for Cayce to enter a trance and to give the printer an astrological reading. Whatever hesitancies the waking Cayce evinced over arcane subjects vanished while he was in his trance state. Cayce expounded on the validity of astrology even as "the Source"—what Cayce called the ethereal intelligence behind his readings—alluded to misconceptions in the Western model. Toward the end of the reading, Cayce almost casually tossed off that it was Lammers's "third appearance on this [earthly] plane. He was once a monk."[33] It was an unmistakable reference to reincarnation—just the type of insight Lammers had been seeking.

In the weeks ahead, the men continued their readings, probing into Hermetic and esoteric spirituality. From a trance state on October 18, Cayce laid out for Lammers a whole philosophy of life, dealing with karmic rebirth, man's role in the cosmic order, and the hidden meaning of existence. It was a modern gnostic vision:

In this we see the plan of development of those individuals set upon this plane, meaning the ability (as would be manifested from the physical) to enter again into the presence of the Creator and become a full part of that creation. Insofar as this entity is concerned, this is the third appearance on this plane, and before this one, as the monk. We see glimpses in the life of the entity now as were shown in the monk, in his mode of living. The body is only the vehicle ever of that spirit and soul that waft through all times and ever remain the same.[34]

These phrases were, for Lammers, the golden key to the mysteries: a theory of eternal recurrence, or reincarnation, which identified man's destiny as inner refinement through karmic cycles of rebirth, then reintegration with the source of Creation. This, the printer believed, was the hidden truth behind the Scriptural injunction to be "born again" so as to "enter the kingdom of Heaven."

"It opens up the door," Lammers told Cayce in Sugrue's account. "It's like finding the secret chamber of the Great Pyramid." He insisted that the doctrine that came through the readings synchronized the great wisdom traditions: "It's Hermetic, it's Pythagorean, it's Jewish, it's Christian!" To him, it was a revelation of universal gnostic spirituality. Cayce himself was unsure what to believe. "The important thing," Lammers reassured him, "is that the basic system which runs through all the mystery traditions, whether they come from Tibet or the pyramids of Egypt, is backed up by you. It's actually the right system. . . . It not only agrees with the best ethics of religion and society, it is the source of them."[35]

Lammers's enthusiasms aside, the religious ideas that emerged from Cayce's readings did articulate a syncretic and compelling theology. Cayce's teachings sought to marry a Christian moral outlook with the cycles of karma and reincarnation central to Hindu and Buddhist ways of thought, as well as the Hermetic concept of man as an extension of the Divine. Cayce's references elsewhere to the causative powers of the mind—"the spiritual is the LIFE; the mental is the BUILDER; the physical is the RESULT"—melded his cosmic philosophy with tenets of New Thought, Christian Science, and mental healing. If there was an inner philosophy unifying the world's religions, Cayce came as close as any modern person to defining it.

CAYCE'S "SOURCE"

Religious traditionalists could rightly object: Just where are Cayce's "insights" coming from? Are they the product of a higher vision, or merely the overactive imagination of a religious outlier? Or, worse, the type of muddle-fuddle produced at sleepover-party Ouija sessions?

Cayce himself wrestled with these questions. His response was that all of his ideas, whatever their source, had to square with gospel ethics in order to be judged vital and valid, which is a principle found, sometimes indirectly, in gnostic writings. Cayce addressed this in a talk that he delivered in his normal waking state in Norfolk, Virginia, in February of 1933, just before he turned fifty-six:

> Many people ask me how I prevent undesirable influences entering into the work I do. In order to answer that question let me relate an experience I had as a child. When I was between eleven and twelve years of age I had read the Bible through three times. I have now read it fifty-six times. No doubt many people have read it more times than that, but I have tried to read it through once for each year of my life. Well, as a child I prayed that I might be able to do something for the other fellow, to aid others in understanding themselves, and especially to aid children in their ills. I had a vision one day which convinced me that my prayer had been heard and answered.[36]

Cayce's "vision" is described differently by different biographers. Sugrue recounts the episode occurring when Cayce was about twelve, in the woods outside his home in western Kentucky. Cayce himself places it in his bedroom at age thirteen or fourteen. One night, this adolescent boy who had spoken of childhood conversations with "hidden friends," and who hungrily read through Scripture, knelt by his bed and prayed for the ability to help others.

Just before drifting to sleep, Cayce recalled, a glorious light filled the room and a feminine apparition appeared at the foot of his bed telling him: "Thy prayers are heard. You will have your wish. Remain faithful. Be true to yourself. Help the sick, the afflicted."[37]

Cayce did not realize until years later what form his answered prayers would take—and even in his twenties it took him years to adjust to being a medical clairvoyant. As his new activities took shape, he labored to use Scripture as his moral vetting mechanism. Yet he consistently attributed his information to the "Source"—another subject on which he expanded at Norfolk:

> As a matter of fact, there would seem to be not only one, but several sources of information that I tap when in this sleep condition.
>
> One source is, apparently, the recording that an individual or entity makes in all its experiences through what we call time. The sum-total of the experiences of that soul is "written," so to speak, in the subconscious of that individual as well as in what is known as the Akashic records. Anyone may read these records if he can attune himself properly.[38]

Cayce's notion of the "Akashic records"—today a core part of New Age spirituality—derives from ancient Vedic writings, in which *akasha* is a kind of universal ether. This idea of universal records was popularized to Westerners in the late nineteenth century through the work of occult philosopher, world traveler, and Theosophy co-founder Madame H. P. Blavatsky, who we briefly met earlier. A generation before Cayce, Blavatsky told of a hidden philosophy at the core of the historic faiths—and of a cosmic record bank that catalogs all human events. In Blavatsky's 1877 study of occult philosophy, *Isis Unveiled*, the Theosophist described an all-pervasive magnetic ether that "keeps an unmutilated record of all that was, that is, or ever will be."[39] These astral records, wrote Blavatsky, preserve "a vivid picture for the eye of the seer and prophet to follow." Blavatsky equated this archival ether with the "Book of Life" from Revelation.

Returning to the topic in her massive 1888 study of occult history, *The Secret Doctrine,* Blavatsky depicted these etheric records in more explicitly Vedic terms (having spent several preceding years in India). In the first of her two-volume study, Blavatsky referred to "Akâsic or astral-photographs"—inching closer to the term "Akashic records" as used by Cayce.[40]

Cayce was not the first channeler to credit the "Akashic records" as his source of data. In 1908, a retired Civil War chaplain and Church of Christ pastor named Levi H. Dowling said that he clairvoyantly channeled an alternative history of Christ in *The Aquarian Gospel of Jesus the Christ.* In Dowling's influential account, the Son of man travels and studies throughout the religious cultures of the East before dispensing a message of universal, gnostic faith that encompasses all the world's traditions. Dowling, too, attributed his insights to the "Akashic records," accessed while in a trance state in his Los Angeles living room.

Cayce, like Blavatsky, equated *akasha* with the Scriptural Book of Life. This was an example of how Cayce harmonized the exotic and unfamiliar themes of his readings with his Christian worldview. In a similar act of gnosis, he reinterpreted the ninth chapter of the Book of John, in which Christ heals a man who had been blind from birth, to validate ideas of karma and reincarnation. When the disciples ask Christ whether it was the man's sins or those of his parents that caused his affliction, the Master replies enigmatically: "Neither hath this man sinned, nor his parents: but that the works of God should be made manifest in him" (John 9:3). In Cayce's reasoning, since the blind man was born with his disorder, and Christ exonerates both the man and his parents, his disability must be karmic baggage from a previous incarnation.[41]

In another effort to unite the poles of different traditions, Cayce elsewhere associated his esoteric search with Madame Blavatsky's. On four occasions he reported being visited by a mysterious, turbaned spiritual master from the East—one of the *mahatmas,* or great souls, whom Blavatsky said had guided her.[42] You'll recall that Neville also claimed tutelage under a mysterious teacher, a recurrent theme of New Age spirituality.

GNOSTIC LEGACY, NEW AGE LEGACY

Neither Cayce nor Sugrue lived long enough to witness the full reach of Cayce's ideas. The psychic died at age sixty-seven in Virginia Beach on January 3, 1945, less than three years after *There Is a River* first appeared. Sugrue updated the book that year. After struggling with years of illness, the biographer died at age forty-five on January 6, 1953, at the Hospital for Joint Diseases in New York.[43]

The first popularizations of Cayce's work began to appear in 1950 with the publication of *Many Mansions,* an enduring work on reincarnation by Gina Cerminara, a longtime Cayce devotee. But it was not until 1956 that Cayce's name took full flight across the culture, with the appearance of the sensationally popular *The Search for Bridey Murphy,* by Morey Bernstein. Sugrue's editor Sloane, having since warmed to parapsychology, published both Cerminara and Bernstein.[44]

Bernstein was an iconic figure. A Coloradan of Jewish descent, and an Ivy League-educated dealer in heavy machinery and scrap metal, he grew inspired by Cayce's career—partly through the influence of Sugrue's book—and became an amateur hypnotist. In the early 1950s, Bernstein conducted a series of experiments with a Pueblo, Colorado, housewife who, while under a hypnotic trance, appeared to regress into a past-life persona: an early nineteenth-century Irish country girl named Bridey Murphy. The entranced homemaker spoke in an Irish brogue and recounted to Bernstein comprehensive details of her life more than a century earlier.

Suddenly, reincarnation—an ancient Vedic concept about which Americans had heard little before World War II—was the latest craze, ignited by Bernstein, an avowed admirer of Cayce, to whom the hypnotist devoted two chapters in his book.[45]

In the following decade, California journalist Jess Stearn further ramped up interest in Cayce with his 1967 bestseller, *Edgar Cayce, The Sleeping Prophet.* With the mystic Sixties in full swing, and the youth culture embracing all forms of alternative or Eastern spirituality—from Zen to yoga to psychedelics—Cayce, while not explicitly tied to any of this, rode the new vogue in alternative spirituality. During this time, Hugh Lynn Cayce reemerged as a formidable custodian of his father's legacy, presiding over the expansion of the Virginia Beach–based Association for Research and Enlightenment, and shepherding to market a new wave of instructional guides based on the Cayce teachings, from dream interpretation to drug-free methods of relaxation to the spiritual uses of colors, crystals, and numbers. Cayce's name became a permanent fixture on the cultural landscape.

The 1960s and '70s also saw a new generation of channeled literature—Cayce himself originated the spiritual use of the term *channel*[46]—from higher intelligences such as Seth, Ramtha, and even the figure of Christ in *A Course in Miracles.* The last was a profound and enduring lesson series, channeled beginning in 1965 by Columbia University research psychologist Helen Schucman.

A concordance of tone and values existed between Cayce's readings and *A Course in Miracles.* Cayce's devotees and the *Course's* wide array of readers discovered that they had a lot in common; members of both cultures blended seamlessly, attending many of the same seminars, growth centers, and metaphysical churches.

Likewise, a congruency emerged between Cayce's world and followers of the Twelve Steps of Alcoholics Anonymous. Starting in the 1970s, Twelve-Steppers of various stripes became a familiar presence at Cayce conferences and events in Virginia Beach.

Cayce's universalistic religious message dovetailed with the purposefully flexible references to a Higher Power in the "Big Book," *Alcoholics Anonymous,* written in 1939.

Alcoholics Anonymous cofounder Bill Wilson, his wife Lois, his confidant Bob Smith, and several other early A.A.s were deeply versed in mystical and mediumistic teachings.[47] Whether they viewed Cayce as an influence is unclear.* But all three works—the Cayce readings, *A Course in Miracles,* and *Alcoholics Anonymous*—demonstrated a shared sense of religious liberalism, an encouragement that all individuals seek their own conception of a Higher Power, and a permeability intended to accommodate the broadest expression of religious outlooks and backgrounds.

▲

The free-flowing tone of the therapeutic spiritual movements of the twentieth and early twenty-first centuries had a shared antecedent, if not a direct ancestry, in the Cayce readings. Cayce's readings themselves resounded ancient themes of gnosticism. In all of the figures and movements we have encountered, we see episodes of gnosis that shaped the spiritual culture of New Age, and united some of the ideals and hopes of ancient and modern seekers.

Other than the presumed consistency of human nature across millennia, we possess relatively little sense of psychological or intimate connection to spiritual movements of the ancient past. But within the New Age's qualities of syncretic search, transcendental yearning, and belief in expanded human awareness, it is possible to detect an indirect retention of attitudes prevalent among the gnostics. New Age is often seen as a kind of flimflam movement.[48] But if viewed in the proper context, and without exaggeration, this intersection provides greater historical and spiritual insight into perennial qualities found within the New Age spiritual search today.

---

*See my postscript for an update on this question.

POSTSCRIPT

Since I published this article, an archivist at the Edgar Cayce Foundation in Virginia Beach, VA, graciously sent me a newly catalogued letter that Bill Wilson wrote to Edgar Cayce's son, Hugh Lynn Cayce, on November 14, 1951.

Wilson wrote, "Long an admirer of your father's work, I'm glad to report that a number of my A.A. friends in this area [New York City], and doubtless in others, share this interest." He went on to comment revealingly about contacts that Hugh Lynn proposed between the Cayce organization and A.A.:

> As you might guess, we have seen much of phenomenalism in A.A., also an occasional physical healing. But nothing, of course, in healing on the scale your father practiced it . . . At the present time, I find I cannot participate very actively myself. The Society of Alcoholics Anonymous regards me as their symbol. Hence it is imperative that I show no partiality whatever toward any particular religious point of view—let alone physic [sic] matters. Nevertheless I think I well understand the significance of Edgar Cayce and I shall look forward to presently hearing how some of my friends may make a closer contact.

Hugh Lynn apparently forwarded the letter to A.R.E.'s New York City center, in whose records it was found.

NOTES

1. van den Broek 2006, 403–16

2. Brakke 2010, 1–28.

3. DeConick 2016, 11–12.

4. Horowitz 2018a.

5. van den Broek 2006, 403.

6. DeConick 2016, 79–90.

7. Horowitz 2014, 116.

8. Fowden 1986, 1993, 14, 25.

9. Deslippe 2011, 18–29.

10. Smoley 2018, ix–xxv.

11. Horowitz 2009, 210.

12. Three Initiates (aka Atkinson) 1908, 113–35.

13. James 1902, 2002, 90–143.

14. Far West Undertakings 1977, vi.

15. Far West Undertakings, 1977, 4.

16. Three Initiates (aka Atkinson) 1908, 211.

17. Salaman, van Oyen, Wharton, and Mahé 1999, 2000 57.

18. Anonymous (aka Valentin Tomberg) 1980, 1985, 2002, 21–26.

19. Copenhaver 1992, 2.

20. Copenhaver 1992, 5.

21. Horowitz 2016.

22. Horowitz 2005, xi–xx.

23. Neville (aka Neville Goddard) 1966, 65.

24. Horowitz 2014, 161–68.

25. Horowitz 2018b, 140–41.

26. Horowitz 2018b, 33, 141.

27. Neville (aka Neville Goddard) 1966, 17.

28. Neville (aka Neville Goddard) 1961, 141–56.

29. Horowitz 2005, xx.

30. *New York Times* (no byline) 1910, 63.

31. Horowitz 2009, 227–45.

32. Ephron 1968, 105.

33. Cayce 1923, reading 5717–1

34. Sugrue 1942, 1945, 230.

35. Sugrue 1942, 1945, 228.

36. Cayce 1946, 23.

37. Cayce, 1997, 1999, 2002, 17.

38. Cayce 1946, 23.

39. Blavatsky 1877, 178.

40. Blavatsky 1888, 18.

41. Sugrue 1942, 1945, 277.

42. Bro 1989, 2011, 358–59, 403, 431, 438.

43. Sugrue (Patricia) 2014, interview.

44. Ephron 1968, 100, 105.

45. Horowitz 2009, 241.

46. Cayce 1923, reading 257–1.

47. Horowitz 2014, 128–35.

48. Horowitz 2018a.

BIBLIOGRAPHY

Anonymous (aka Valentin Tomberg). 1980, 1985, 2002. *Meditations on the Tarot: A Journey into Christian Hermeticism*. New York: Tarcher/Penguin.

Blavatsky, H. P. 1877. *Isis Unveiled: A Master-Key to the Mysteries of Ancient and Modern Science and Theology*, Vol. I: *Science*. New York: J. W. Bouton.

Blavatsky, H. P. 1888. *The Secret Doctrine: The Synthesis of Science, Religion, and Philosophy*, Vol. I: *Cosmogenesis*. London: Theosophical Publishing Company.

Brakke, David. 2010. *The Gnostics: Myth, Ritual, and Diversity in Early Christianity*. Cambridge, London: Harvard University Press.

Bro, Harmon Hartzell. 1989, 2011. *A Seer Out of Season: The Life of Edgar Cayce*. Virginia Beach, Va.: A.R.E. Press.

Cayce, Edgar. May 24, 1923. Reading 257–1.

Cayce, Edgar. October 11, 1923. Reading 5717–1.

Cayce, Edgar. 1946. *What I Believe*. Virginia Beach, Va.: A.R.E. Press.

Cayce, Edgar. 1997, 1999, 2002. *My Life as a Seer: The Lost Memoirs,* compiled and edited by A. Robert Smith. New York: St. Martin's Press.

Copenhaver, Brian P. 1992. *Hermetica: The Greek Corpus Hermeticum and the Latin Asclepius in a New English Translation with Notes and Introduction*. Cambridge: Cambridge University Press.

DeConick, April D. 2016. *The Gnostic New Age: How a Countercultural Spirituality Revolutionized Religion from Antiquity to Today*. New York: Columbia University Press.

Deslippe, Philip, ed. 2011. *The Kybalion: The Definitive Edition*. New York: Tarcher/Penguin.

Ephron, Nora, August 11, 1968. "Publishing Profits for Profit." *New York Times*. 100, 105.

Far West Undertakings. 1977. *Hermetica*. London, San Francisco: Far West Press.

Fowden, Garth. 1986, 1993. *The Egyptian Hermes: A Historical Approach to the Late Pagan Mind*. Princeton, N.J.: Princeton University Press.

Horowitz, Mitch, ed. 2005. *The Neville Reader: A Collection of Spiritual Writings and Thoughts on Your Inner Power to Create an Abundant Life*. Marina del Rey, Calif.: DeVorss & Company.

Horowitz, Mitch. 2009. *Occult America: The Secret History of How Mysticism Shaped Our Nation*. New York: Bantam.

Horowitz, Mitch. 2014. *One Simple Idea: How Positive Thinking Reshaped Modern Life*. New York: Crown.

Horowitz, Mitch, November 6, 2016. "So You Wanna Be a New Age Star?" *Medium*.

Horowitz, Mitch, April 30, 2018a. "In Defense of New Age." *Medium*.

Horowitz, Mitch. 2018b. *The Miracle Club: How Thoughts Become Reality*. Rochester, Vt.: Inner Traditions.

James, William. 1902, 2002. *The Varieties of Religious Experience: A Study in Human Nature*. New York: Modern Library.

Neville (aka Neville Goddard). 1961. *The Law and the Promise*. Marina del Rey, Calif.: DeVorss & Company

Neville (aka Neville Goddard). 1966. *Resurrection*. Marina del Rey, Calif.: DeVorss & Company.

New York Times (no byline), October 9, 1910. *Illiterate Man Becomes a Doctor When Hypnotized: Strange Power Shown by Edgar Cayce Puzzles Physicians*, 63.

Salaman, Clement, Dorin van Oyen, William D. Wharton, and Jean-Pierre Mahé. 1999, 2000. *The Way of Hermes: New Translations of The Corpus Hermeticum and The Definitions of Hermes Trismegistus to Asclepius*. Rochester, Vt.: Inner Traditions.

Smoley, Richard, ed. 2018. *The Kybalion: Centenary Edition*. New York: Tarcher/Penguin.

Sugrue, Patricia (daughter of Thomas Sugrue), 2014, phone interview, Cambridge, Massachusetts.

Sugrue, Thomas, 1942, 1945. *There Is a River: The Story of Edgar Cayce*. New York: Tarcher/Penguin.

Three Initiates (aka William Walker Atkinson). 1908. *The Kybalion: Hermetic Philosophy*. Chicago: Yogi Publication Society.

Van den Broek, Roelof. 2006. "Gnosticism I: Gnostic Religion." Pages 403–16 in *Dictionary of Gnosis and Western Esotericism* edited by Wouter J. Hanegraaff in collaboration with Antoine Faivre, Roelof van den Broek, Jean-Pierre Brach. Brill.

13

HERMES RESURRECTED

What Hermetic Literature Reveals to Contemporary Seekers

This piece appeared on October 11, 2017, at Patheos, *an online religious studies journal. I believe that Hermeticism, the late ancient Greek-Egyptian mystical philosophy, helps untangle some of the difficulties faced by contemporary seekers, particularly in the area of New Thought or mind metaphysics.*

Does Hermetic literature hold any meaning for today's seekers?

I sometimes suspect that we use the word "Hermetic"—a term for late ancient Greek-Egyptian mystical texts attributed to the mythical man-god Hermes Trismegistus, or thrice-greatest Hermes—as a kind of marker, intended to connote a venerable ancestor to modern mysticism, and thus giving our current spiritual pursuits the sheen of historical vintage.

But, the truth is, Hermeticism is a living philosophy, which ought to be read, debated, and engaged in. The Hermetic texts, mostly those found in the *Corpus Hermeticum* and the dialogue called *Asclepius,* can serve the needs of a twenty-first century person in search of metaphysical ideas and clarity.

Hermeticism is of immediate value, much like the more arcane books of the Hebrew scriptures. Although certain Hebrew rites, rituals, and genealogical recordkeeping may seem period-bound, or of little more than liturgical significance to any but the religiously orthodox, such passages provide a framework for luminous ethical and spiritual insights. Similarly, elements of the late-Egyptian Hermetic books also reflect traditions of formalism, ritual, and recital—and these elements likewise frame passages of penetrating relevance to current seekers. This fact has not always been apparent due to the longstanding paucity of quality translations, a deficit that is thankfully being redressed in our time.*

The central and most enduring theme of the Hermetic literature—and one that left its mark on the ancient and Renaissance worlds, and, indirectly, on our contemporary culture of New Thought and mind metaphysics—is that the human mind is an extension and imitation of *Nous,* the Higher Mind, which serves as the divine creative force behind all that is.

This perspective finds particular resonance in books I and XI of the seventeen tracts that make up the *Corpus Hermeticum.* In book I, sometimes called the Divine Pymander of Hermes Trismegistus, we learn of the mind's causative abilities: ". . . your mind is god the father; they are not divided from one another for their union is life."† As we come to realize our creative capacities, we grow closer in nature and perspective to the Eternal: ". . . he who has understood himself advances toward god."

Book XI goes further in urging man's awareness of how his mind, through its abilities to visualize all things, originate new concepts, and surpass physical boundaries, reflects innate divinity:

See what power you have, what quickness! If you can do these things, can god not do them? So you must think of god in this way,

---

*Of particular note are *Hermetica* translated by Brian P. Copenhaver (Cambridge University Press, 1992) and *The Way of Hermes* translated by Clement Salaman, Dorine van Oyen, and Jean Pierre-Mahé (Inner Traditions, 1999, 2000).
†In this essay, I use Copenhaver's translation.

as having everything—the cosmos, himself, (the) universe—like thoughts within himself. Thus, unless you make yourself equal to god, you cannot understand god; like is understood by like. Make yourself grow to immeasurable immensity, outleap all body, outstrip all time, become eternity and you will understand god. Having conceived that nothing is impossible to you, consider yourself immortal and able to understand everything, all art, all learning, the temper of every living thing.

In the student-teacher dialogue called *Asclepius,* which is often grouped as an adjunct to the *Corpus Hermeticum,* man's estimate is even further elevated. We first learn that "one who has joined himself to the gods in divine reverence, using the mind that joins him to the gods, almost attains divinity." Using a variant of the famous Hermetic formula, "as above, so below" (enunciated in another text called *The Emerald Tablet*), this dialogue counsels: "Forms of all things follow kinds. . . . Thus, the kind made up of gods will produce from itself the forms of gods." This adds a deeper resonance to man being made in God's image, as found in Hebrew scripture.

Hermes goes on to teach his disciple Asclepius that man, at his highest, is actually on par with the gods: "Because of this, Asclepius, a human being is a great wonder, a living thing to be worshipped and honored: for he changes his nature into a god's . . ." Hermes ultimately evaluates man as even greater than the gods because, while a god's nature is fixed in immortality, the striving and aware man is ever in process of becoming and fulfilling his highest nature: "In short, god made mankind good and capable of immortality through his two natures, divine and mortal, and so god willed the arrangement whereby mankind was ordained to be better than the gods, who were formed only from the immortal nature . . ."

Moreover, man, in his reverence and worship, performs necessary acts of caretaking of the gods: "He not only advances toward god; he also makes the gods strong."

In considering man's potential, the modern reader of Hermetic literature may find himself facing a question that also faces contemporary students of New Thought: given the causative powers ascribed to our minds, and the manner in which thought relates to the highest source of creation, why do we suffer physical decline, illness, and bodily death? Indeed, the most Hermetic of all New Thought teachers, Neville Goddard (1905–1972), instructed that your mind is God, and all that you experience is the product of your imagination—so, again, why must we "die as princes?" as the psalmist puts it?

The *Corpus Hermeticum* offers a reconciling response. Man, for all his potential greatness, is nonetheless conscripted to dwell within a "cosmic framework" where physical laws must be suffered and limitations experienced. "The master of eternity," Hermes tells Asclepius, "is the first god, the world"—or great nature—"is second, mankind is the third." Man may be the greatest of beings in God's schema of creation, but he nonetheless remains bound to other aspects of the creative order.

In book I we learn: "mankind is affected by mortality because he is subject to fate"—fate being a term for nature's governance—"thus, although man is above the cosmic framework, he became a slave within it."

These views of man's greatness and weakness, the forces in which he functions, and his higher possibilities are considered with surprising adroitness in the 1908 occult classic, *The Kybalion*. Published under the tantalizingly Hermetic pseudonym "Three Initiates," the slender but powerful book is a reasonable iteration of certain Hermetic concepts, as well as a vehicle for its author's personal insights into New Thought psychology.

In essence, *The Kybalion* adds specific techniques to the overarching Hermetic principle that the mind of the individual is an adjunct to the Mind of God, through which man may not only create but also aspire to his eventual return to the source from which he was created.

For those seeking a guiding, cosmic philosophy, as well as the reconciliation of certain vexing ideas within New Thought and other modern mystical schools, I recommend reading the Hermetic literature hand in hand with Neville, *The Kybalion,* and other mature New Thought works.

You will also discover within the Hermetic texts, particularly *Asclepius,* a poignant and, incidentally, accurate prophecy of Ancient Egypt's decline, and the demise of its lexicon of gods. But with today's renewed interested in Hermeticism, and the arrival of a new generation of supple translations, we may be entering a phase of Hermetic rebirth. This renewal, however, comes with a caveat, one deeply grounded in Hermetic tradition: if Hermes is to be resurrected, such an operation must occur within you.

14

THE DEVIL AND MR. JONES

In Defense of New Age

I delivered this talk on March 29, 2018, at the aforementioned Gnostic America conference at Rice University. I was grateful to its organizers for allowing me to dispense with the traditional academic approach of reading from a paper— my formal paper appeared earlier as "The New Age and Gnosticism"—and instead present this extemporaneous address defending the validity of New Age spirituality. Although some circumstances, personal and otherwise, have changed since this talk, I have preserved it as it was delivered.

My mother-in-law, Terri Orr, retired several years ago as an associate dean at Harvard Medical School. She's a remarkable woman for many reasons, but among them she's a seeker in certain New Age and mystical ideas not often associated with the ranking echelon of Harvard's administration. In addition to being a devout Catholic, Terri is interested in the channeled text *A Course In Miracles,* and she is dedicated to both the Twelve Steps and to variants of positive-mind metaphysics.

Her second husband, Jerry Packer, a Jewish man, also from Harvard, was a lawyer and quite conservative. When Jerry was going through some life changes, he found his way to a popularization of *A Course In Miracles* called *Love Is Letting Go of Fear* by psychologist Gerald G. Jampolsky.

Jerry told me one night, very energetically, how much the book had helped him. I was touched to hear this, not only because I am interested in people's experiences with New Age texts, but also because Jerry was conservative in every way, yet he enthused over how a modern mystical work *changed his life* (he specifically used that phrase).

Later that evening, while Jerry was clearing the dinner dishes, my mother-in-law came up to me and said lovingly but with wry humor that the book had not made living with him a picnic: "It may have changed his life, but it certainly hasn't changed mine!"

This is often how popular religious and mystical teachings play out in people's lives. A reader or seeker encounters a psycho-spiritual book, lecture, weekend seminar, or audio program, and feels absolutely flooded with discovery. In such cases, a person sometimes feels permeated by a kind of "divine influx," a phrase used by Swedish mystic and scientist Emanuel Swedenborg and later adopted by Ralph Waldo Emerson. Those around them, with whom they are in relationships, do not always feel or recognize the change. But, to the individual, these experiences can be profound.

I will define New Age shortly, but let me note that its books and ideas often arise when a writer or channeler reports a transcendent communique or transmission—that is, an experience of gnosis—which he communicates to others. Most religious traditions, old or new, begin this way. Over time, a canon of literature, liturgy, and practices develop around the experience. Not infrequently, faction splits occur and someone breaks off to start a parallel movement. This pattern plays out repeatedly in religious history. In fact, several years ago there were competing groups who saw themselves as custodians of *A Course In Miracles,* and they were fighting a copyright battle in federal court. The judge remarked that for people whose entire theology is based in forgiveness, the claimants did not seem to be doing a good job of it. But we are human, and these struggles occur within every religious movement.

Much of the material that is now considered New Age began through an experience of gnosis, of a perceived higher transcendent awareness.

Very often, an individual like Columbia University research psychologist Helen Schucman, who acted as the scribe and channel for *A Course In Miracles,* or Edgar Cayce, a celebrated medical clairvoyant in the first part of the twentieth century—Cayce coined the term *channel* in a spiritual sense—will receive a message, either from within or without, and people come to agree that the individual experienced some kind of new covenant, dispensation, or scripture. Readers of *A Course In Miracles* often regard it as a text of almost scriptural importance—Schucman identified the voice in the work as Jesus. Those who follow the Big Book, or *Alcoholics Anonymous,* a work that did not come from any divine transmission—although it did begin with the experience of Bill Wilson recovering in a hospital and having a religious or spiritual awakening—also regard it as a work of near-scriptural significance (though it is not a substitute for any sacred text). I respect that outlook very deeply.

I respect such modern teachings, and the veneration in which followers hold them, because you can often measure the results of these ideas in the conduct and day-to-day experience of the individual. This has been largely neglected and written out of much of our journalistic and scholarly consideration of new religious movements. In 1970, philosopher Jacob Needleman published *The New Religions,* which was largely a book of field work. Needleman's book is structured around interviews with participants in various new religious movements, such as Transcendental Meditation, Zen, different yogic and Vedantic schools, and so on. I think most journalists, scholars, and historians have neglected this kind of religious field work; that is, of talking to and interacting with participants in these movements. This has left a huge gap of understanding in our culture, to the extent that probably few terms in American life today are considered as demeaning or as much a mark of frivolity as "New Age." People flee from the label. It is almost like being called a fundamentalist. No one will claim it.

I lay claim to the term New Age, and define myself by it. Since many journalists and scholars neglect proximity to practitioners of various New Age methods and teachings, it has become easy for them, for reasons I will consider, to equate the term with everything that is fickle, unserious, trendy, and immature in spiritual life. Yet there are labels I refuse to cede entirely to the critics. I also regularly use the terms occult, positive thinking, and ESP. I do so because I believe these somewhat sullied terms possess historical integrity; they *mean* something, and help define historic movements and modalities. If such terms are misunderstood, then I say labor to make them understood.

There exists a polarity today in how New Age is defined. It is described on one hand, often within the mainstream, as a mishmash of shallow and trendy spiritual ideas. On the other extreme, sometimes from within its own ranks, people say that New Age is perennial wisdom, that it is a term to describe ageless insights—"New Age is old age," you will hear. I think it is none of those things. I do not believe it is useful to describe a culture or movement from its polarities. In another outlook, some even argue that New Age cannot be described, that it is so amorphous it is like trying to grab smoke. But New Age can be described, and simply: it is a radically ecumenical culture of therapeutic spirituality. It is that plain. The movement is very broad, and includes a wide array of spiritual, physical, and healing-oriented modalities—but, in short, that is what it is: a radically ecumenical culture of therapeutic spirituality. The term New Age grew popular in the 1970s, partly through the influence of the monthly *New Age Journal.* In its earliest use, the term was benign or honorable. But it soon took on negative connotations within the larger culture. Part of the reason, in addition to the lack of hands-on proximity of those writing about it, is that New Age culture has generally done a poor job of producing scholars, journalists, and formidable public voices from within its own ranks.

I was discussing this issue recently with religion scholar Catherine Albanese. We both noted that other new religious movements, particularly Mormonism and Christian Science, have produced significant scholars; and institutionally those movements possess impeccable record keeping, beautiful libraries, and a strong command of technology. If you visit the Mary Baker Eddy Library maintained by the Christian Science

Church in Boston, for example, you will enter a first-class library; it ranks with any in the world in terms of archival practices and technology. Brigham Young University maintains outstanding digital archives, which put within easy reach documents that would have been extremely difficult to find a generation ago. By contrast, if you attend a weekend seminar at a New Age center, you will be lucky if the greeter at the door can tell you where the bathroom is. I am being glib, of course, but there is a serious problem of accountability and professionalism within New Age growth centers and media. (And the bathroom story has occurred.)

Now, there are extremely well-run growth centers. The Edgar Cayce center in Virginia Beach, called the Association for Research and Enlightenment, is managed impeccably well, at every level. The Theosophical Society of America campus in Wheaton, Illinois, is remarkably well run. So is the Esalen Institute. But those are among a handful of exceptions.

Generally speaking, and I have no wish to name names, there is a poorly developed culture of both intellectual search and, frankly, administrative competence within the New Age. I am ill at ease saying that because I have located myself within that culture for about twenty years as a writer, speaker, publisher, and seeker. And, believe me, I have traversed the map. Until recently, I was vice-president of a publishing division at Penguin Random House that specialized in metaphysical books. I have written on alternative spirituality within both mainstream and New Age cultures, and spoken on it coast to coast and internationally, so I hope you will not think I am venturing a casual opinion. I have been out there. And the New Age does, by and large, have a poor atmosphere of intellectual inquiry, as well as business and administrative acumen. The question is: why? Why are other new religious movements, like Christian Science and Mormonism, distinguished by far greater levels of professionalism and study? Are the critics correct that we are just a carnival of trendy and fickle religious ideas, and hence attract fuzzy-headed participants? I cannot conclude that the critics are right. I simply cannot conclude that because I have seen too many examples to the contrary. And I have seen too many instances where the therapeutic and spiritual ideas and methods that emerge from New Age culture prove meaningful in the lives of a wide range of people. Moreover, New Age ideas have opened our culture to many things held vital by large numbers of people, which would not have found a foothold in America if not for the platform and launchpad that New Age has provided. Almost anything having to do with natural medicine or alternative health, for example, be it macrobiotics, acupuncture, hatha yoga, Transcendental Meditation, or any kind of mind-body stress reduction, first entered society from the margins of what would have been called New Age.

The founder of Transcendental Meditation, the Maharishi Mahesh Yogi, ventured to California in 1959—occult explorer Madame H. P. Blavatsky predicted in 1888 that the West Coast would be the birthplace of the New Age—and he began teaching Transcendental Meditation, which is now widely practiced and accepted. At the time, people were able to make sense of this man, and his cultural transmission, because they were already involved in various proto-New Age and alternative spiritual subcultures. They had some familiarity with figures like Madame Blavatsky and Swami Vivekananda, and thus sufficient orientation to understand: "Oh, this is a man bearing wisdom from the East—let's see what he has to teach." There existed a cultural capacity to receive this figure. This kind of episode occurs again and again in American religious history. Since the mid-twentieth century, various alternative spiritual offerings got picked up, popularized, remade, and, very often, exported again—and these ideas and practices usually entered society through the fringes of New Age culture, even if they did not have their inception there.

I am sometimes asked: "Don't you find it irritating that there is such a poor intellectual climate in New Age? Don't you find a lot of weirdos? Aren't there a lot of flakes?" My response is that you must be willing to put up with some of that if you want to be in proximity to the staging ground where innovation occurs. Innovation often enters society from its periphery, and you do not know where it will go. If Steve Jobs grew inspired to wage a technological revolution, in part, by imbibing psychedelics and studying Vedanta and Zen, how did such things become available to a suburban kid growing up in a tract house in Northern California? These things did not fall from the sky. They came from somewhere. They required a staging ground, and an incipient audience, however small, to usher them into the mainstream.

Hence, it is inadequate to say, "Oh God, the New Age is just an aquarium of weirdness." It is not an aquarium; it is a channel, it is an inlet—and a lot passes through it, some of which blossoms across America and other parts of the world. Alternative ideas require an entry point, and that is what New Age is.

Given all that, why *isn't* there a better culture of inquiry within the New Age? That is, a more mature and rigorous style of thought, discourse, historical study, and writing? I think it has something to do with how successful the New Age has been in taking a sledgehammer to conventional concepts of hierarchies. Hence, someone like Helen Schucman, a research clinician who claimed to be an atheist (although the story is more complicated when you peel back the layers), or a Southern Bible-Belt kid like Edgar Cayce who grew up in rural Kentucky, or any number of the people whose names are widely known or obscure, can lay claim to the mantle of prophecy. The New Age has been so effective in practicing a style of anti-hierarchy and personal gnosis, that, as a byproduct, it has disproportionately attracted people who prefer not to, or find it difficult to, function within professional and administrative norms. That does not mean this population is a majority, but it is well represented.

I view this situation as a side effect of the culture's success. If we define gnosticism, in the classical sense, as a syncretic, un-hierarchical, widely dispersed, somewhat elastic, ecumenical form of spiritual seeking, encompassing many sects and variants, with no top-down seat of authority, it is possible to conclude that New Age, in a way, replicates that attitude and outlook, though without a direct family tree of connection. As blunt as I am trying to be in this presentation, and as admittedly general as I am being, one cannot get carried away with a negative analysis of the New Age. It is vitally important not to slide over to the obfuscating polarity of concluding: "Oh, the New Age is a bunch of woo-woo silliness." Yet this polarized attitude prevails in the mainstream, and has for some time.

I was moved recently to hear a presentation at Rice University by religious studies professor Gregory Shaw, in which he spoke of the enduring influence of Emerson and the Transcendentalists. I noted at the time that if it were not for New Age culture, many new editions of Emerson and Thoreau would not get published and read, since those figures, and others from world literature, such as the Persian poet Rumi, have experienced a renewed vogue within New Age. Greg shrewdly quoted the early twentieth-century social critic G. K. Chesterton, whose 1908 book *Orthodoxy* bemoaned the impact of the new spirituality: "That Jones shall worship the god within him turns out ultimately to mean that Jones shall worship Jones."

When we first hear things like that from a cultural icon like Chesterton, it sounds like a knockout blow against any kind of free-floating conceptions of contemporary spirituality. It seems like a staggering punch against what we have come to call "cafeteria religion." Such a statement appears to topple the notion that a spiritual search can involve eating off multiple and self-selected plates, which devolves, Chesterton warned, into Jones worshiping Jones.

Unfortunately, the New Age has not produced many people to respond to Chesterton's outlook, which is now widely echoed, including by *New York Times* columnist Ross Douthat and others who consider themselves rapier critics of New Age. Yet it is easy to rebut the charge of delusion or narcissism. Because the knockout punch, if you want to enter a debate of ideas, invites a counterblow—and Chesterton left himself open to an enormous one, without even realizing it. Since Chesterton set the template for how many social critics continue to view New Age, I will use a contemporary example to respond to his sentiment.

The social critic Barbara Ehrenreich recently wrote a book called *Bright-Sided,* which was a polemic against the culture of positive thinking, which Barbara is convinced is laying waste to our nation. She sees the notion that thoughts are causative as deteriorative and unrealistic, economically and socially. Barbara promoted her book several years ago on *The Daily Show,* when it was hosted by Jon Stewart. Stewart asked her about religion or spirituality making a difference in people's lives: "If Jesus makes you stop drinking, isn't that okay?" Now, I think Barbara is, in some ways, very unfamiliar and shallowly read in her subject, which I have considered in *The Miracle Club,* but she is nonetheless extremely quick witted. She replied: "No, I never think delusion is okay." The audience applauded and they quickly moved on. But here is the rub: how do you determine whether something is delusion, which to me means a catastrophically ruinous illusion, other than by measuring it through a person's conduct of life? *The Conduct of Life* was the title of one of Emerson's last essay collections.

Only by measuring an individual's experiences, in terms of his or her conduct, can you reach a reasonable, empirical, rational judgment of whether an ethical, religious, or philosophical system proves beneficial in someone's life. And there are certainly ways of measuring such things: recovery from addiction, recovery from diseases—whether emotional, physical, or psychological—the ability to see through projects in life, the ability to act with a sense of personal agency, the maintenance of relationships, the maintenance of careers, the maintenance of some kind of financial self-sufficiency, and the ability to stay out of the legal system. These are some measurements.

Now, an individual's entanglements in life have many contributing factors. There are political factors, economic factors, environmental factors, and so on. But if the serious person testifies that Jesus, or Universal Force, or Divine Influx, or whatever you may call it, has helped him stop drinking, and there exists a "before and after" that empirically bears that out, then you have a testimony to the effectiveness of a philosophy in a person's life. Calling that a delusion, or Jones merely worshiping Jones, is subjectivity. It is like saying, "Chocolate ice cream is evil." It just means nothing. It is not a statement at all. It is not a knockout blow. It is irrelevant.

I contend that to understand New Age as a gnostic and spiritual expression, students, scholars, journalists, and observers must place themselves in closer proximity to what they are studying. Moreover, I call upon my friends in the New Age movement, of which I am a part, to take seriously the crisis of intellectual inquiry often found within New Age. I call out the New Age movement to produce some of its own scholars and significant public voices, so that when a Barbara Ehrenreich or G. K. Chesterton starts to rail against Jones, there is someone to defend Jones.

PART IV

Incarnations

A man's attitude goes some ways. The way his life will be.

MULHOLLAND DRIVE, 2001

15

OCCULT AMERICAN

Rediscovering Manly P. Hall

Now past the second decade of the twenty-first century, it is clear that greater numbers of people are discovering occult scholar Manly P. Hall and his encyclopedia arcana, The Secret Teachings of All Ages, *than did during the author's lifetime, which ended in Los Angeles in 1990. Hall's career is a kind of Rorschach onto which observers project their own wishes or fears. Some enthusiasts view Hall as an illumined teacher or reincarnated sage. In 2020, a writer in* The New Republic *(a university writing instructor no less) clipped and pasted some of my historical writing on "Manley" P. Hall and construed him as the connecting joint of mysticism and right-wing politics, a point I never made. Since 2010, I have, however, probed the connections between Hall and Ronald Reagan.* Since a not-quite-classifiable figure like Manly P. Hall is easily misunderstood, I produced this piece to frame some of my research into, and personal perceptions of, the dean of esoteric scholarship.*

I will never forget the first time I heard the stately name: *Manly P. Hall.* It was a summer day about twenty years before this writing. I was having

---

*E.g., "Reagan and the Occult," *Washington Post,* April 10, 2010.

lunch with friends in New York City, where the esoteric scholar Hall (1901–1990) once lived and began researching his "Great Book," *The Secret Teachings of All Ages,* at the city's cathedral-like public library, where I am a writer-in-residence today.

It was early in my studies of occult and esoteric traditions. "Who should I be reading?" I asked my friends, both longtime seekers. One, named Pythia—the same name, I later learned from Hall's work, as the oracle at Delphi—said: "Manly P. Hall," lingering over every syllable. I felt the kind of electrical charge you sometimes experience when you know you are about to make a life-shifting discovery. I had to learn who was behind that imposing name; I felt an inner conviction that such knowledge would prove personally meaningful. My conviction turned out right: Hall's work helped chart the course of my career.

Hall was the first writer who helped me understand that studying the metaphysical dimensions of history could be a vocation in itself. In fall of 2005, I delivered my first full-scale talk, "The Occult Philosophy in American Life," at the Mayan-Egyptian-Art Deco campus he founded in Los Angeles, the Philosophical Research Society (PRS). My presentation that day formed the basis for my first book, *Occult America,* and much else that followed.

Without Hall's influence, I am not sure I would have found my way as a historian of alternative spirituality. Although Hall's name is rarely heard in academia today (this is slowly changing), I believe that his writing and persona have quietly moved many scholars of esotericism toward their work. University of Chicago historian of ancient religions Mircea Eliade, whose scholarship brought new respect to the study of Gnostic and esoteric belief systems in the twentieth century, told friends that as a young man Hall's writing ignited his own love for symbol and myth.

TRANSCENDENTAL HISTORY

Hall spent seven decades, most of them in Los Angeles, writing about the esoteric and inner dimensions of the United States, and much else besides.

Hall's view of American history could be called transcendental. It was neither liberal nor conservative, populist nor elitist; and the writer rarely concerned himself directly with politics, elections, or current events, other than to remark on the need for environmental stewardship and moderation in civic life (which can only lead us to imagine how he would have despaired over the nature of today's perpetual attack-mode).

Within Hall's writings on American history, particularly his 1944 book *The Secret Destiny of America,* appears the principle that the United States serves—at its finest moments—as a vessel for primeval ideals of democracy, self-development, individual searching, and personal liberty. Hall located these principles, in their earliest form, within ancient esoteric traditions. He believed that such aims were preserved within the work of illumined intellects, like Francis Bacon and Sir Walter Raleigh, as well as covert fraternities, including Freemasonry and Rosicrucianism (the latter probably not an actual brotherhood but a thought movement), and enacted, albeit with egregious gaps, by America's founders, many of whom were either Masons, such as Washington and Franklin, or were intimately steeped in ethical and individualist philosophy, such as Paine and Jefferson.

This perspective ignited the patriotic imagination of a surprising range of figures, including President Ronald Reagan. I first discovered in 2010 that some of Hall's ideas and language about the inner meaning of America began appearing in Reagan's writing and speechmaking from the earliest years of his political career up through his presidency. As we will see, it is likely that the two met in their hometown of Los Angeles while Reagan was governor. In this sense, Hall's influence traveled far beyond esoteric circles. The most powerful case in point appears in his impact on one of the twentieth century's most consequential politicians.

THE MYSTIC AND THE PRESIDENT

During Reagan's two terms as governor of California, from 1967 to 1975, whispers and speculation circulated about the ex-actor's penchant for lucky numbers, superstitions, and newspaper horoscopes. But it was unknown that the esoteric scholar Hall, and particularly his occult back-story of America, made a lasting impact on the man who became our for-tieth president.

As is typical of many actors, Reagan was no stranger to occult lore. He was friendly with Eden Gray, a onetime costar who went on to write the nation's first popular guides to Tarot. Later on, as governor, Reagan was friends with psychic Jeane Dixon (he and Nancy broke with the prophetess after she failed to foresee his rise to the White House) and was especially close to Santa Monica stargazer Carroll Righter, who in 1969 became the first, and only, astrologer to appear on the cover of *Time* magazine.

Deep into the second term of Reagan's presidency, in the spring of 1988, stories about Ronald and Nancy Reagan's interest in the occult broke into full view. A tell-all memoir by disgruntled ex-chief of staff Donald Regan definitively linked Nancy to a San Francisco astrologer named Joan Quigley, who closely monitored the president's calendar and appointments. Speaking at a press briefing, White House spokesman Marlin Fitzwater attempted to quickly dispel the matter by acknowl-edging that, yes, the Reagans were fans of astrology, but they never used it for policy decisions; the spokesman also conceded the president's pen-chant for "lucky numbers" or numerology. To many political observers, the revelations cemented press speculations that arose when Reagan, as governor-elect, scheduled his first oath of office at the eyebrow-raising hour of 12:10 a.m., which critics saw as an effort to align the inaugural with promising heavenly signs.

But a bigger and more substantive piece of the story went miss-ing. In speeches and essays that he produced decades apart, Reagan revealed the unmistakable mark of Hall's writing and phraseol-ogy. Judging from a tale of Hall's that Reagan borrowed and often repeated, the president's interests in the esoteric went far beyond the daily horoscope. And this returns us to the book-lined Los Angeles sanctum of Manly P. Hall.

▲

In 1944, within the stucco walls of his "mystery school" in Griffith Park, Hall produced a historical work at first little-known beyond his immediate circle. *The Secret Destiny of America*—based on Hall's earlier lectures and essays—caught the eye of the future president, then a middling movie actor gravitating toward politics. The book's wording became a mainstay of Reagan's speeches.

The Secret Destiny of America describes how America was the product of a "Great Plan" for religious liberty and self-governance, launched by an ancient order of arcane philosophers and secret societies. In Hall's original 1943 essay, he recounts a rousing speech delivered by an "unknown speaker" before the signers of the Declaration of Independence. Hall also told an earlier version of this story in his 1928 opus, *The Secret Teachings of All Ages*.

The "mysterious man," Hall wrote, invisibly entered and exited the locked doors of the Philadelphia statehouse on July 4, 1776, delivering an oration that bolstered the wavering spirits of the delegates. "God has given America to be free!" commanded the stranger, urging the men to overcome their fears of the noose, axe, or gibbet, and to seal destiny by signing the great document. Newly emboldened, Hall wrote, the delegates rushed forward to add their names. They looked to thank the man, only to discover that he had vanished from the locked room. Was this, Hall wondered in 1944, "one of the agents of the secret Order, guarding and directing the destiny of America?"

At a 1957 commencement address in Illinois at his alma mater, Eureka College, Reagan, then a corporate spokesman for GE, sought to inspire students with this leaf from occult history. "This is a land of destiny," Reagan said, "and our forefathers found their way here by some Divine system of selective service gathered here to fulfill a mission to advance man a further step in his climb from the swamps." Reagan then retold, without attribution, the tale of Hall's unknown speaker. "When they turned to thank the speaker for his timely words," Reagan concluded, "he couldn't be found and to this day no one knows who he was or how he entered or left the guarded room."

Reagan revived the story several times, including in 1981, when *Parade* magazine asked the new president for a personal essay on what Independence Day meant to him. Longtime aide Michael Deaver delivered the piece with a note saying, "This Fourth of July message is the president's own words and written initially in the president's hand," on a yellow pad at Camp David. Reagan retold the legend of the unknown speaker—this time using language very close to Hall's own: "When they turned to thank him for his timely oratory, he was not to be found, nor could any be found who knew who he was or how he had come in or gone out through the locked and guarded doors."

Continuing on Hall's theme, Reagan spoke of America's divine purpose and of a mysterious plan behind the nation's founding. "You can call it mysticism if you want to," he told the Conservative Political Action Conference (CPAC) in Washington, D.C., in 1974, "but I have always believed that there was some divine plan that placed this great continent between two oceans to be sought out by those who were possessed of an abiding love of freedom and a special kind of courage." Reagan repeated these words almost verbatim before a television audience of millions for the Statue of Liberty centenary on July 4, 1986.

▲

Where did Manly P. Hall uncover the tale that made such an impact on a president and his view of American purpose and destiny? In actuality, the episode originated as "The Speech of the Unknown" in a collection of folkloric stories about America's founding, published in 1847 under the title *Washington and his Generals, or Legends of the Revolution* by American social reformer and muckraker George Lippard. Lippard, a friend of Edgar Allan Poe, had a strong taste for the gothic—he cloaked his mystery man in a "dark robe." He also tacitly acknowledged inventing the story: "The name of the Orator . . . is not definitely known. In this speech, it is my wish to compress some portion of the fiery eloquence of the time."

Regardless, the parable took on its own life and came to occupy the same shadow land between fact and fiction as the parables of George Washington chopping down a cherry tree, or young Abe Lincoln walking miles to return a bit of a change to a country-store customer. As with most myths, the story assumed different attributes over time. By 1911, the speech resurfaced in a collection of American political oratory, with the robed speaker fancifully identified as Patrick Henry.

For his part, Hall seemed to know little about the story's point of origin. He had been given a copy of the "Speech of the Unknown" by a since-deceased secretary of the occult Theosophical Society, but with no bibliographical information other than it being from a "rare old volume of early American political speeches." The speech appeared in 1938 in the Society's journal, the *Theosophist,* with the sole note that it was "published in a rare volume of addresses, and known probably to only one in a million, even of American citizens."

It is Hall's language that unmistakably marks the Reagan telling. Indeed, there are indications that Reagan and Hall may have even met to exchange ideas. In an element unique to Hall's version, the mystic-writer attributed the tale of the unknown speaker to the writings of Thomas Jefferson. When Reagan addressed CPAC he added an attribution—of sorts: Reagan said the tale was told to him "some years ago" by "a writer, who happened to be an avid student of history . . . I was told by this man that the story could be found in the writings of Jefferson. I confess, I never researched or made an effort to verify it."

Gnostic scholar Stephan A. Hoeller, for many years a close associate and friend of Hall's, and a frequent speaker at PRS, affirmed the likelihood of a Reagan and Hall meeting. Hoeller told me that while he was on the Griffith Park campus one day in 1971, early in Reagan's second term as governor, he spotted a black limousine with a uniformed chauffeur standing outside it. Curious, he approached the man and asked, "Who owns this beautiful car?"

"At first," Hoeller recalled, the driver "hemmed and hawed and then said, 'Oh, it's Governor Reagan—he is in a meeting with Mr. Hall."

Hall's longtime librarian, Pearl M. Thomas, confirmed the account to Hoeller. "They know each other quite well," he recalled Thomas saying. She further told him that Reagan had "called him here at the office several times. But we are not supposed to talk about this."

Hall was known for discretion and avoidance of Hollywood chatter and social climbing; there is no record of his speaking directly about the governor. But when Reagan began his ascent to the White House and his name arose in conversation, Hoeller recalled, the mystic smiled and said, "Yes, yes, we know him."

Hoeller, a distinguished man of old-world bearing, eschews hyperbole. He concluded: "There are definitely several indications that there was contact and influence there." The scholar's recollections square with the timing of Reagan's 1974 remarks before CPAC.

▲

Given the fanciful origins of the "unknown speaker," one may wonder what worth, if any, the tale has as history. It is important to remember that myths, ancient and modern, reflect psychological truth and the teller's self-perception, sometimes more so than events themselves. Myths reveal who we aspire to be, and warn us against what we may become. Those on which we dwell reveal character.

Hall captured an element of what philosopher Jacob Needleman calls "the American soul" within the story. Reagan certainly thought so. And the codes and stories in which Reagan spoke form the skeleton key to the inner man—a fact intuited by President Gerald Ford, who called Reagan "one of the few political leaders I have ever met whose public speeches revealed more than his private conversations."

ESOTERICIST AS HISTORIAN

Other elements of Hall's Americana were more factually verifiable than the unknown speaker. Indeed, the writer sometimes gave voice to rejected ideas that time later validated. This is the case with Hall's description of the Oracle at Delphi in *The Secret Teachings of All Ages*. Hall first published his epic codex to symbolic philosophy in 1928, at the remarkably young age of twenty-seven. At the time, many mainstream scholars and historians dismissed as fantasy the classical portrait of the Delphic oracle as a female medium seated on a tripod in a cavern imbibing fumes and foretelling the future. The image was considered more drama than fact. Yet Hall, reading deeply into esoteric sources, affirmed the scene's historical accuracy. About a decade after Hall's death in 1990, archaeological discoveries at Delphi bore out his vision and restored this classical description to widely accepted history.

My point in documenting these varied episodes is that we do no service to Hall's memory, or to his uniqueness as a thinker, to raise him on a pedestal, as some of his students wish to do. Nor is it closer to accurate to paint Hall as a purveyor of white-supremacist manifest destiny, as one professor recently did from that hallowed court of wisdom, Twitter.

In my books *Occult America, One Simple Idea,* and elsewhere, I have written critically about aspects of Hall's career. He sometimes overrelied on folkloric or single sources, including in his writing about the influential German-American mystic Johannes Kelpius (1667–1708), with some legend mixed in. But to neglect Kelpius, as many historians once did, would mean ignoring an important if subtle facet of American history.

The facts are these: the mystic Kelpius and his small circle of followers fled religious persecution in Central Europe in 1693, arriving in the colonies the next year to establish a monastic hermitage in Philadelphia on the banks of the Wissahickon Creek. The mystical community helped to establish the colonies' reputation as a safe harbor for religious radicalism, and to attract other experimenters to its shores. Hence, Kelpius's influence is seminal, and is slowly being rediscovered by historical scholars today. Although Hall includes several fanciful episodes from the monk's life, involving secret caskets and alchemical explosions, his work kept this important figure from being written out of modern history at the time when Kelpius's reputation was overlooked. Hall vouchsafed the Hermetic monk's importance, and today no account of the development of America's religious culture is considered complete without at least noting him.

In this sense, to understand Hall, and to constructively read and write about him, requires taking full account of his strengths and weaknesses as a historical thinker. You do not read Manly P. Hall for a timeline of consensus-based history, or for a blow-by-blow rendering of what occurred. Rather, Hall saw history as a transcendent arc of ideas. His work is an esoteric key to the meaning behind people, ideas, and events. His historical telling is sometimes parabolic—revealing the internal currents and ideas of a certain time and place, and often of our own. Hall's historicism helps us find new layers in our nation's self-conception.

MASONIC REPUBLIC?

In light of what I have written, it is also important to understand Hall's "secret society" thesis, in which he describes how esoteric ideals were preserved within the vessel of clandestine fraternities and societies, and later put into governance in the new republic.* Aspects of his thesis are over-dramatized. Yet, in the broadest strokes, Hall's outlook provides a vital and not wholly inaccurate insight into an element of American history that most mainstream historians and scholars overlook. Key facets of Hall's "secret society" vision can be seen in the veritable influence of Freemasonic ideals on America's founders.

Indeed, Hall was among the first modern historians to grasp Freemasonry's impact on early America—and the facts are richer and more significant than anything that entertainment or conspiracy

---

*I further explore this history in the chapter "How I Learned to Stop Worrying and Love the Illuminati" in Part V.

would hold. As a radical thought movement that emerged from the Reformation, Freemasonry was one of the first widespread and well-connected organizations in modern life to espouse religious toleration, ecumenism, internal democracy, and personal liberty—principles that the fraternity helped spread among key American colonists.

It may seem anomalous for liberal principles to arise from within a "secret society," but skullduggery was never Masonry's primary aim. In an age of religious conflict in seventeenth-century Europe—when an individual caught running afoul of church strictures could suffer persecution or worse—Freemasons clung to secrecy less out of esoteric drama than political expedience. Many Masons believed in a search for religious truth as it existed in all civilizations, including those of a pre-Christian past, and they drew upon ancient and occult symbols, from pentagrams to luminescent eyeballs, as codes for ethical development and progress. Reactions from church authorities ranged from suspicion to hostility. European Masons had good reason to be discreet.

It was in a young America that Masonic ideals fully took flight—sometimes in unexpected ways. In Boston in 1778, local freemen of color affiliated as Masons under the banner of African Lodge No. 1. The African Lodge later became known as Prince Hall Masonry, so named for the order's founder, Prince Hall, a freed slave and leatherworker.* Hall became the first Black American named a Grand Master. Despite the African Lodge's segregated status, Prince Hall Masonry was a bastion of abolitionism. Its leader affixed his name to some of the republic's earliest anti-slavery petitions in 1777 and 1778. As such, African Lodge No. 1 represented the first Black-led abolitionist movement in American history.

---

*The founding of Prince Hall Masonry is often dated to 1775. But historians John L. Hairston and E. Oscar Alleyne have recently and definitively established its founding year as 1778. Details and primary documents appear in their revelatory monograph, *Landmarks of Our Fathers: A Critical Analysis of the Start and Origin of African Lodge No. 1* (The Quill and the Sword Publishing, 2016).

Whatever its airs of mystery and images of skulls, pyramids, and all-seeing eyes, Freemasonry's most radical, even dangerous, idea was the encouragement of different faiths within a single nation. Early in his first term, Washington communicated these ideals in a letter of August 18, 1790, to the congregation of a Rhode Island synagogue:

> It is now no more that toleration is spoken of as if it was the indulgence of one class of people that another enjoyed the exercise of their inherent natural rights. For happily, the government of the United States, which gives to bigotry no sanction, to persecution no assistance, requires only that they who live under its protection should demean themselves as good citizens . . .

In other words, in the new nation, minority religions were not just guests at the table, but full householders.

As Manly P. Hall noted, Washington and other early-American Freemasons rejected a European past in which one overarching authority regulated the exchange of ideas. This outlook is further suggested in one of the greatest symbols associated with Freemasonry: the eye-and-pyramid of the Great Seal of the United States, familiar today from the back of the dollar bill.

The Great Seal's design began on July 4, 1776, on an order from the Continental Congress and under the direction of Benjamin Franklin (another Freemason), Thomas Jefferson, and John Adams. The Latin maxim that surrounds the unfinished pyramid—*Annuit Coeptis Novus Ordo Seclorum*—can be roughly, if poetically, translated as: "God Smiles on Our New Order of the Ages." Although the symbol is not directly from Freemasonry, it embodies Masonic philosophy to the core: the pyramid, or worldly achievement, is incomplete without the blessing of Providence. And this polity of man and God, as Masonic philosophy held, required a break with the religious order of the Old World and a renewed search for universal truth. In its symbols and ideas, Masonry conveyed a sense that something new was being born in America: that the individual's conscience was beyond denominational affiliation or government command.

Historically, Masonry's voice and principles informed America's founding commitment to the individual pursuit of meaning, as Manly P. Hall also understood. Taking a leaf from Hall's thesis, it is not going too far to suggest that many Masons foresaw the nascent republic as a place destined to protect the individual search for meaning—from majority rule, from foreign meddling, and from sectarian restriction. That ideal represents Freemasonry's highest contribution to our national life. This noble, meaningful aspect of Masonic philosophy runs throughout Hall's work.

▲

I believe that Hall's historical writing makes it possible for readers today to rediscover a neglected dimension of our shared history and purpose. He also wrote extensively about undercurrents of esoteric thought and spiritual insight found within the Native American cultures. Hall considered these topics with veneration when such cultures were often ignored or caricatured within mainstream letters.

Hall's vision of America is a nation born from, and in the ongoing process of fulfilling, primeval ideals of individual agency and the search for meaning. In illuminating our best principles, Hall provides a way to measure our insufficiencies and failures, and also an internal obelisk by which to recalibrate the heights we wish to attain.

16

SEEING IN THE DARK

David Lynch Uncut

I spoke with filmmaker David Lynch for the May 18, 2017, episode of public radio's Interfaith Voices, *which I guest hosted. We explored the role of fear in Hollywood, Transcendental Meditation, catching ideas, and negativity. Here is the uncut, unexpurgated version of our discussion, including off-air comments.*

David: Have to enjoy the smoke before the interview.

Mitch: This will be like the old Tom Snyder show; you can smoke during this.

D: Yeah, I was on a Tom Snyder show one time.

M: Really?

D: He's from Philadelphia. Actually we both, unbeknownst to each other, came out to California at exactly the same time from Philadelphia.

M: Is that right? Did he share your warm feelings toward Philly?

D: I think his feelings were a bit warmer.

M: *Introduction:* The director and artist David Lynch is often credited with breaking down the wall between Hollywood movie making and arthouse cinema. Known for projects including *Twin Peaks, Mulholland Drive, Blue Velvet, Wild At Heart,* and beyond, David is speaking to us today from his Los Angeles home. We are marking the release of the tenth anniversary edition of his book *Catching the Big Fish,* where he explores creativity and his longtime commitment to Transcendental Meditation. David, thanks for being with us.

D: You're very welcome, Mitch.

M: Can you begin by reading the opening of *Catching the Big Fish?*

D: I'd be happy to try to read that. Here goes:

> Ideas are like fish. If you want to catch little fish, you can stay in the shallow water. But if you want to catch big fish, you've got to go deeper. Down deep, the fish are more powerful and more pure. They're huge and abstract. And they're very beautiful. I look for a certain kind of fish that is important to me, one that can translate to cinema. But there are all kinds of fish swimming down there. There are fish for business, fish for sports. There are fish for everything. Everything, anything that is a thing, comes from the deepest level. Modern physics calls that level the Unified Field. The more your consciousness—your awareness—is expanded, the deeper you go toward this source, and the bigger the fish you can catch.

M: What's the biggest fish you've ever caught?

D: I've caught some beautiful fish, beautiful to me. Beauty is in the eye of the beholder. So, everything I've ever written or made so-called on my own came from ideas that I caught. I always say we really don't do anything original, we just are blessed with catching some ideas. And then we know what to do, based on the idea. The key is to fall in love with that idea and then follow that idea, stay true to that idea, and then do the best you can, and lo and behold, something comes out into the physical world.

M: In *Catching the Big Fish,* you write that when pursuing a project of any kind, it's critical for the project's success to honor the idea, the inceptive idea, at the heart of it. How can an artist facing various pressures and forces stay focused on that original idea?

D: It's very easy. When you catch an idea, you see it, and you hear it, and you feel it, and it's very important that you write that idea down in such a way that when you read the words later, that idea comes back as complete as possible. And so, you have the idea written down; you can always read those words, or you don't really have to all the time; you have that idea in your head, in your heart. To stay true to that, and all the steps along the way to realizing something, you keep checking back to see if you're true to that idea. And I always say, also along the way, stay on your toes, because new ideas can come in; a thing is not finished 'til it's finished; other ideas can come swimming in, some you can save for later. They don't relate to what you're working on now, but others, you say, "Oh my goodness, this thing was not complete, look at this idea." And the thing jumps, and you know, you're thankful for that idea.

M: In the ten years since you wrote *Catching the Big Fish,* what has changed in your outlook as an artist, or on life?

D: Well, everything is always changing, they say. So, one thing that is changing for sure, is that digital cinema came along. That said goodbye to celluloid and opened up a whole other thing, which gives people more control over the image and the sound and it's a beautiful world, the digital world. Of course, when you look at celluloid and film emulsion and still-photograph emulsions, and photographs from that, it's organic and deeply, deeply, deeply beautiful. And digital sometimes just can't quite get that yet. But it's still a beautiful medium for the amount of control we have over it. That's been a big change. And then another change is: the arthouse cinema died away, and there are no more art-houses. I say now that cable television is the new arthouse.

M: When you're working with digital, is there ever an issue with the technology or the resolution being almost too good? Is it more difficult as an artist to capture some of the mood that you want when digital video picks up just everything?

D: Well, there's tricks that you can do, there's so many plugins, there's so many things to manipulate the image. You can add film grain to it, you can do a bunch of things. Digital, the way it is now, sort of catches the surface, and emulsion seemed to get in there way deeper and kind of made things alive, and I'm hoping that digital one day will get that abil-ity to go deeper. But you can still manipulate the image to get a great mood and a great look, so it's okay.

M: Over the past decade, you've spoken a great deal about your experi-ence of meditation. Why did you originally start meditating?

D: I started meditating for two reasons. One, I heard the word "enlight-enment" and I wondered if it was really true that human beings had this potential to become enlightened. And I wanted to know, kinda, what enlightenment was all about, if it was just an Eastern thing, or if it was true for people, if that was a full potential of every human being. And also there's the phrase, "true happiness is not out there, true happi-ness lies within," and I wondered where the *within* was. And it seemed that we just think of ourselves as our body, and I wondered where in the world in the body could this thing be. And I started thinking about this phrase, "true happiness lies within," and I felt a truth to it, but I didn't know how to go within; I didn't even know where the within was. Anyhow, one thing led to another, and I found Transcendental Meditation as taught by Maharishi Mahesh Yogi. And I learned this technique on July 1, 1973, at about ten thirty in the morning, and I just loved that experience, and have been meditating twice a day, every day since. And it's money in the bank for the human being. It changes things for the good. I'm really getting sick of all the suffering and negativity in this world, and all they gotta do is get this technique, dive within, and things get really good. It happens for everybody who gets this technique, and it's time to get the word out, Mitch—it's really ridiculous what's going on.

M: Inasmuch as you can describe it, walk us through the process of meditating.

D: There are many forms of meditation; everybody knows that, and some work better than others. For instance, Maharishi said—for Yogananda, who teaches Kriya Yoga—he said: Yogananda brought the airplane method. I, Maharishi, bring the rocket-ship method. It's the superhighway to the goal, and it is easy and effortless. And because it's easy and effortless, a lot of people said, "it's a Mickey Mouse form of meditation, it's baloney, it's for children; the real serious guys do hard work in their meditation, twelve hours a day." But, Maharishi's technique, it's easy and effortless because that's the way you slip into the transcendent. It's not a *trying* thing; trying keeps you next to the surface. It doesn't give transcending, and transcending is the key to everything. Experiencing that deepest level, that level of bliss, of intelligence, of creativity, of love, of energy, of peace. People are tired, they're depressed, they're filled with tension and stress, and they make a mess of things. You picture this deepest level as unbounded light. You start enlivening that, and darkness, negativity, starts to flee away. And it happens. Easily, and effortlessly. It takes about four days to learn this technique from a legitimate teacher. Someone on the corner tells you they can teach you Transcendental Meditation, say, "Thanks Jack, but I want the real thing." You go and find a legitimate teacher of Maharishi Mahesh Yogi's Transcendental Meditation. It's about an hour and a half a day for four days, and then you understand the technique, you understand how to use the mantra, and you've got this technique for the rest of your life. All you gotta do, then, is stay regular, and watch life get better and better and better.

M: I think part of the problem with our spiritual and intellectual culture today is that if something works, we are immediately suspicious of it. We're suspicious of simple things. Which I think is a problem.

D: Well, it is a big problem. The proof is in the pudding, in the tasting. So, it's difficult to describe the beautiful experience, the bliss of transcending to people who haven't experienced it. But it's true that there is a treasury within each one of us human beings. With Transcendental Meditation you can access that treasury easily and effortlessly for the first time and every time, and this transcendent is an unbounded field. It's always and forever been there; one name for it is *atma,* meaning the self. It's the big self—"know thyself," the line is. This is what they're talking about. It's a field, it's so beautiful, so powerful; it's a field of total knowledge, all the laws of nature are in this field; it's eternal, it's immortal, it's immutable, it's infinite, it's unbounded, and all of everything that is a thing has emerged from this field, this fantastic eternal field. And you can experience it with this technique. And when you experience it, bliss comes in, love comes in, peace comes in, intelligence comes in, creativity comes in, energy comes in, and you start really enjoying life, and you look around and everything looks better. Your health improves, you see a bigger and bigger picture. People don't look like enemies, they look like friends. You start getting ideas, you start thinking more positive. The things that used to stress you don't stress you so much. Sometimes they make you giggle. You feel good, you want to buy a bunch of people coffees, you want to put your arm around people, you want to enjoy life.

M: How has meditation impacted your work as a filmmaker and an artist?

D: Okay, the ideas, as you can look at it, flow through a conduit, and stress squeezes that conduit, tension squeezes it, depression squeezes it, hate squeezes it, anger squeezes it. Now a lot of people—I gotta say one thing, Mitch—a lot of artists say, "I don't wanna get a technique that makes me like everybody else, and makes me calm, and I lose my drive, I lose my edge, I don't have any more power or any individuality anymore." This is what I thought about. *Au contraire.* You get more of *you.* You get more energy to do the things, the ideas. There are billions of ideas and you'll find the one you love, and you'll find 'em on a deeper and deeper level when you start expanding that consciousness. And this thing of righteous anger is fine—you can be against something, really truly against something, and fight for something you believe in. You'll have more energy to do that. You'll have more power, more edge to really get in and get the thing the way you want it. Suffering is the enemy to creativity. Negativity is the enemy to creativity. If you're depressed, you can't create. If you've got diarrhea and vomiting, as I say, you don't feel like creating. You gotta feel good, you gotta have energy, you gotta have, you know, all these ideas rolling. We start transcending, that conduit widens out, the stress goes. All these things that have been squeezing it, they go away. The ideas start just flowing. You start enjoying things and you love the doing of the thing. Enjoy the doing. So many people do stuff, but they don't enjoy the doing of it. And I always say, that's your life going by. It's important to enjoy the doing of something. Jeez, Louise!

M: Speaking of the doing, one of your most acclaimed movies is *Mulholland Drive,* from 2001, which is a story that unfolds in contemporary Hollywood. There was a time in my life—and I'm actually re-experiencing that right now—where I thought literally every day, sometimes several times a day, about the scene in *Mulholland Drive,* where Adam, this hotshot director, encounters a mysterious man who asks to see him, The Cowboy. And we're going to play a short piece of that scene for our listeners. I was wondering if first, you could set this up for us, just tell us what people would see if they were looking at it.

D: Well, it's nighttime, high up on the Hollywood Hills, in a corral where the cowboys that worked in the Westerns hung out. And Adam has to go up there. He enters the corral, it's all dark, and this light buzzes on. He turns around, and here comes The Cowboy.

> COWBOY
>
> Howdy.

> ADAM
>
> Howdy to you.

> COWBOY
>
> Beautiful evening.

> ADAM
>
> Yeah.

> COWBOY
>
> Sure want to thank you for coming all the way up to see me from that nice hotel downtown.

> ADAM
>
> No problem. What's on your mind?

> COWBOY
>
> Well now, here's a man who wants to get right down to it. Kinda anxious to get to it, are ya?

> ADAM
>
> Whatever.

> COWBOY
>
> A man's attitude . . . a man's attitude goes some ways, the way his life will be. Is that somethin' you might agree with?

> ADAM
>
> Sure.

COWBOY

Now did you answer because you thought
that's what I wanted to hear or did you
think about what I said and answer cause
you truly believe that to be right?

ADAM

I agree with what you said . . . truly.

COWBOY

What'd I say?

ADAM

That a man's attitude determines to a
large extent how his life will be.

COWBOY

So since you agree, you must be a person who
does not care about the good life.

ADAM

How's that?

COWBOY

Well just stop for a little second and
think about it. Can ya do that for me?

ADAM

Okay, I'm thinkin'.

COWBOY

No, you're not thinkin'. You're too busy being
a smart aleck to be thinkin'. Now I want ya to
think and stop bein' a smart aleck. Can ya try
that for me?

M: Now, personally speaking, I find a whole philosophy of life in that scene. I think if we lived on another planet and had no information about life except for this scene, and this was all that reached us, we would make it. We would find a way to make it. What The Cowboy says informs a lot of the work that I'm doing right now about the power of thought. How do you view the power of an attitude, and do you think we're all too busy being smart alecks?

D: Well, there's a lot of smart aleck stuff going on these days, but, the thing is, the key is, Mitch, you can talk about people changing their attitudes, and you can make laws that kinda indicate what a good attitude is, and you should have that. But the thing is that the torment and the beliefs and the way is inside the people. And you can't change that unless you get down on a deeper level—and you gotta get underneath the problem, Einstein said, in order to solve the problem. You can't get deeper than the unified field—that transcendent, the ocean of pure consciousness, the being. So you, you teach people Transcendental Meditation. All this negativity flies out, all the gold comes in and attitudes change, but it's not because of some law or somebody telling you to change your attitude—it's natural. It just changes. And people don't, for instance, feel like blowing someone's head off anymore, they just don't want to do that anymore. They don't wanna rob any bank, they don't wanna beat their wife. You know, they might have enjoyed beating their wife last week, but now they don't wanna do that anymore.

M: Do you believe that our thoughts are causative in some way?

D: Yeah, everything starts with thinking, thinking goes to speaking, and speaking goes to action. Like a lot of times, action, you go to kill somebody, but then that's a little bit better way of saying, "I would like to kill you"—and there's another way where you don't say that, you don't do that, but you think that. And then there's another way where you clean out all that and you don't even think that. That thought doesn't even come up— you're just filled with a great, great love for everybody, for everything.

M: One of your earliest movies is *Eraserhead,* from 1977. It takes us through the world of a man who faces strange things in life, including caring for a freakish baby. I grew up on this movie and it meant a great deal to me and to my friends. My personal outlook as a viewer, speaking only for myself, is that it deals with gnostic themes. The ancient gnostics believed that we live under a kind of ersatz or fraudulent god, not the true God, and in the movie we see a deformed deific figure pulling levers like a deformed god who creates flawed beings. You had told me back in 2006 that *Eraserhead* is your most spiritual movie, which absolutely blew me away. What do you mean when you use the word *spiritual*? What does that term mean to you?

D: Spiritual, I guess, means truthful. You know, there is, like they say, one truth. And we're all like detectives trying to find that one truth. And there's scientists looking all the time for truths, and they call that objective science. And what I believe is objective science will get really far down in there, they'll really get down close to the truth. And be able to explain it. But the ultimate thing is subjective science. The last step to knowing the whole thing happens inside the human being, and that's the thing that is spiritual, and the truth, the thing we're all looking for.

M: In *Catching the Big Fish,* you write that much of the movie business today is run on fear and uncertainty. Why is it that way?

D: Well, there's a lot of reasons. There's this love of money, for one thing, and then there's stress on top of that, fear of losing their job, making a profit, second guessing what the audience wants for any kind of product. It's a world of fear and stress, and a lot of times the workplace, because of these things, is not a pleasant place at all. And people run their business on fear, so the people, the employees, are afraid. And that conduit of ideas is gonna get squeezed—they're filled with stress, they take this home, they take it out on their wife, and their kids are affected. The whole house is affected, and the kids are bringing home stress, and the wife's bringing home stress, and it's a kind of vicious circle. But somebody who runs a business, who gives all the employees Transcendental Meditation, and takes it for himself or herself—what's gonna happen is that the workplace is gonna start getting happy. Stress is gonna start going. People are gonna start getting more ideas, people are gonna want to go the extra mile for the boss, and they're gonna feel real good about helping the company— and they're gonna come home and the kids are going to be so happy to see them, just like Santa Claus coming home, there'll be so much happiness. And they'll even take part in washing the dishes, maybe, if they get happy enough. That hasn't happened to me, though.

M: That'll have to be an experiment at my house. A lot of your films have haunting imagery: the Dwarf, speaking backwards, in *Twin Peaks;* the severed ear discovered in a field at the beginning of *Blue Velvet.* And I still cannot get to sleep at night when I see Robert Blake's white-faced, grinning character from *Lost Highway.* What is it that scares you, personally?

D: Well, I think death is pretty frightening to people, so I guess that's the ultimate thing, you know, suffering and death. That'll get ya.

M: In *Catching the Big Fish,* you wrote that feelings of anger for—

D: In total enlightenment they say all fear goes away. That's something very beautiful for each and every human being. Doesn't matter, every human being has this potential. Education, they say, you know, we want to bring out the students' full potential—but they're not talking about enlightenment, they're talking about getting them a job or something. But imagine education that truly unfolds the human beings', the students', full potential. That is consciousness-based education. They learn all these things that can help 'em get a job and do all that, but also they'll learn how to dive within, get more creative, get more intelligent, get more happy, get more love, get more inner peace, get more energy. And think of the power you're giving 'em. Put them on the big superhighway to enlightenment. They're unfolding their full, full, full potential. They get happy. Their grades go up, the fighting stops, the bullying stops, the teacher burnout stops. Teachers start to love to teach again. The school gets happy, it gets blissful. Students help each other out. And that school becomes like a little lighthouse for the neighborhood. They're pumping out happiness. They say every human being is like a lightbulb—if you're filled with negativity you blow that out like light from a lightbulb. If you're filled with bliss and love and energy and happiness and creativity, all these things that come up when you transcend, you'll broadcast that out. And you'll affect the environment in a positive way. This can happen. Every school should have this quiet time program. Every school. And this is something, Mitch, you gotta get out and get happening, with your books.

M: I'm working on it. In *Catching the Big Fish,* you wrote that you were experiencing feelings of anger at a certain point in your life, before you learned to start meditating. Do you still struggle with that today?

D: No, I'm not really that angry about anything. It's like I say, life gets more like a game. There's lots of people that are angry, and I just say that the anger, you know, you get angry enough and it causes a disease. And there's all these stress-related illnesses. So there're illnesses that maybe aren't connected to stress, who knows why those come, but you can get rid of stress-related illness by transcending every day. Stress goes away. The things that used to stress you don't stress you so much. And the old stresses that are hooked in there like barbed wire, ingrained all through your body, these stresses, they start to dissolve, evaporate. You start feeling so good, so stress-free. And stress-related illness isn't going to get you. There's people that things happen to and they get really, really sad, or really, really angry, and then a little bit down the road they get some kind of strange disease. Save yourself, get this technique, and start enjoying life.

M: Do you believe there are dark forces in the world as palpable things?

D: Yes, there are dark forces in the world, for sure; you just gotta look around, you can feel it. You can feel things going on. You might not be able to see it, but you can feel it. And we're in a time right now where we're kind of in a transition from a dark, dark time to a beautiful bright light, positive, golden time. But there's a lot of negativity that's gotta go; and there's always been the very, very good, and the very, very bad swimming in the same sea. And it's just a question of balance.

M: Describe for us your perfect day.

D: Perfect day? Lots of ideas, energy to realize the ideas, tools to get the ideas done. And some very, very good coffee along the way.

M: Speaking of coffee, how do you avoid exhaustion or burn out when you're crashing on a deadline?

D: You meditate regularly; people are very fatigued these days, and when you're tired you do not feel good. And even if you just sit for a moment, you just start falling asleep, you're so tired. And you're grouchy. And the world looks dark and miserable. You start transcending every day, and that fatigue starts to lift. Energy starts replacing it, and you're wide awake, more and more wide awake each day, and it's money in the bank.

M: Have you ever seen a ghost, a UFO, or something you can't explain?

D: No, I haven't.

M: What would you say gives you your greatest satisfaction as an artist? And has it changed as you've aged?

D: I love working, and so I need ideas to know what to work on, and I love getting ideas that I love. It's a beautiful thing. For a long time, I didn't have the money to, I didn't have the tools to build something that I got an idea for. That's very frustrating, and many people are in that boat. You've gotta find a way to realize your ideas; there's huge satisfaction in realizing an idea. But where there's a will there's a way.

M: Now, one of the big parts of *Catching the Big Fish* that affected me most, personally, is where you wrote about the importance of an artist having a set up: If you're a painter you gotta have your canvases and paints ready to go. If you're a writer, you've gotta be ready to write down ideas. Has there ever been a crisis point in your life where you didn't feel you could have a set up, and you just weren't able to actualize certain ideas—and what did you do about it?

D: Yeah, as I just told you, I didn't have any money in the early days, and I lived on $200 a month, delivering the *Wall Street Journal*. But my rent was only $85 a month, I only worked five hours a week, and I had a little bungalow, and I had all the things I wanted but except for canvas and paints and to do big things. So I had to do small things, like drawings instead of paintings, and even if I got an idea for a big painting, I didn't have the money to get the stuff to do it.

M: So sometimes it's a matter of doing things on the scale that you can afford?

D: Exactly right. And then, if you're fortunate, you'll find that something will come along that will give you more money to get those things you need.

M: After meditating, how does the world look differently to you? Physically?

D: The world looks better and better and better. If you're, you know, happy inside, you know, feeling good, the world—they say the world is as you are. If you're tired and depressed and filled with stress, the world looks one way. It's like this, there's Thursday morning, you get up, the alarm goes off, you're absolutely bagged. The last thing you wanna do is get out of bed; you wanna go back to sleep so bad. You're not feeling good. You get up, the coffee is cold, somebody didn't turn the thing on, you're late for work, there's nothing but traffic. You get to work; the whole place is stressed, feeling just like you. Then you oppose that with Saturday morning: you wake up, you get to sleep in, and the sunshine is going outside, birds are chirping, and you have the whole day to do whatever you want. There's a wood shop waiting for you down there, or a painting studio, or whatever. And you just—it's a different feeling. Everything looks good. Another example is: you're madly in love with someone, and you're in the car driving, somebody cuts in front of you, so what. You just keep on driving happily, you're in love, nothin' bothers you. Somebody left you, your heart is broken. You're so upset, you're so distraught, you're so tormented by this. Somebody cuts in front of you, you wanna kill the fuckin' guy.

M: Everybody's laughing. Can we say "fucking" on NPR? I guess we'll find out.

D: I don't know, bleep it out. Sorry.

M: What advice would you give to yourself back when you were twelve or thirteen years old? If that were possible?

D: Well, I'd say: don't lose faith.

M: That's beautiful. I know you've got a crunch for time—is there anything else you'd like to say to us?

D: Pardon?

M: I know you're on a crunch for time . . .

D: No, you've done a great interview, Mitch.

M: Thank you, man. Is there anything else you'd like to add, anything else you'd like to leave people with?

D: Well, I'd like to tell people that it's enough suffering; get this technique for yourself, Transcendental Meditation as taught by Maharishi Mahesh Yogi. Get it for your family, get it for your friends, and let's all start living together like they say in a Vedic sentence—"the world is my family." Start enjoying diversity, start enjoying unity in the midst of diversity. Peace on earth. Heaven on earth. And get this going right away. Talking isn't gonna do it, laws aren't gonna do it. Watching CNN is just gonna depress you. Get this technique and get going on it right away. If you can't afford it—because the teachers need to get paid, they're full-time teachers—write a letter to the David Lynch Foundation, and we're trying to raise money so we can give this technique to people who can't afford it and who want it. Get it for your kid's school. Get it for your place of work. And start saying goodbye to suffering and negativity in this world.

M: There's a line of verse that you sometimes read to your audiences when you speak to them. Is that something you can say to us now?

D: Sure, that's a four-line verse. I'll say it now, okay?

M: Thank you, yes.

D: *May everyone be happy. May everyone be free of disease. May auspiciousness be seen everywhere. May suffering belong to no one. Peace.*

M: David, thank you so much.

D: You got it, Mitch. Take care, buddy.

M: God bless—be well.

D: God bless you, Mitch.

17

THE MAN WHO DESTROYED SKEPTICISM

Scourge of Psychics James Randi Was No Skeptic;
Our Culture Is Poorer as a Result

Widely celebrated for his skepticism, stage magician and psychic-buster James Randi (1928–2020) was, in my estimation, less a crusading debunker of woo than a culture warrior for materialist thought. Over the course of his nearly four-decade career, Randi degraded our ability to discuss and consider contentious issues in science, and to bring measured thinking to questions of the extra-physical. Written amid a flood of otherwise heroizing obituaries, this article questioned Randi's legacy. It met with a good deal of support—and a chorus of vituperative and, in some cases, coordinated pushback, a Randian tactic that I expected. In the end, the United States has probably lost more than a generation of progress in clinical research of ESP due to the efforts of Randi and his supporters. We as a culture will pick up the pieces; I hope starting here. This article appeared at Boing Boing *on October 26, 2020.*

Several years ago I was preparing a talk on the life of occult journeyer Madame H. P. Blavatsky (1831–1891) for the Rubin Museum of Art in New York City. Someone on Facebook asked sardonically: "Will James Randi be there?" My interlocutor was referencing the man known worldwide as a debunker of psychical and paranormal claims. (That my online critic was outspoken about his own religious beliefs posed no apparent irony for him.)

Last week marked the death at age ninety-two of James "The Amazing" Randi, a stage magician who became internationally famous as a skeptic—indeed Randi rebooted the term "skepticism" as a response to the boom in psychical claims and research in the post-Woodstock era. Today, thousands of journalists, bloggers, and the occasional scientist call themselves skeptics in the mold set by Randi. Over the past decade, the investigator himself was heroized in documentaries, profiles, and, now, obituaries. A *Guardian* columnist eulogized him as the "prince of reason."*

I mourn Randi's passing for those who loved him, and there were many. But his elevation to the Mount Rushmore of skepticism obfuscates a basic truth. In the end, the feted researcher was no skeptic. He was to skepticism what Senator Joseph McCarthy was to anticommunism—a showman, a bully, and, ultimately, the very thing he claimed to fight against: a fraud. This has corroded our intellectual culture—in a Trumpian age when true skepticism is desperately needed.

▲

Born Randall James Hamilton Zwinge in Toronto in 1928, Randi became a celebrated stage magician and escape artist, who appeared in prestigious venues and on television shows, including an episode of *Happy Days*. His stage aesthetics and devices were often brilliant and original. Randi toured with rock icon Alice Cooper in 1973, designing a mock beheading-by-guillotine for the proto-metal star. When claiming the garland of skepticism in the early 1970s, the MacArthur-winning Randi announced his intention to expose phony faith healers and grifter psychics.

---

*"Farewell James Randi, prince of reason. Now who'll mock the quacks and anti-vaxxers?" by Catherine Bennett, October 25, 2020.

Today, many people know Randi from the award-winning 2014 documentary, *An Honest Liar*. But the laudatory and engaging profile tells its story in a fashion that skeptics traditionally decry: including only the magician's successful exposes (some of which were more questionable than the film allows)* and obfuscating his darker and more lasting impact: making it more difficult for serious university-based and academically trained researchers to study ESP and mental anomalies, and to receive a fair hearing in the news media. Indeed, Randi ultimately cheapened an important debate over how or whether extra-physical mentality can be studied under scientifically rigorous conditions and evaluated by serious people.

In a typical example, the *New York Times* ran a 2015 piece about a recent wave of fraudulent and flawed psychology studies;† its lead paragraph cited a 2011 precognition study, "Feeling the Future," by Cornell University psychologist Daryl J. Bem—without justifying why it was grouped with polluted research or even further referencing Bem's study in the article. (I wrote to the *Times* to object. The paper has used several of my letters and op-eds, often on controversial subjects—this time, crickets.)

In the pioneering days of scholarly psychical research in the United States, roughly between the 1930s and 1960s, Duke University housed a highly regarded center for the study of ESP, founded by researchers J. B. and Louisa Rhine. Yet today the Rhine Research Center functions off-campus as a nonprofit organization and, while individual researchers and a handful of university labs soldier on, many college textbooks brand ESP research a pseudoscience,‡ often citing Randi's work as the

---

*E.g., see the critically important paper "Reflections on 'Project Alpha': Scientific Experiment or Conjuror's Illusion?", *Zetetic Scholar* (1987) by Marcello Truzzi, a constructive and vital voice of skepticism to whom I return. It is posted on the website for The Australian Institute of Parapsychological Research.

†"Many Psychology Findings Not as Strong as Claimed, Study Says" by Benedict Carey, August 27, 2015.

‡E.g., see: "The coverage of parapsychology in introductory psychology textbooks: 1990–2002" by James McClenon, Miguel Roig, Matthew D. Smith, Gillian Ferrier, *Journal of Parapsychology* (Spring 2003).

source of that opinion, so the topic is shunned by most academics and journalists who cover them.

As a historian and writer on metaphysical topics, I have spent time among fraudulent mediums, and I share Randi's outrage at their manipulations. I have no issue with his or others' targeting of stage psychics and woo-woo con artists—I join in it.* But Randi made his name, and influenced today's professional skeptics, by smearing the work of serious researchers. This includes Rhine, who, in founding the original parapsychology lab at Duke with his wife and co-researcher Louisa, labored intensively—and in a scientifically conservative manner that reverse-mirrored Randi's work—to devise research protocols for testing psychical phenomena.

In one of Randi's freely distributed classroom guides for teachers, *Do You Have ESP?* (2012), he misleadingly stated that Rhine had reported only positive results in his ESP trials. In fact, in the early 1930s, when Rhine's lab opened, it was standard practice in the behavioral and life sciences to discount experiments with null or negative results. But Rhine was one of the first academic researchers to recognize this common practice as a problem, and then to explicitly reject it. By 1940, with the publication of *Extra-Sensory Perception After Sixty Years,* Rhine's lab took a leading role in reporting *all* results, positive and negative, ahead of the curve of other researchers.

Randi's contemporaneous parapsychology skeptics, including science writer Martin Gardner and University of Oregon psychologist Ray Hyman, differed from Randi's uncritical dismissals by offering qualified respect to Rhine and his protégé Charles Honorton, with whom Hyman coauthored a 1986 paper in the *Journal of Parapsychology* validating Honorton's research methods[†] In a moment of intellectual probity, the skeptic Gardner wrote of Rhine in his 1952 book *Fads and Fallacies in the Name of Science:* "It should be stated immediately that Rhine is

---

*E.g., see my article "How to Spot a Sketchy Spiritual Guru," *Medium,* June 19, 2018.
[†]"A Joint Communiqué: The Psi Ganzfeld Controversy," *Journal of Parapsychology* (December 1986).

clearly not a pseudoscientist to a degree even remotely comparable to that of most of the men discussed in this book. He is an intensely sincere man, whose work has been undertaken with a care and competence that cannot be dismissed easily, and which deserves a far more serious treatment." (Another notable contemporary was sociologist Marcello Truzzi—a self-described "constructive skeptic"—who criticized Randi's methods in the paper cited earlier. Truzzi coined the maxim popularized by astronomer Carl Sagan: "Extraordinary claims require extraordinary proof.")

To Randi, such moderate tones were alien. When criticizing the parapsychology research of University of Arizona psychology professor Gary E. Schwartz, for example, Randi repeatedly accused the researcher of believing in Santa Claus and the tooth fairy, and taunted him with the Trump-worthy sobriquet "Gullible Gary."* Randi showed no compunction about brutalizing reputations and ignoring complexities. Indeed, Randi showed willingness to mislead the public about testing certain paranormal claims—while simultaneously touting his "results" and trashing reputations. Such was the case with his public rebuttal to Cambridge University biologist Rupert Sheldrake. Sheldrake's theory of "morphic resonance" proposes that "memory is inherent in nature." The biologist has written that "morphic fields of social groups connect together members of the group even when they are many miles apart, and provide channels of communication through which organisms can stay in touch at a distance. They help provide an explanation for telepathy."† To this Randi retorted: "We at JREF [James Randi Educational Foundation] have tested these claims. They fail."

Yet Sheldrake complained that Randi ignored his requests to see the test data. In 2014, reporter Will Storr of Britain's the *Telegraph* followed up with Randi and received a series of dog-ate-my-homework excuses—until the reporter realized that the Amazing Randi was either misleading him about the existence of tests, or was proffering an incredibly

---

*See Schwartz's letter to Randi at the Survival Science 50 Megs website.
†"Morphic Resonance and Morphic Fields—an Introduction" at Rupert Sheldrake's website.

byzantine (and inconsistent) backstory that the results "got washed away in a flood."* Unbelievable as Randi's responses were, he continued running down the biologist in public. This is what sociologist Truzzi dubbed "pseudoskepticism": rejection absent investigation.

Amid Randi's persistent and questionable media dings, academics began to recoil. John G. Kruth, executive director of the Rhine lab, experienced the chill firsthand in the 1980s. "As the old guard began to age out of the field," he said, "there were very few opportunities for new researchers to study parapsychology . . . younger students typically had to travel abroad or design their own study programs."

Beyond scholarly circles, Randi set the template for a zealous band of professional skeptics, many of whom are science journalists or bloggers who focus on niche takedown pieces of people who study any form of ESP, mediumship, or anomalies. Even more damaging over the last decade has been a group of self-described "Guerrilla Skeptics"—winners of the 2017 James Randi Educational Foundation (JREF) Award—who wage a kind of freewheeling digital jihad on Wikipedia, tendentiously revising or trolling pages about scientific parapsychology and the lives of its key players.

"While there are lots of anonymous trolls that have worked hard to trash any Wikipedia pages related to psi, including bios of parapsychologists," said Dean Radin, chief scientist at the Institute of Noetic Sciences in northern California, one of a few remaining scholarly parapsychology labs, "this group of extreme skeptics is proudly open that they are rewriting history . . . any attempt to edit those pages, even fixing individual words, is blocked or reverted almost instantly."

Another case was Randi's yearly "million-dollar challenge," often held in Las Vegas, in which he tempted psychics with a cash prize. For years it was an annual charade to which virtually no serious observer or claimant would venture near.† Journalist and NPR producer Stacy

---

*"James Randi: debunking the king of the debunkers" by Will Storr, *Telegraph,* December 9, 2014.
†E.g., see: "A Critical Look at Randi's Million Dollar Challenge" by Craig Weiler, January, 2, 2011, at The Weiler Psi Blog website.

Horn, who wrote about Rhine's lab at Duke University in her 2009 book *Unbelievable,* queried Randi in June 2008 about his million-dollar prize. She told me:

> I had an exchange with Randi because I was going to have the following sentences about his million-dollar prize in my book:
>
> "To date, Randi's million-dollar prize has not been awarded, but according to Chris Carter, author of *Parapsychology and the Skeptics,* Randi backs off from any serious challenge. 'I always have an out,' he has been quoted as saying."
>
> I sent that to Randi to ask him if he really said that . . . He wrote back saying that the quote was true, but incomplete. What he really said was, "I always have an 'out'—I'm right!"
>
> It seemed like he thought he was being amusing, but I didn't really know a lot about him yet. But it also seemed to indicate that the million-dollar prize might not really be a serious offer. So I asked him how a decision was made, was there a committee, and who was on it? He replied, "If someone claims they can fly by flapping their arms, the results don't need any 'decision.' What 'committee'? Why would a committee be required? I don't understand the question."
>
> At that point I wrote him off and decided to not mention his prize in my book since it just seemed like a publicity stunt for Randi.

The *Telegraph*'s Storr wondered what—besides organizing the yearly Vegas conference (discontinued in 2015)—Randi's nonprofit JREF actually *does:*

> More recently I've begun to wonder about his educational foundation, the JREF, which claims tax exempt status in the US and is partly dependant on public donations. I wondered what actual educative work the organisation—which between 2011 and 2013 had an average revenue of $1.2 million per year—did. Financial documents reveal just $5,100, on average, being spent on grants.

There are some e-books, videos, and lesson plans on subjects such as fairies on their website. They organise an annual fan convention. James Randi, over that period, has been paid an average annual salary of $195,000. My requests for details of the educational foundation's educational activities, over the last 12 months, were dodged and then ignored.

The two years that follow, according to public filings, show executive compensation at an average of over $197,000, more than 20 percent of the Foundation's total yearly revenue.* According to a contemporaneous analysis of 100,000 nonprofit CEO salaries, this figure nearly triples the average compensation in JREF's revenue class.†

Randi proved hugely adept at sound bites. Most researchers and scientists do poorly with sound bites. Such devices contributed to his being lionized in news coverage‡ by observers who seemed genuinely unaware of his unwillingness to distinguish between parapsychologists who perform juried and meticulous work, such as scientists Dean Radin and Rupert Sheldrake, versus the average storefront psychic. The "broad smear" and polarized thinking typify most professional skepticism today.

Indeed, when encountering the efforts of clinicians, such as Rhine and Radin, Randi often played "move the goalpost." Physicists Bruce Rosenblum and Fred Kuttner made this pertinent historical observation in their book *Quantum Enigma: Physics Encounters Consciousness:* "Greek science had a fatal flaw. *It had no mechanism to compel consensus.* The Greeks saw experimental tests of scientific conclusions as no more relevant than were experimental tests of political or aesthetic positions. Conflicting views

---

*See the James Randi Educational Foundation listing available from the Nonprofit Explorer on the Pro Publica website.
†See: "High Pay for Nonprofit Execs? Analysis of 100,000 Salaries" by Linda Lamptin, June 5, 2012 on the Blue Avocado Website.
‡E.g., see: "The Unbelievable Skepticism of the Amazing Randi" by Adam Higginbotham, *New York Times Magazine,* November 7, 2014.

could be argued indefinitely." Randi and his admirers embraced this flaw as a polemical device, often wearing down scientists and winning over journalists with perpetual, repeat-loop disparagement of ESP research and other science they disfavored, no matter how valid the methods.

▲

We urgently need good skeptics today. We are living under the cloud of a president who spreads QAnon conspiracy theories and 5 a.m. Twitter smears, while questioning the gravity of Covid, the reality of climate change (as Randi did, too*—along with a proclivity for eugenics†), and the facts of responsible news coverage. Even in our truth-challenged times, however, Randi never stopped baiting researchers and punching down at eccentrics who may have been self-deluded about their psychical abilities.

Yes, Randi may have bagged some con artists along the way. Senator McCarthy may have caught a few authentic Soviet sympathizers or spies. But at what cost? Each man laid tracks for future demagogues who proved less interested in defending facts than in promulgating smears and half-truths for personal benefit.

I sympathize with those who want to challenge credulity and generalized references to psychical phenomena—and all the more with researchers and investigators who expose frauds. I sympathize, too, with those who have lost a man, a friend, and a spouse. But to the intellectual community, and anyone concerned with critical inquiry in general, Randi's legacy should serve as a cautionary tale, and a call to restore sound practices when discussing or writing about contentious topics in science or any field. These are things that a showman can deter but never erase.

---

*James Randi, "AGW Revisited," December 15, 1999, James Randi Educational Foundation website.
†"James Randi: Let Survival of the Fittest 'Act Itself Out' on Those with Low IQ and 'Mental Aberrations'" by Greg Taylor, *Daily Grail,* February 14, 2013.

PART V

Damned History

By the damned, I mean the excluded.
CHARLES FORT,
THE BOOK OF THE DAMNED, 1919

18

THE WAR ON WITCHES

And How to End It

July 4, 2014, marked a personal milestone in my career: I published an op-ed in the New York Times. *I am almost embarrassed to admit it, but this was something for which I hungered—reflecting perhaps too great an attachment to mainstream approval. Seeking respectability is, as I noted earlier from Krishnamurti's insight, the greatest barrier to personal growth. After acceptance, I waited months until publication of my piece on modern-day witch hunts—the real kind, in which accused spellcasters are persecuted, physically attacked, and often killed. Shortly before it appeared, just as we were rounding the final corner of a long editing process, an opinion editor told me, "Look, you know we don't publish pieces like this often, so when the factchecker contacts you, be completely ready to verify and backup everything." I was ready. I had so much source material at hand, and had supplied it sufficiently in advance, that the factchecker had barely a single question.*

The experience left me a bit rueful, however. A lot of what appears on the op-ed pages of influential publications is based on cultural affinities. In fact, mediocre or under-researched pieces sometimes sail through because they are congenial to the outlook of assigning editors. The Times put my op-ed through months of editing and rewrites—yet I believe, with as much objectivity as I can muster, that the original version was actu-

ally a bit better than the final product. For that reason, I have opted to reproduce the original here.

More important: this piece calls attention to the persistent problem of violence against accused witches and others who practice outsider spirituality, or who are believed to. It shows what ultimately occurs when communities punish thoughts, identity, and ideas—and how such violence can be ended. The effort at combatting global violence against witches attained a milestone in 2021 when the United Nations Human Rights Council passed a resolution specifically calling attention to the crisis and urging member states to take legal action against it.

———————————

Violence against accused "witches" remains a grim fact of life in the twenty-first century. And it is growing worse.

In an era of Broadway hits such as *Wicked,* and *Buffy*-style television programs that feature appealing young witches, we like to think of witch hunts as something that petered out after the mob murders in Salem, Massachusetts, in the early 1690s. But late this past January, a Queens, New York, man was arrested for beating his girlfriend and her twenty-five-year-old daughter to death with a hammer, telling police that the women were "witches" who had been "performing voodoo and casting spells" on him.*

Voodoo, more properly known as Vodou, is an authentic Afro-Caribbean faith based in deity worship and ritual, practiced in New York and many American cities. Other belief systems that retain or reinvent ancient nature worship and spell practices sometimes go under the names of Wicca or neo-paganism.

It is too early to know whether the Queens victims had ties to Vodou or any related systems of faith. Accusations like those made by the suspected murderer, who is under psychiatric evaluation, rarely contain any shade of truth—but such language, even when the product of psychosis or delusion, is being heard with alarming and growing

———————

*The murderer, Carlos Amarillo, was given two consecutive life sentences in 2017.

frequency around the world today as an incitement to violence.

The past several years have witnessed a spate of news coverage of disturbingly similar acts of violence against accused witches in Africa, the Pacific, Latin America, and immigrant communities in the United States and Western Europe. While the last international efforts to track such violence appeared in a United Nations Refugee Agency Report in 2009 and a UNICEF report in 2010—both of which found a rise, especially in Africa, of violence and child abuse linked to witchcraft accusations—recent reports suggest a deepening and disturbing pattern of torture, mutilations, mob attacks, and murder, often claiming women as victims.

Early last year, a mob in Papua New Guinea burned alive a young mother, Kepari Leniata, who was accused of sorcery. Violent mobs took the lives of at least two other Papua New Guinea women accused of witchery in 2008 and 2009. In all these cases the victims were publicly burned before crowds of hundreds, who in Ms. Leniata's case reportedly blocked police. "These are becoming all too common in certain parts of the country," complained Prime Minister Peter O'Neill.

As a result, the southwestern Pacific nation—where fear of witches is widespread in rural areas (and can also be found among police, who sometimes display indifference to this violence)—last year repealed a 1971 law that permitted attackers to cite intent to combat witchcraft as a legal defense. But progress is slow. Although police charged a man and woman in the 2013 killing of Ms. Leniata, Amnesty International issued a statement in February protesting the absence of convictions.

Related violence—ranging from rape to murders to the parental abandonment of children accused of witchcraft—has been reported from South Africa to India. In early 2012, two horrific murders, each claiming women, occurred in Columbia and Nepal following accusations of witchery. Indeed, one of the grimmest aspects of these crimes is their brutality. Victims are often burned alive, as in the Papua New Guinea and Nepal cases; beaten to death, as in Columbia; or are beheaded or stoned, as has been reported in Indonesia and sub-Saharan Africa.

United Nations officials have described such murders as running into the tens of thousands worldwide, while beatings and banishments could run as high as the millions. "This is becoming an international problem—it is a form of persecution and violence that is spreading around the globe," Jeff Crisp, head of the UN's refugee agency, told a panel in 2009, the last year in which an international body studied the worldwide dimensions of this problem.

One human rights expert in Australia estimates that witchcraft-related violence in the South Pacific is directed five-to-one against women. But children are increasingly victims in other parts of the world, particularly Central and West Africa.

The UN's Office of the High Commissioner for Human Rights reported that most of the 25,000 to 50,000 children who live on the streets of Kinshasa, the capital of the Democratic Republic of Congo, ended up there after abandonment by families who accused them of witchcraft or possession. Accusations against "child witches" are fairly new. According to human rights researcher Aleksandra Cimpric, who has studied witchcraft-related violence in the Central African Republic, some of the earliest cases took hold around 2006.

No one is quite sure why this is happening now, but experts point to overpopulation, stresses on parents who are forced to relocate to cities to seek work, and the intense difficulties of raising children amid raw poverty. Particularly vulnerable are children who suffer from disabilities or protracted illnesses, which are sometimes seen as signs of demon possession. These superstitions are stoked by local "healers" who charge parents to exorcise evil spirits.

The attacks on children are not limited to the economically deprived regions of the sub-Sahara. In 2012, England's *Daily Mail* reported "a rise in sadistic murders and attacks on children accused of witchcraft," noting eighty-one "sorcery cases" within the last decade, mostly in South Asian and African immigrant communities. These included the 2012 torture and murder of a fifteen-year-old boy, Kristy Bamu, in East London, at the hands of his older sister and her boyfriend, both Congolese nationals, who accused him of sorcery after he wet his bed.

(Such events are sometimes considered a sign of *kindoki,* or witchcraft, in the Congolese Lingala language.)

The episode spiraled into accusations of possession and witchery, during which the boy's attackers, over a period of several days, knocked out his teeth with a hammer, smashed floor tiles over his head, slashed him with knives, and finally drowned him in icy bathtub water.

British police are now receiving special training in understanding and anticipating witchcraft-related abuse.

The Western violence tells a particular story, insofar as it seems to occur either within immigrant communities, as with the London killing, or within pockets of Caribbean or Hispanic communities, as with the recent Queens, New York, killing, where there exists a presence, culturally and in occasional personal practice, of Santeria, Vodou, or some of the Latin-Caribbean traditions that are associated with witchcraft or spell work. Hence, this violence can be seen to "migrate" today across varying lines of geography.

Nor are such murders limited to mob violence or acts of sadistic vigilantism. Some legal systems sanction the killing of accused witches. In 2011, Saudi Arabian courts, in two separate incidents, sentenced a man and woman to beheading after convictions for sorcery. In 2013, Saudi courts sentenced two Asian housemaids to 1,000 lashings and 10 years in prison on charges of casting spells against their employers.

In a case that attracted international attention, a Lebanese TV personality, Ali Hussain Sibat, was arrested in Saudi Arabia in 2008 and sentenced to beheading for sorcery. Apprehended by that nation's notorious religious police while on a pilgrimage in Medina, Mr. Sibat was targeted for hosting a popular television show in his native Lebanon, "The Hidden," where he would make psychic predictions and prescribe love potions and spells. After an outcry by Amnesty International and other human-rights watchers, Saudi courts in 2010 stayed Mr. Sibat's execution, but sentenced him to a fifteen-year prison term.

Today Mr. Sibat remains imprisoned despite "many promises from the Lebanese government and from the president of the Lebanese republic to release him" through talks with Saudi Arabia, said his Lebanon-based lawyer, May El Khansa.*

As in Africa, the wave of anti-witchery violence in Saudi Arabia is fairly new. That nation's religious police, the Committee for the Promotion of Virtue and the Prevention of Vice, devised an Anti-Witchcraft Unit in 2009, resulting in the arrests of 215 accused conjurors in 2012.

This sudden interest in witchery can probably be traced to the royal family's attempts to appease its religious inquisitors by keeping them busy targeting a defenseless (and probably mislabeled) handful of individuals. The religious police terrorize various segments of Saudi society while remaining a politically popular force among the nation's most fervently conservative constituencies. (Not surprisingly, the *Harry Potter* series is banned in the desert monarchy.)

▲

In analyzing this global phenomenon, it is tempting to point to poverty and scapegoating as chief causes. And such forces are undoubtedly at work. But Africa and the southwestern Pacific have a long history of economic despair, while much of this violence, especially against children, has evidently worsened since 2000. The current violence—and its sheer brutality—suggests forces other than ancient superstitions and suspicions. The congregations in Africa, the brutality against children, the incidents within immigrant communities, and some of the violence against women in the Pacific—much of it appears due to contemporary triggers.

As was once seen among lynch mobs in America's Deep South, twenty-first century witch hunters are mainly young men who appear to believe that they are earning a certain degree of community prestige by cleansing undesirables and enforcing social mores—especially in Africa, where large parts of the continent experience the destabilizing currents

---

*Mr. Sibat's lawyer proved unreachable after my article appeared. I never found out why. It may be that foreign attention was deemed unhelpful. In any case, with the help of Human Rights Watch researcher Adam Coogle, I learned through a June 9, 2016, article in *al-Akhbar,* an anti-Saudi monarchy publication based in Beirut, that Mr. Sibat had been freed.

of rapid urbanization, migration, family diffusion, and the fraying of the social fabric that is sometimes brought on by disease, HIV, and gross disparities in wealth.

Another factor, again seen in central Africa and its immigrant communities, is the advent of fervent revivalist churches in which self-styled pastor-prophets rail against witchery and demon-possession, sometimes specializing in—and often charging for—the casting out of evil spirits. One of Nigeria's most popular Pentecostal preachers, Helen Ukpabio, has written in her book *Unveiling the Mysteries of Witchcraft* that "if a child under the age of 2 screams in the night, cries and is always feverish with deteriorating health, he or she is a servant of Satan." This kind of rhetoric heightens paranoia in societies already struggling with a wide range of social and economic ills.

And, finally, some experts point to fraud and graft, noting that many victims in the Pacific and Africa are widows, single mothers, or unmarried women, who, lacking in family or community protection, can be isolated and targeted, leaving them open to banishment or murder on the thinnest of charges, while their homes and property are seized by the accused's killers.

▲

Although this brutality persists across a wide range of settings and societies, it must not be accepted as a tragic repetition of old aggressions. Concrete measures can ease this violence:

- Laws against accusing children of witchcraft are needed throughout Africa and the southwestern Pacific. Such a law has already been enacted in Ms. Ukpabio's home state in Nigeria.
- Western branches of Pentecostal and Charismatic congregations should work with their African and immigrant counterparts to understand the tragedy and hatred that can spiral from "exorcisms." Pentecostal and Charismatic congregations in the U.S. do have contact with (and some influence over) newer congregations in central Africa, where some revivalist pastors stir up fury against witchcraft

and perform for-profit exorcisms. The current persecution of gays in Uganda likewise stems from an upcropping of fervent ministries. While no African congregation wants to feel dictated to by the West, there is a place for informational exchanges, cultural pressure, and Western ecclesiastical and ordaining bodies enacting prohibitions against for-profit exorcisms.

- Nations must combat police indifference to such crimes, especially in societies that traditionally harbor beliefs about "black magic," where police may be less inclined to punish those who attack perceived witches. The British government has issued instructional materials to police and social workers in immigrant communities; these could be exported and adapted to the needs of other nations.

- Witchcraft should be effectively decriminalized in nations where such prohibitions exist, such as the Solomon Islands, where witch hunts are also reported. Papua New Guinea has taken a right step in this direction, last year repealing a law that allowed attackers to claim anti-witchery as a defense. (Of less promise is that the nation extended its death penalty to those convicted of sorcery-related killings.)

- The United Nations and international human-rights organizations should begin compiling yearly statistics on these crimes so that the scale of this crisis can be properly understood.

- Perhaps most importantly, witchcraft-related violence should be branded as hate crimes by international courts, NGOs, and anywhere in the world (including the United States) where anti-hate statutes exist, either on national or municipal levels. A pillar of modern hate-crime statutes is that a victim need only be *perceived* as a member of a given group when that identification serves as a pretext to violence. Branding today's anti-witchery violence as a hate crime is vital to recognizing and combating this criminality.

The accusation of witchcraft has become an international flashpoint for mob violence. It is time to put the ghosts of Salem to rest. Twenty-first century witch hunts must end.

19

HOW I LEARNED TO STOP WORRYING AND LOVE THE ILLUMINATI

If there is one major way in which my work differs from much mass media on the occult, it is my rejection of conspiracy theorizing and speculation about secret societies. This article is adapted from a chapter in my 2020 book, The Seeker's Guide to The Secret Teachings of All Ages, *which began as a lecture at the Philosophical Research Society in Los Angeles. I believe this essay provides historical clarity to those who seek it at an anger-filled moment in American life. I am deeply concerned over the degree of QAnon-adjacent thought that occurs on the alternative spiritual scene. Conspiracism, as I define it here—and I always define it simply—is man's perpetual hunt for a hidden enemy. And this hunt nearly always results in an enemy being found, not infrequently among people accused of witchcraft, as just explored, or of "Satanism," a favorite trope of QAnon congregants. (In that vein, see my comment on the Satanic Panic in the essay "My Will Be Done.") Conspiracy theorizing is not the work of independent thinkers. It is the work of those who endanger independent thinkers.*

The question of "secret societies" is one of the most controversial and dramatic in all of esoteric spirituality. In a sense, it is particularly controversial at this moment in the twenty-first century because we are living through a period in America, and in other parts of the world, where people are suffused with a kind of *us-versus-them* mentality.

A certain degree of conspiracist thought has always been popular within American history, going back to the anti-Masonic scares of the early nineteenth century.* We seem to be experiencing an upsurge of this kind of conspiracist thinking today, in which a "hidden hand" is thought to be manipulating our destiny.

It is worth commenting on that before getting into the question and the history of secret societies. I think that within American culture today, there is a deep and justified hunger for *transparency*.

People feel like there are holes in the straight story, people feel like there are forces at work—financial and governmental—that do not have anywhere near their best interests at heart, and they feel manipulated and locked out of decision-making processes. I think this instinct is correct. But I think this instinct also gets perverted and misdirected into conspiracist thought, in which a perhaps historically real but fictitiously reimagined secret society (the Illuminati, most frequently) is cited as wielding nefarious control over human affairs. People speak in terms of different groups, like the Council on Foreign Relations; Bohemian Grove; the Bilderberg Group; Skull and Bones; the Deep State; Freemasonry, of course; and other organizations; some historically real, but reimagined along the lines of being a secret force in human affairs.

The problem I have with this outlook is that it frequently results in the us-versus-them mentality that I mentioned. It is, in certain ways, almost antithetical to the spiritual search, because the conspiracy model locates problems in the world as existing *out there,* among *them;* and those of us who are trying to expose the problem—so goes the mood that you find within conspiracist culture—are somehow always the *good guys.* It is never the mirror that we look in for the problem. It is never, or rarely, our own relationships that we scrutinize. Or our own ethics. But rather, the notion is that *some other* force that is out there somewhere perpetuates

---

*See my *Occult America* (Bantam, 2009).

manipulations and mechanizations that oppose the best interests of human flourishment. This, in the ultimate sense, perpetuates an angry, tribal mentality. This way of thought almost never leads to policy ideas or reforms; or to an understanding of the economic forces that strip the individual of decision-making ability, economic forces that often conceal their profit-making apparatus, so that the individual does not realize when he is being taken advantage of (such as by health insurers). Rather, the conspiracist model tends to cement a view of life in which the epicenter of good is usually located in *me,* the observer, and the epicenter of bad is always *out there* in a secretive, shadowy apparatus.

Not that one shouldn't be concerned with unseen policies, economic manipulation, and a paucity of social equality—those things are urgent. But I contend that anything that directs us, first and foremost, away from self is ultimately antithetical to the search. I believe that the wish for greater transparency—and the suspicion that we are being moved around by larger forces, and that we deserve greater insight and decision-making capacity—is healthy and important. It is justified.* But I very often find that *instead* of looking at, say, the pricing policies of pharmaceutical companies, or at predatory credit-card or mortgage lenders, or at the grossly inflated profits reaped by health-insurance companies that continually narrow the range of benefits payable to the consumer, or at the problems of banking deregulation, which contributed to the mortgage crisis and, hence, the Great Recession of 2008, the reverberations of which are still being felt today—instead of looking at such things, considering such things, asking about such things, and determining corrective *policies,* which are entirely within reach, we get waylaid into delving into chimeras, into notions of secret societies or occult power centers, where no solutions or causes lie. And often where nothing lies. If I were an unaccountable Big Pharma executive, I would consider conspiracy theories my best friend. Keep looking *over there*—and not at me. Or at yourself.

---

*This chapter was written prior to the Covid lockdown. I believe that public health decisions should be transparent and that the public has a vital say in shaping them.

WHITHER THE ILLUMINATI?

The notion that secret fraternities or societies are controlling things is not only simplistic, and not only (usually) in our present day part of a repeating loop of references, premises, and suppositions—in that vein, I cannot tell you how many times I hear people use the term *Illuminati* without any definition or historical grounding—but conspiracist culture often *misdirects the human gaze from the real problems and complexities* of abuse of power in our economic and governmental system. Again, the emotional hunger behind conspiracy theorizing is *right;* it is a hunger for transparency. But that hunger gets misdirected by a kind of ideologically entrenched conspiracist thought—an obsessive search for a hidden hand—and devolves into an us-versus-them schema, usually ending in paranoia of a kind, and frequently devolving into theories that demean or dehumanize other individuals and groups.

Eventually, almost all conspiracy theories, as they are practiced in the twenty-first century, lead to an exaltation of self and a suspicion of other. That is the primary problem I have with the conspiracist outlook when it is practiced as a kind of dogma.

None of this is to say that there have not been secret societies of a sort in human history, and that these secret societies have not wielded influence.

Humanity has always had a penchant for forming into fraternities, mutual aid societies, and communities of interest. And humanity, of course, always has a penchant for intrigue and self-interest; so, to some extent, those factors will always be present in whatever community or grouping we find ourselves. But what we are really concerned with here is the *actuality and role* of secret societies as a veritable force for ideas, insight, and the preservation of esoteric ritual, rite, and practice throughout the last several hundred years of history. That is an entirely legitimate area of inquiry when done with a sense of critical thought and historicism.

Now, Manly P. Hall, in *The Secret Teachings of All Ages,* and at other times, actually took a very positive measure of what we would call secret societies, including Freemasonry. Manly was a Freemason himself. He wrote several books extolling the virtues of Freemasonry as an initiatory organization dedicated to the refinement of the individual through ancient symbols and passion plays, which encrypted ideas about ethical development and the inner proportions and possibilities of the individual.

Historically speaking, Freemasonic practices include dramas and rites that depict the passage of the individual from ignorance to understanding; mastery of esoteric symbols as codes to development; internal democracy; abstention from tale-bearing or rumor mongering; and the principle that legitimate rank and privilege do not come without personal advancement. These are some of the ideals actually practiced within Freemasonry historically; this sufficiently attracted Manly, so that he became a Freemason in 1954, and in 1973 he was awarded the honorary 33rd-degree in the Scottish Rite, its highest designation. One of the last talks he delivered before his death in 1990 was to a gathering of Freemasons in Los Angeles.

Manly also took positive measure of the historical movement called Rosicrucianism, or the Rosicrucians. This name is adopted by a variety of modern groups. And, as we will see, historically Rosicrucianism may have been more of a thought movement than an actual organization.

Manly also made reference to that most controversial of groups, the Illuminati—frequently encountered today on late-night radio and online posts, but rarely understood as an authentic historical entity. Since the Illuminati is the source of so much contemporary misunderstanding, that is where I will begin. Indeed, every time I step onto a basketball court, some well-intentioned kid will see my tattoos and ask, "Are you a member of the Illuminati?" And it is not even clear what anybody means when they put that question to you. I have been accused of being the public face or PR agent for something called the Illuminati; I am supposed to be their cover, or so the story goes on certain websites.

The Illuminati, in our day, has become a catchall phrase for some sort of nefarious hidden force. Supposedly, all kinds of influential figures belong to this group—from Barack Obama to Jay-Z to Lady Gaga to Pope Francis—and some of these people are thought to disclose their affiliation through the use of symbols in their songs or media, or during Super Bowl halftime shows. Why exactly the Super Bowl or a Disney movie would be a venue to suggest one's secret allegiances, I am not sure; but the idea behind these stories is that we are being manipulated, and, again, it is *those guys,* the *Illuminati*—always someone else, someone other than the being who gazes back at me from the mirror—who is the source of the problem. And people sometimes associate the beautiful symbol of the eye and pyramid on the back of our dollar bill, about which I will say more, as some sort of code or symbol for the Illuminati.

In a sense, the real story is very different, but no less remarkable. I always tell people that actual history is, in many regards, more extraordinary than anything fantasy holds. We could learn so much if only we really wanted to probe the *actualities of history,* rather than engage in fantasizing, which admittedly—and this is another attraction of conspiracy theory—is dramatic; it is entertaining, it is alluring, it is fun. It is much more fun than understanding why your health insurance company is capable of declining perfectly valid claims—or that insurers have done market research, I aver, that finds that if you deny a certain number of valid claims and make people wait a certain number of minutes on hold, ten percent or some odd number of people will just go away in exhaustion. If you want to find evil, look there. So much in our financial life requires greater transparency; and yet, the policy requirements are difficult and sometimes confounding. Instead, we get lost talking about groups like the Illuminati.

There was, indeed, a real organization called the Illuminati. It was founded in Bavaria in 1776 by a philosopher and lawyer named Adam Weishaupt (1748–1830). Weishaupt was a remarkable and interesting man. He was a radical democrat, who believed ardently in separation of church and state; he believed that rank, privilege, and aristocratic status should not translate into license to hold governmental, legal, or parliamentary positions; he believed that government should be representative; and he believed that every individual should have the freedom to pursue his own religious ideals. He believed in radical ecumenism. Weishaupt felt that the ideals of the ancient religions of Egypt, Greece, and Rome could be revived and used as initiatory rites to refine the individual in the modern age. He practiced a kind of mystical or primeval Christianity, although he rejected *organized* Christendom and the economic benefits granted to the Church.

At the time, the government of Bavaria—like many governments across Europe—was completely intertwined with an official state church; the two formed a DNA strand of power. Hence, state-sponsored religion was given enormous legal and economic benefits, all of which Weishaupt wanted to abolish. If some of this sounds familiar, bear in mind that it is not accidental that Weishaupt founded the Illuminati in Bavaria in 1776—a date that was very important to him, because he identified with some of the most radical ideals of the American founders, especially those of Thomas Paine and, to a degree, Thomas Jefferson (although Weishaupt was much more interested in initiatory religion and spirituality than Jefferson). And Jefferson knew about Weishaupt, about which I will have more to say.

Weishaupt was also friendly with the philosopher Goethe, who was a member of the order; possibly with the composer Mozart, who belonged to a Freemasonic lodge steeped in Illuminati members;* and with a wide range of artists, philosophers, and political reformers who agreed with his ideas about the establishment of a civic democracy, the protection of the individual search for meaning, and the separation of church and state authority. Those were Weishaupt's *primary* ideals. He wanted to form revolutionary cells within Bavarian society, and in other parts of Europe, to oppose the church-state complex, and to help disseminate, agitate, and advocate for these reformist-radical ideas within monarchical societies.

---

*For references to this milieu, see Katharine Thompson's rare and impeccably researched, *The Masonic Thread in Mozart* (Lawrence and Wishart, 1977). Also see *The Bavarian Illuminati* by René Le Forestier, translated by Jon E. Graham (Inner Traditions, 1914, 2022).

Weishaupt also had, as I mentioned, a deep personal interest in the rites and rituals of the mystery traditions of Persia, Egypt, Rome, and Greece. He was interested in the ideas that grew out of the occult Renaissance across Europe. He was interested in the Hermetic literature, which we discussed earlier. He believed, quite rightly, that threads of ideas and symbolism had reached modern people from deepest antiquity, and that these threads could sometimes be found within the Hermetic writings, within some of the occult practices that developed and were refined during the Renaissance, and within the rites and rituals of Freemasonry, a group that he venerated.

In short, Weishaupt devised a plan to form a renegade Freemasonic movement, which was called the *Illuminati*—the illumined ones. He intended to assemble a cluster of like-minded political radicals to secretly infiltrate Freemasonic lodges, which is why I call him a renegade Freemason. In so doing, Weishaupt intended to remake these lodges into vehicles for political reform or revolution.

Now, seen from one perspective, Weishaupt had good reason to be secretive. The Bavarian government brutally punished its political enemies; in Bavaria and other parts of Europe at the time, if you were considered a provocateur who advocated overthrowing the prevailing church-state order, you could meet with harassment, arrest, jailing—or worse. Hence, there were reasons for secrecy that went beyond the drama of "secret societies." Because of this, Weishaupt was attracted to another secretive body—clandestine might be a better way of putting it. Freemasonry not only operated, in many respects, below the radar of government authority, but had the same taste and penchant for occult and esoteric symbolism, and for the rituals and rites of personal initiation and refinement, that Weishaupt did. The agitator considered it a perfect marriage.

That is one part of the picture. There also arises the ethical question of conducting your political program under the screen of secrecy. Mahatma Gandhi, who had early involvements with the Theosophical Society and was a lifelong admirer of the occult movement, stated that he never actually joined any esoteric organization because he believed that secrecy is ultimately at odds with true democracy. Thomas Jefferson, a contemporary of Weishaupt, saw it differently: although Jefferson had no taste for esoteric spirituality, he nonetheless wrote admiringly about the revolutionary. In a letter of January 31, 1800, Jefferson defended Weishaupt, noting that the renegade essentially believed in the refinement of the individual and in the practice of some of the civil reforms that had proceeded in the U.S.

Jefferson concluded that if Weishaupt lived in the new republic, clandestine behavior would be unnecessary: "if Wishaupt [sic] had written here, where no secrecy is necessary in our endeavors to render men wise & virtuous, he would not have thought of any secret machinery for that purpose." But Jefferson believed that because Weishaupt lived in a more politically and religiously oppressive society, a degree of secrecy was forced upon him.

Within this atmosphere, Weishaupt began his program to infiltrate Masonic lodges and transform them into political vehicles. Is it defensible to enter any organization with an ulterior purpose? I have given you two points of view on the matter. Personally, I believe in transparency. But I am speaking from a twenty-first century perspective. Someone living in an oppressive, church-state apparatus in 1776 could easily and justifiably see things differently. In any case, Weishaupt's efforts did not get very far. He interjected himself into a few lodges, he wrote a few tracts, he attracted a few confederates, but he also quickly aroused the suspicion of the state. The Duke of Bavaria, Charles Theodore, orchestrated a series of laws to decimate the Illuminati: in 1784, the monarchy outlawed all non-approved societies; in 1785, the government specifically disbanded the Illuminati; in 1787, members of the Illuminati could suffer the seizure of their property; and in 1790, the Duke's government issued its final edict outlawing the Illuminati. These democratic reformers were harassed, exiled, and jailed. After 1790, the scent trail of the Illuminati goes completely cold.

Of course, some like to say that the Illuminati merely went deeper underground. That is speculation, at best. Consider that the next time historical writers addressed the question of the Illuminati was to theorize that the secret sect lay behind the French Revolution—a conspiracy theory that Jefferson, who was ambassador to France at the outbreak of the revolution, called "perfectly the ravings of a Bedlamite" in his letter of January 31, 1800. A variety of pamphleteers began to argue that this overwhelming revolution could not possibly have swept away the old order overnight; there had to be some hidden mechanism behind it. Thus reenters the Illuminati, now cast as an all-powerful conspiratorial villain, and described in almost completely fictitious terms. Consider: the Bavarian government outlawed the Illuminati within about nine years, and the group was brutally disbanded and dispersed, but pamphleteers following the French Revolution insisted that the old order just could not have dissolved so quickly.

Revolutions and dramatic political reforms have a discordant, deeply disorienting effect on anyone attached to the old order. People are sometimes shocked that the old world they once knew could be upended and vanish so quickly. Rarely do they take the time to look at or understand the cumulative social causes that provided an antecedent, which can be traced out and predicted if an observer applies scrutiny to the matter. Nonetheless, it can feel shocking when change finally occurs, regardless of the buildup; it can feel sudden, jarring, and disorienting. It is easier, simpler, and more tempting to understand that change as having been the product of some kind of hidden plan or schism, rather than social conditions that proved inevitably unsustainable.

Even when events are cumulative, change itself seems sudden. If you backtrack a year from the mortgage crisis of 2008, which triggered the Great Recession, it is possible to detect (at least in hindsight) that trouble was on the horizon, that so much of the securities industry and its mortgage-lending apparatus was unsustainable. But few voices, including financial "experts" at leading brokerage houses, made any such observation. And when the crash occurred over the course of a weekend, there was panic. The events themselves felt *sudden;* it felt like prosperity had gone boom-and-bust, almost literally in the space of seventy-two hours. I watched a relative, a partner at a major bank, rush into work on a Sunday shell-shocked at what was occurring. Suddenly, a vast banking concern like Bear Stearns closed down. Bear Stearns was a household name in the banking world, and it crashed and vanished in about seventy-two hours. And that is just one financial institution.

Financial change, unexpected election results, and mass protests can be part of a great contextual chain, yet the event itself can still feel sudden. Hence, for figures who had been attached to the aristocracy or the church structure, or their sympathizers, the French Revolution felt unreal. And it was easy to redirect attention to a neighboring "secret society" that had been outlawed by another aristocratically based government, and that could be considered the hidden hand behind this supposedly inexplicable reversal. And this cycle of conspiracism continued. The Illuminati theory was revived after the Russian Revolution, after Vatican II, and after other disruptive social events in Europe into the early twentieth century.

A variant of the hidden-hand concept was inadvertently revived by President George H. W. Bush (1924–2018). In two addresses to joint sessions of Congress—on September 11, 1990, at the start of the first Iraq War, and on March 6, 1991, at the war's end—the elder Bush described the emergence of a "new world order." His use of this phrase at the dawning of the digital era caught the ear of conspiracy theorists, who interpreted it as code for world domination by groups like the Illuminati, or a hidden global cabal.

If you read the speeches themselves, Bush, validly or not, was making reference to the possibility that, with the conclusion of the first Iraq War, there could be a new era of commerce, peace treaties, cultural exchange, and so on; it was a bit of fanciful idealism. He drew upon a phrase, New World Order—or New Order of the Ages—that appears in Latin in the Great Seal of United States, a topic explored earlier in the essay "Occult American." Bush's phrasing, which has now been surpassed by "Deep State," was interpreted as a catchphrase for unseen forces, and it drummed up a new chapter of conspiracy theorizing around the Illuminati, a group that has not actually existed for close to 250 years.

Those are the facts of the Illuminati's existence and the perpetuation of its mythos. As noted, I think we should seek to understand the group's radical democratic ideals, and its attachment to the occult and esoteric traditions of antiquity, as an *alternative* to a church order that had grown grotesquely calcified. I think Weishaupt should be understood as a radical political reformer, in the same way we consider a figure like Thomas Paine—even if one has misgivings, as I do, about Weishaupt's secrecy. This was Manly P. Hall's understanding of the Illuminati, and my wish is that students could be educated about this history, so that they might find such a group inspiring, if flawed, rather than frightful and fantastical.

ENTER FREEMASONRY

Likewise, there are a lot of dramatic ideas around Freemasonry, which rivals the Illuminati in its reputation for skullduggery, most of it unfounded. Freemasonry, on which I commented earlier, is a historically fascinating and, in some ways, justly mysterious group, because even within the Freemasonic order itself, where you can find some truly first-class historians, there is no consensus as to the order's origins. The group's founding remains the subject of debate. Masonry may be the only modern organization for which that is true.

On an idealistic level, some will say that Freemasonry goes back to the builders of Solomon's Temple; some will say it goes back to the builders of the pyramids; some will say, more traditionally speaking, that it goes back to the stone-making guilds, the cathedral-building guilds, of the Middle Ages. I believe there is historical validity to that latter outlook. I am not sure that it covers *all* the bases, because there are aspects of Freemasonry that are deeply esoteric in nature, and we may never have the full story. But it is possible that the order began among the great cathedral builders, at least in part.

Regarding the timeline of Masonry's development, we possess a few important and tantalizing signposts. One of the most significant is the diaries of British esotericist and antiquarian Elias Ashmole (1617–1692). Ashmole wrote in his diaries of 1646 about being inducted into an order of Masons, and that this induction ceremony had a spiritual and esoteric quality. This account is very useful, because it is one of the first and earliest explicit references to Freemasonic practice found on the European continent. It was not until more than a generation later, in 1717, that the Grand Lodge of England actually emerged aboveground with the public declaration of its existence. That is the crucial year in the history of Freemasonry. These dates are significant bookends because— while they are certainly not the only pertinent dates and other, earlier references than Ashmole can be linked to Freemasonry—the Ashmole diaries are inarguably clear; they make it plain that he was inducted into a Masonic order of esoteric spiritual outlook.

Freemasonry, like the Illuminati, has always had a tense and uncomfortable relationship with church authority, in Europe in particular, because Masonry as it emerged on the public scene in the 1700s promulgated a belief in God and a radical ecumenism but *existed outside of the authority* of any church structure.* And, as it happened, there were major figures who emerged from the folds of Freemasonry, including the Italian democratic revolutionary Giuseppe Garibaldi (1807–1882), who fought militarily against church authority in Italy and other parts of Europe. It is important to remember that even into the 1870s, there were still monarchies in control in Europe. And this was true into the 1900s in Russia. It was not until the 1870s, under pressure from unifying Italian democrats, that the church officially disbanded its private army and militia, allowing for the emergence of a democratic republic of Italy. Garibaldi, a Freemason and revolutionary, militarily opposed

---

*In a papal bull of 1738, Pope Clement XII denounced Masonry; Pope Leo XIII issued an anti-Masonic encyclical in 1884, which was reaffirmed in 1983 by Cardinal Ratzinger (the future Pope Benedict XVI); and even the usually temperate Pope Francis condemned "Masonic lobbies" in a 2013 interview.

the church; there was a civil war going on in what is today the modern state of Italy, which hinged on the effort to disband the Vatican as a separate and independent military fiefdom. To put it simply, religious or monarchical military power was a fact of life in Europe into the late-nineteenth century, and in Germany and Russia into the twentieth century. Masonry generally opposed this.

That an organization—of students, scholars, merchants, bankers, farmers, political figures, and artists—would group together in a manner outside of church authority was no small matter. Again, this also gives you some idea of why clandestine behavior was sometimes necessary—for much of their history, Masons were functioning outside of sanctioned authority. Yes, there was a certain drama to Masonry's attachment to secrecy; there was a certain esoteric quality to it—although I would defend anybody's right to assemble in private—but there was also a political necessity. For generations, Masonry in Europe promulgated principles that you could not easily pursue aboveground; indeed, you could suffer severe consequences, as did the Illuminati, which was rendered illegal.

Like the Illuminati, Freemasonry also promulgated the belief that the ancient mystery religions—of Persia, Egypt, Greece, and Rome—had left behind certain scent trails and threads, which Masons believed they could piece together and reassemble into rites and rituals. Masons also sought to revive a variant of the rites of the Hebrew priests, who presided over the Temple of Solomon and the Tabernacle in the Wilderness in the early religious structures of the Hebraic world. Freemasons attempted to forge these surviving threads into ceremonies, dramas, and passion plays that would foster the ethical development of the individual. They drew upon occult symbolism—the pyramid, the all-seeing eye, the obelisk, the skull and crossbones, the pentagram, the Star of David—which Manly P. Hall writes about in *The Secret Teachings of All Ages*. These symbols were seen as keys that could ignite self-understanding.

I think, in a certain sense, that Freemasonic ideals reached their fullest fruition in the life and the experience of some of America's most idealistic founders. It was in the United States, rather than in Europe, that Freemasonry was able to express its fullest political and spiritual vision—with glaring contradictions, of course. And because Freemasonic lodges tended to reflect local customs and mores, in Europe, where there was greater class and social stratification, Masonry tended to evince a greater degree of clubiness and mutual aid, and this probably remains so today. I do not perceive that kind of cliquishness as a large part of current Freemasonic culture in the United States; but I think some of that attitude has more or less persisted in parts of Europe.

In the past couple of generations, there have been certain scandals in Europe—including in Italy and England—where people who were fellow Freemasons within law enforcement or finance were involved in certain acts of collusion, or so the accusations went. I take those charges seriously, not because they suggest something innate to Freemasonry so much as they do to human nature in general: all of our endeavors, all of our groupings, carry the risk of devolving into the practice of self-service, or the perpetuation of local prejudices. That is a fact of human life and it occurs everywhere; that it would occur within Freemasonry is no surprise.

But the essential ideals of Freemasonic practice in Europe were to create a spiritual and intellectual order that existed outside the dogma or doctrine of church and state. Masonry's great innovation was *radical ecumenism;* any individual could join, provided he voiced belief in one Creator, and (so went the ideal) people from any walk of life could be a member and attain rank and privilege only as they passed through the degrees, passion plays, rites, and rituals that had been structured to reward responsibility rather than bloodline. In other words, Freemasonry, in its ideal, was supposed to be a radical meritocracy. And it generally practiced internal democracy, electing its leaders based on members' preferences rather than inheritance. These were radical ideas in the early 1700s; they sound to us like Civics 101 today, but at that time they were threatening to the established order.

TRIUMPH OF THE ROSICRUCIANS?

In addition to the Illuminati and Freemasons, the best-known so-called secret society in modern history is Rosicrucianism. Manly P. Hall writes a great deal about Rosicrucian doctrines and philosophy in *The Secret Teachings of All Ages.* There are, in fact, many self-styled Rosicrucian organizations that cropped up on the alternative spiritual scene in the United States and other parts of the world beginning in the early twentieth century, and that continue today. But Rosicrucianism as a historical fact can be traced to the years 1614 to 1616, during which time there appeared in Germany three anonymously written manuscripts that caused a great sensation.

The first manuscript, appearing in 1614 (but circulating as early as 1610), was called the *Fama Fraternitatis,* roughly meaning "the story of our brotherhood." It declared the existence of what came to be regarded as an "invisible college" of esoteric seekers who had as their aim the promotion of a healthful, just civic society—where there would be free hospitals, free education, and the free practice of religion, and Christian, Muslim, and Jew could all live together. And, again, if these ideas sounded radical in the early practices of Freemasonry, you can imagine how much more radical they must have sounded in 1614 in post-Renaissance, aristocratic Europe.

About a year later, there appeared another secret manuscript circulating in Germany, the *Confessio Fraternitatis,* or *Confessions of the Rosicrucian Brotherhood.* The work gave further voice to and explanation of this hidden fraternity, which was said to have emerged from the initiatory travels of a mysterious pilgrim, Father C. R. (for Christian Rosenkreuz). According to the mythos of this fraternity, Father C. R. was interred in a mysterious tomb bathed with white light and containing ciphers, codes, and messages that communicated to his brothers the existence of an ageless wisdom—a perennial philosophy that taught the principles of self-refinement and, again, that called for the establishment of a just civic order and social polity, and the creation of hospitals and colleges. Supposedly, this "invisible college" of Rosicrucians was an unseen force that would propel society forward. This is probably what inspired Adam Weishaupt more than a century later to found the Illuminati.

And in 1616, there appeared the third and final Rosicrucian manuscript of the era, the *Chemical Wedding of Christian Rosenkreuz*. The *Chemical Wedding* was a spiritual allegory, somewhat in the vein of the later *The Pilgrim's Progress,* in which a young man, Christian Rosenkreuz, is called to a palace to help oversee a magical wedding between a king and a queen. Embedded within this allegory is a late-Renaissance understanding of the Hermetic literature and the nature of psychological alchemy. One of the key ideals of alchemy—and something that you will see repeated again and again in alchemical woodcuts and drawings from the Renaissance—is the *unifying of male and female forces* within the individual; uniting the capacity, classically speaking, for intellect and emotion, intuition and industry, and suggestion and birth. The notion is that the masculine and feminine sides of human nature must become rejoined into the *divine hermaphrodite*—an amalgam of Hermes (the god of writing, commerce, and intellect) and Aphrodite (the keeper of wisdom, beauty, and art). The marriage of the divine hermaphrodite is voiced within the principles of psychological alchemy, symbolized within the joining of polarities in Hermetic philosophy, and retold as an allegory in the Rosicrucian tract. The young Christian—a seeker, pilgrim, and philosopher—is to help the king and the queen, the metaphorical man and woman, rejoin and become the one great being that fell into two pieces after the fall from Paradise.

It is worth asking: Was there any Rosicrucian order? Was there an actual Rosicrucian brotherhood? It is not entirely clear. Rosicrucianism, I think, can be more accurately understood as a *thought* movement. Certainly there were key figures behind it—these unsigned manuscripts came from the hand of *someone*—and it may have been a cluster of people who were interested in promoting revolutionary and spiritual ideas, without necessarily being part of an actual order or brotherhood.

That does not make what they did any less valid, any more than an idea is valid because it is old or new, popular or obscure. Some historians have theorized that Rosicrucianism may have been composed of disgruntled followers of the magician John Dee (1527–c.1608/9), who was forced into exile after the death of Queen Elizabeth in 1603. More recent research has pointed to a circle of radical Protestant thinkers and mystics.*

Others have theorized Rosicrucian ties to Freemasonry, including the groundbreaking British historian Frances Yates (1899–1981). In her 1972 book *The Rosicrucian Enlightenment,* Yates argued compellingly that Rosicrucianism formed the earliest vestiges of esoteric ideas that later emerged as Freemasonry. The timeline matches up, because the Rosicrucian manuscripts appeared in the early 1600s; the diaries of Elias Ashmole appeared not much later, in 1646; some other, roughly contemporaneous references appeared in literature, poetry, and religious expression. Mentions of the "Rosie Crosse" and *"Mason word"* (emphasis in the original) appear in a 1638 poem by Henry Adamson, "The Muses Threnodie" or "Mirthful Mournings," published in Edinburgh: "For we be brethren of the Rosie Crosse:/ We have the *Mason word* and second sight." Indeed, Ashmole himself, who copied the *Fama* and *Confessio* by hand, "Petitioned" (in his term) the unseen Rosicrucians for membership. In brief, what is called Freemasonry, in the form of the Grand Lodge of England, emerged aboveground in 1717, about a hundred years after the last Rosicrucian manuscript appeared. That leaves sufficient gestation for Rosicrucianism to have transformed from a thought movement to an actual initiatory brotherhood—which continues today, and which I explore further in the essay "Occult American." This is real occult history—not fantasy, but the true currents of the unseen quest to know.

---

*For the Dee theory, see *The Rosicrucian Enlightenment* (Routledge, 1972) and *The Occult Philosophy in the Elizabethan Age* (Routledge, 1979) both by Frances Yates. For later research, see *The Invisible History of the Rosicrucians* by Tobias Churton (Inner Traditions, 2009).

What I have outlined is part of the actual history of so-called secret societies, more of which can be read about and understood in *The Secret Teachings of All Ages;* in the work of Francis Yates (who is a wonderful historian, whose work should be engaged by any student and lover of Manly P. Hall); and in anthologies like *The Secret History of America.* And, of course, you can find quality translations of the Rosicrucian manifestos, and I encourage you to read those as well.*

It is critical to understand that these groups really did exist and do exist, but not to get lost in the lurid misrepresentations that populate paranoid postings online. Rather, one must look at these groups and ask: What were they really doing? What were their ideals? And how can their successes, shortcomings, and outlook help inform and propel forward our own highest ideals today?

---

*I particularly admire *Rosicrucian Trilogy: Modern Translations of the Three Founding Documents* by Joscelyn Godwin, Christopher McIntosh, & Donate Pahnke McIntosh (Weiser, 2016).

20

A DIABOLICAL DEVICE

In Search of Ouija

This article represents one of my first forays into occult history. It appeared under the title "OUIJA!" in the arts journal Esopus *in fall 2006 and was later shortened and reprinted by a National Endowment for the Humanities publication. It appears here in its original form. When I wrote the piece, Parker Brothers, which today manufactures Ouija, proved skittish to discuss one of its most storied products. The toy company probably feared that calling attention to what was then a quietly selling curio (sales revived with Ouija franchise movies in 2014 and 2016) could trigger religiously driven boycotts or blowback. At the time, the company made scant mention of Ouija on its website, and a public affairs executive ignored my queries. I sent a letter to Parker's president asking why a family-themed company would not respond to a writer from an arts journal asking about one of its legendary products. The close-lipped spokesperson responded immediately.*

Ouija. For some, the rectangular board evokes memories of late-night sleepover parties, shrieks of laughter, and toy shelves brimming with Magic Eight Balls, Frisbees, and Barbie dolls.

For others, Ouija boards—known more generally as talking boards or spirit boards—have darker associations. Stories abound of fearsome entities making threats, dire predictions, and even physical assaults on innocent users after a night of Ouija experimentation.

And the fantastic claims do not stop there: Pulitzer Prize–winning poet James Merrill vowed until his death in 1995 that his most celebrated work was written with the use of a homemade Ouija board.

For my part, I first discovered the mysterious workings of Ouija nearly twenty years ago, during a typically freezing-cold winter on eastern Long Island. While heaters clanked and hummed within the institutional-white walls of my college dormitory, friends allayed boredom with a Parker Brothers Ouija board.

As is often the case with Ouija, one young woman became the ringleader of board readings. She reprised the role of spirit medium that had typically fallen to women in past eras, when the respectable clergy was a male-only affair. Under the gaze of her dark eyes—which others said gave them chills—the late-night Ouija sessions came into vogue.

Most of my evenings were given over to editing the college newspaper, but I often arrived home at the dorm to frightening stories: the board, one night, kept spelling out the name "Seth," which my friends associated with evil (probably connecting it with the rebellious Egyptian god Set, who is seen as a Satan prototype). When asked, "Who's Seth?" the board directed its attention to a member of the group, and repeatedly replied: "Ask Carlos." A visibly shaken Carlos began breathing heavily and refused to answer.

Consumed as I was with exposing scandals within the campus food service, I never took the opportunity to sit in on these séances—a move I came to regard with a mixture of relief and regret. The idea that a mass-produced game board and its plastic pointer could display some occult faculty, or could tap into a user's subconscious, got under my skin. And I was not alone: in its heyday, Ouija outsold Monopoly.

Ouija boards have sharply declined in popularity since the 1960s and 70s, when you could find one in nearly every toy-cluttered basement. But they remain among the most peculiar consumer items in American history. Indeed, controversy endures to this day over their origin. To get a better sense of what Ouija boards are—and where they came from—requires going back to an era in which even an American president dabbled in talking to the dead.

SPIRITUALISM TRIUMPHANT

Today, it is difficult to imagine the popularity enjoyed by the movement called Spiritualism in the nineteenth century, when table rapping, séances, medium trances, and other forms of contacting the "other side" were practiced by an estimated 10 percent of the population. It began in 1848, when the teenaged sisters Kate and Margaret Fox introduced "spirit rapping" to a lonely hamlet in upstate New York called Hydesville.

While every age and culture had known hauntings, Spiritualism appeared to foster actual communication with the beyond. Within a few years, people from every walk of life took seriously the contention that one could talk to the dead. For many, Spiritualism seemed to extend the hope of reaching loved ones, and perhaps easing the pain of losing a child to one of the diseases of the day. The allure of immortality or of feeling oneself lifted beyond workaday realities attracted others. For others still, spirit counsels became a way to cope with anxiety about the future, providing otherworldly advice in matters of health, love, or money.

According to newspaper accounts of the era, President Abraham Lincoln hosted a séance in the White House—though more as a good-humored parlor game than as a serious spiritual inquiry.* Yet at least one vividly rendered Spiritualist memoir places a trance medium in the private quarters of the White House, advising the President and Mrs. Lincoln just after the outbreak of the Civil War.

MAKING CONTACT

In this atmosphere of ghostly knocks and earnest pleas to hidden forces, nineteenth-century occultists began looking for easier ways to

---

*I explore the historicism of the Lincoln séances in *Occult America* (2009).

communicate with the beyond. And in the best American fashion, they took a do-it-yourself approach to the matter. Their homespun efforts at contacting the spirit world led toward something we call Ouija—but not until they worked through several other methods.

One involved a form of table rapping in which questioners solicited spirit knocks when letters of the alphabet were called out, thus spelling a word. But this proved a tedious and time-consuming exercise. A faster means was by "automatic writing," in which spirit beings could communicate through the pen of a channeler; but some complained that this produced many pages of unclear or meandering prose.

One invention directly prefigured the heart-shaped pointer that moves around the Ouija board. The *planchette*—French for "little plank"—was a three-legged writing tool with a hole at the top for the insertion of a pencil. The planchette was designed for one person or more to rest their fingers on it and allow it to "glide" across a page, writing out a spirit message. The device originated in Europe in the early 1850s; by 1860 commercially manufactured planchettes were advertised in America.

Two other items from the 1850s are direct forebears to Ouija: "dial plates" and alphabet paste boards. In 1853, a Connecticut Spiritualist invented the "Spiritual Telegraph Dial," a roulette-like wheel with letters and numerals around its circumference. Dial plates came in various forms, sometimes of a complex variety. Some were rigged to tables to respond to "spirit tilts," while others were presumably guided—like a planchette—by the hands of questioners.

Alphabet boards further simplified matters. In use as early as 1852, these talking-board precursors allowed seekers to point to a letter as a means of prompting a "spirit rap," thereby quickly spelling a word. It was, perhaps, the easiest method yet. And it was only a matter of time until inventors and entrepreneurs began to see the possibilities.

BALTIMORE ORACLES

More than 150 years after the dawn of the Spiritualist era, contention endures over who created Ouija. The conventional history of American toy manufacturing credits a Baltimore businessman named William Fuld. Fuld, we are told, "invented" Ouija around 1890. So it is repeated online and in books of trivia, reference works, and "ask me" columns in newspapers. For many decades, the manufacturer itself—first Fuld's company and later the toy giant Parker Brothers—insinuated as much by running the term "William Fuld Talking Board Set" across the top of every board. The conventional history is wrong.

The patent for a "Ouija or Egyptian luck-board" was filed on May 28, 1890, by Baltimore resident and patent attorney Elijah H. Bond, who assigned the rights to two city businessmen, Charles W. Kennard and William H. A. Maupin. The patent was granted on February 10, 1891, and so was born the Ouija-brand talking board.

The first patent reveals a familiarly oblong board, with the alphabet running in double rows across the top, and numbers in a single row along the bottom. The sun and moon, marked respectively by the words "yes" and "no," adorn the upper left and right corners, while the words "Good bye" appear at the bottom center. Later on, instructions and the illustrations accompanying them, prescribed an expressly social—even flirtatious—experience: two parties, preferably a man and woman, were to balance the board between them on their knees, placing their fingers lightly upon the planchette. ("It draws the two people using it into close companionship and weaves about them a feeling of mysterious isolation," the box read.) In an age of buttoned-up morals, it was a tempting dalliance.

TRUE ORIGINS

The Kennard Novelty Company of Baltimore employed a teenaged varnisher who helped run shop operations, and this was William Fuld. By 1892, however, Charles W. Kennard's partners removed him from the company amid financial disputes, and a new patent—this time for an improved pointer, or planchette—was filed by a nineteen-year-old Fuld. In years to come, it was Fuld who would take over the company and affix his name to every board.

Based on an account in a 1920 magazine article, inventor's credit sometimes goes to an E. C. Reichie, alternately identified as a Maryland cabinetmaker or coffin maker. This theory was popularized by a defunct Baltimore business monthly called *Warfield's,* which ran a richly detailed—and at points, one suspects, richly imagined—history of Ouija boards in 1990. The article opens with a misspelled E. C. "Reiche" as the board's inventor and calls him a coffin maker with an interest in the afterlife—a name and a claim that have been repeated and circulated ever since.

Yet this figure appears virtually nowhere else in Ouija history, including on the first patent. His name came up during a period of patent litigation about thirty years after Ouija's inception. A 1920 account in New York's *World Magazine*—widely disseminated that year in the popular weekly the *Literary Digest*—reports that one of Ouija's early investors told a judge that E. C. Reichie had invented the board. But no reference to an E. C. Reichie—be he a cabinetmaker or coffin maker—appears in the court transcript, according to Ouija historian and talking-board manufacturer Robert Murch.

Ultimately, Reichie's role, or whether there was a Reichie, may be moot, at least in terms of the board's invention. Talking boards of a homemade variety were already a popular craze among Spiritualists by the mid-1880s. At his online Museum of Talking Boards, Ouija collector and chronicler Eugene Orlando posts an 1886 article from the *New-York Daily Tribune* (as reprinted that year in a Spiritualist monthly, the *Carrier Dove*) describing the breathless excitement around the new-fangled alphabet board and its message indicator. "I know of whole communities that are wild over the 'talking board,'" says a man in the article. This was a full four years before the first Ouija patent was filed. Obviously, Bond, Kennard, and their associates were capitalizing on an invention—not conceiving of one.

And what of the name Ouija? Alternately pronounced wee-JA and wee-GEE, its origin may never be known. Kennard at one time claimed it was Egyptian for "good luck" (it's not). Fuld later said it was simply a marriage of the French and German words for "yes." One early investor claimed the board spelled out its own name. As with other aspects of Ouija history, the board seems determined to withhold a few secrets of its own.

ANCIENT OUIJA?

Another oft repeated but misleading claim is that Ouija, or talking boards, have ancient roots. In a typical example, Frank Gaynor's 1953 *Dictionary of Mysticism* states that ancient boards of different shapes and sizes "were used in the sixth century before Christ." In a wide range of books and articles, everyone from Pythagoras to the Mongols to the Ancient Egyptians is said to have possessed Ouija-like devices. But the claims rarely withstand scrutiny.

Chronicler-curator Orlando points out that the primary reference to Ouija existing in the pre-modern world appears in a passage from Lewis Spence's 1920 *Encyclopedia of Occultism*—which is repeated in Nandor Fodor's popular 1934 *Encyclopedia of Psychic Science*. The Fodor passage reads, in part: "As an invention it is very old. It was in use in the days of Pythagoras, about 540 BC. According to a French historical account of the philosopher's life, his sect held frequent séances or circles at which 'a mystic table, moving on wheels, moved towards signs, which the philosopher and his pupil Philolaus, interpreted to the audience." It is, Orlando points out, "the one recurring quote found in almost every academic article on the Ouija board." But the story presents two problems: the "French historical account" is never identified; and the Pythagorean scribe Philolaus lived not in Pythagoras's time, but in the following century.

It is also worth keeping in mind that we know precious little today about Pythagoras and his school. No writings of Pythagoras survive, and the historical record depends upon later works—some of which were written centuries after his death. Hence, commentators on occult topics are sometimes tempted to project backward onto Pythagoras all sorts of arcane practices, Ouija and modern numerology among them.

Still other writers—when they are not repeating claims like the one above—tend to misread ancient historical accounts and mistake other divinatory tools, such as pendulum dishes, for Ouija boards. Oracles were rich and varied from culture to culture—from Germanic runes to Greek Delphic rites—but the prevailing literature on oracular traditions supports no suggestion that talking boards, as we know them, were in use before the Spiritualist era.

OUIJA BOOM

After William Fuld took the reins of Ouija manufacturing in America, business was brisk—if not always happy. Fuld formed a quickly shattered business alliance with his brother Isaac, which landed the two in court battles for nearly twenty years. Isaac was eventually found to have violated an injunction against creating a competing board, called the Oriole, after being forced from the family business in 1901. The two brothers would never speak again. Ouija, and anything that looked directly like it, was firmly in the hands of William Fuld.

By 1920, the board was so well known that artist Norman Rockwell painted a send-up of a couple using one—the woman dreamy and credulous, the man fixing her with a cloying grin—for a cover of the *Saturday Evening Post.* For Fuld, though, everything was strictly business. "Believe in the Ouija board?" he once told a reporter. "I should say not. I'm no spiritualist. I'm a Presbyterian—been one ever since I was so high." In 1920, the *Baltimore Sun* reported that Fuld, by his own "conservative estimate," had pocketed an astounding $1 million from sales.

Whatever satisfaction Fuld's success may have brought him was soon lost: on February 26, 1927, he fell to his death from the roof of his Baltimore factory. The fifty-four-year-old manufacturer was supervising the replacement of a flagpole when an iron support bar he held gave way, and he fell three stories backward.

Fuld's children took over his business—and generally prospered. While sales dipped and rose—and competing boards came and went—only the Ouija brand endured. By the 1940s, Ouija was experiencing a new surge in popularity.

Historically, séances and other Spiritualist methods proliferate during times of war. Spiritualism had seen its last great explosion of interest in the period around World War I, when parents yearned to contact children lost to battlefield carnage. In World War II, many anxious families turned to Ouija. In a 1944 article, "The Ouija Comes Back," the *New York Times* reported that one New York City department store alone sold 50,000 Ouija boards in a five-month period.

American toy manufacturers were taking notice. Some attempted knock-off products. But Parker Brothers developed bigger plans. In a move that would place a carryover from the age of Spiritualism into playrooms all across America, the toy giant bought the rights for an undisclosed sum in 1966. The Fuld family was out of the picture, and Ouija was about to achieve its biggest success ever.

The following year, Parker Brothers is reported to have sold more than two million Ouija boards—topping sales of its most popular game, Monopoly. The occult boom that began in the late 1960s, as astrologers adorned the cover of *Time* magazine and witchcraft became a fast-growing "new" religion, fueled the board's sales for the following decades. A Parker spokesperson says the company has sold over ten million boards since 1967.

The sixties and seventies also saw the rise of Ouija as a product of the youth culture. Ouija circles sprang up in college dormitories, and the board emerged as a fad among adolescents, for whom its ritual of secret messages and intimate communications became a form of rebellion. One youthful experimenter recalls an enticing atmosphere of danger and intrigue—"like shoplifting or taking drugs"—that allowed her and a girlfriend to bond together over Ouija sessions in which they contacted the spirit of "Candelyn," a nineteenth-century girl who had perished in a fire. Sociologists suggested that Ouija sessions were a way for young people to project, and work through, their own fears. But many Ouija users claimed that the verisimilitude of the communications were reason enough to return to the board.

OUIJA TODAY

While officials at Parker Brothers (now a division of Hasbro) would not get into the ebb and flow of sales, there is little question that Ouija has declined precipitously in recent years. In 1999, the company brought an era to an end when it discontinued the vintage Fuld design and switched to a smaller, glow-in-the-dark version of the board. In consumer manufacturing, the redesign of a classic product often signals an effort to reverse falling sales. Listed at $19.95, Ouija costs about 60 percent more than standards like Monopoly and Scrabble, which further suggests that it has become something of a specialty item.

In a far remove from the days when Ouija led Parker Brothers' lineup, the product now seems more like a corporate stepchild. The "Ouija Game" ("ages 8 to Adult") merits barely a mention on Hasbro's website. The company posts no official history for Ouija, as it does for its other storied products. And the claims from the original 1960s-era box—"Weird and mysterious. Surpasses, in its unique results, mind reading, clairvoyance and second sight"—have since been significantly toned down. Given the negative attention the board sometimes attracts—both from frightened users and religionists who smell a whiff of Satan's doings—Ouija, its sales likely on the wane, may be a product that Hasbro would just as soon forget.

And yet Ouija receives more customer reviews—alternately written in tones of outrage, fear, delight, or ridicule—than any other "toy" for sale on Amazon (280 at last count). What other "game" so polarizes opinion among those who dismiss it as a childhood plaything, and those who condemn or extol it as a portal to the other side? As it did decades ago in *The Exorcist,* Ouija figures into the recent fright films *What Lies Beneath* and *White Noise.* And it sustains an urban mythology that continues to make it a household name in the early twenty-first century. There would seem little doubt that Ouija—as it has arisen time and again—awaits a revival in the future. But what makes this game board and its molded plastic pointer so resilient in our culture, and, some might add, in our nightmares?

"AN OCCULT SPLENDOR"

Among the first things one notices when looking into Ouija is its vast—and sometimes authentically frightening—history of stories. Claims abound from users who experienced the presence of malevolent entities during Ouija sessions, sometimes even being physically harassed by unseen forces. A typical storyline involves communication that is at first reassuring and even useful—a lost object may be recovered—but eventually gives way to threatening or terrorizing messages. Hugh Lynn Cayce, son of the eminent American psychic Edgar Cayce, cautioned that his researches found Ouija boards among the most "dangerous doorways to the unconscious."

For their part, Ouija enthusiasts note that teachings such as the inspirational "Seth material," channeled by Jane Roberts, first came through a Ouija board. Other channeled writings, such as an early twentieth-century series of historical novels and poems by an entity called "Patience Worth" and a posthumous "novel" by Mark Twain (pulled from the shelves after a legal outcry from the writer's estate), have reputedly come through the board. Such works, however, have rarely attracted enduring readerships. Poets Sylvia Plath and Ted Hughes wrote haunting and dark passages about their experiences with Ouija; but none attain the level of their best work.

So, can anything of lasting value be attributed to the board—this mysterious object that has, in one form or another, been with us for nearly 120 years? The answer is yes, and it has stared us in the face for so long that we have nearly forgotten it is there.

In 1976, the American poet James Merrill published—and won the Pulitzer Prize for—an epic poem that recounted his experience, with his partner David Jackson, of using a Ouija board from 1955 to 1974. His work *The Book of Ephraim* was later combined with two other Ouija-inspired long poems and published in 1982 as *The Changing Light at Sandover*. "Many readers," wrote critic Judith Moffett in her penetrating study entitled *James Merrill*, "may well feel they have been waiting for this trilogy all their lives."

First using a manufactured board and then a homemade one—with a teacup in place of a planchette—Merrill and Jackson encounter a world of spirit "patrons" who recount to them a sprawling and profoundly involving creation myth. It is poetry steeped in the epic tradition, in which myriad characters—from W. H. Auden, to lost friends and family members, to the Greek muse/interlocutor called Ephraim—walk on and off stage. The voices of Merrill, Jackson, and those that emerge from the teacup and board, alternately offer theories of reincarnation, worldly advice, and painfully poignant reflections on the passing of life and ever-hovering presence of death.

The Changing Light at Sandover gives life to a new mythology of world creation, destruction, resurrection, and the vast, unknowable mechanizations of God Biology (GOD B, in the words of the Ouija board) and those mysterious figures who enact his will: bat-winged creatures who, in their cosmological laboratory, reconstruct departed souls for new life on earth. And yet we are never far from the human, grounding voice of Merrill, joking about the selection of new wallpaper in his Stonington, Connecticut home; or from the moving council of voices from the board, urging: in life, stand for something.

"It is common knowledge—and glaringly obvious in the poems, though not taken seriously by his critics—that these three works, and their final compilation, were based on conversations . . . through a Ouija board," wrote John Chambers in his outstanding analysis of Merrill in the Summer 1997 issue of the *Anomalist*.

Critic Harold Bloom, in a departure from others who sidestep the question of the work's source, calls the first of the Sandover poems "an occult splendor." Indeed, it is not difficult to argue that, in literary terms, *The Changing Light at Sandover* is a masterpiece—perhaps *the* masterpiece—of occult experimentation. In some respects, it is like an unintended response to Mary Shelley's *Frankenstein,* in which not one man acting alone, but two acting and thinking together, successfully pierce the veil of life's inner and cosmic mysteries—and live not only to tell, but to teach.

One wonders, then, why the work is so little known and read within a spiritual subculture that embraces other channeled works, such as the Ouija-received "Seth material," the automatic writing of *A Course In Miracles,* or the currently popular Abraham-Hicks channeled readings. *The Changing Light at Sandover* ought to be evidence that something—be it inner or outer—is available through this kind of communication, however rare. It is up to the reader to find out what.

VOICES WITHIN?

Of course, the Merrill case begs the question of whether the Ouija board channels something from beyond or merely reflects the ideas found in one's subconscious. After all, who but a poetic genius like James Merrill could have recorded channeled passages of such literary grace and epic dimension? Plainly put, this was not Joe Schmo at the board.

In a 1970 book on psychical phenomena, *ESP, Seers & Psychics,* researcher-skeptic Milbourne Christopher announces—a tad too triumphantly, perhaps—that if you effectively blindfold a board's user and rearrange the order of letters, communication ceases. A believable enough claim—but what does it really tell us? In 1915, a specialist in abnormal psychology proposed the same test to the channeled entity called Patience Worth, who, through a St. Louis housewife named Pearl Curran, had produced a remarkable range of novels, plays, and poems— some of them hugely ambitious in scale and written in a Middle English dialect that Curran (who did not finish high school) would have had no means of knowing.

As reported in Irving Litvag's 1972 study, *Singer in the Shadows,* Patience Worth responded to the request that Curran be blindfolded in her typically inimitable fashion: "I be aset athin the throb o' her. Aye, and doth thee to take then the lute awhither that she see not, think ye then she may to set up musics for the hear o' thee?" In other words, how can you remove the instrument and expect music?

Some authorities in psychical research support the contention that Ouija is a tool of our subconscious. For years, J. B. Rhine, the veritable dean of psychical research in America, worked with his wife, Louisa, a trained biologist and well-regarded researcher in her own right, to bring scientific rigor to the study of psychical phenomena. Responding to the occult fads of the day, Louisa wrote an item on Ouija boards and automatic writing adapted in the winter 1970 newsletter of the American Society for Psychical Research. Whatever messages come through the board, she maintained, are a product of the user's subconscious—not any metaphysical force: "In several ways the very nature of automatic writing and the Ouija board makes them particularly open to misunderstanding. For one thing, because [such communications] are unconscious, the person does not get the feeling of his own involvement. Instead, it seems to him that some personality outside of himself is responsible. In addition, and possibly because of this, the material is usually cast in a form as if originating from another intelligence."

For his part, the poet Merrill took a subtler view of the matter. "If it's still yourself that you're drawing upon," he said, "then that self is much stranger and freer and more far-seeking than the one you thought you knew." And at another point: "If the spirits aren't external, how astonishing the mediums become!"

TO OUIJA—OR NOT TO OUIJA?

As I was preparing for this article, I began to revisit notes I had made months earlier. These presented me with several questions. Among them: should I be practicing with the Ouija board myself, testing its occult powers in person? Just at this time, I received an email, impeccably and even mysteriously timed, warning me off Ouija boards. The sender, whom I did not know, told in sensitive and vivid tones of her family's harrowing experiences with a board.

As my exchange with the sender continued, however, my relatively few lines of response elicited back pages and pages of material, each progressively more pedantic and judgmental in tone, reading—or projecting—multiple levels into what little I had written in reply (most of which was in appreciation). And so, I wondered: in terms of the influences to which we open ourselves, how do we sort out the fine from the coarse, allowing in communications that are useful and generative, rather than those that become simply depleting?

Ouija is intriguing, interesting, even oddly magnetic—a survey of users in the 2001 *International Journal of Parapsychology* found that one half "felt a compulsion to use it." But, in a culture filled with possibilities, and in a modern life of limited time and energy, is Ouija really the place to search? Clearly, for a James Merrill, it was. But there exists a deeper intuition than what comes through a board, or any outer object—one that answers that kind of question for every clear-thinking person. For me, the answer was no.

It was time to pack up my antique Ouija board in its box and return to what I found most lasting on the journey: the work of Merrill, who passed through the uses of this instrument and, with it, created a body of art that perhaps justifies the tumultuous, serpentine history from which Ouija has come.

21

VISIONS FROM SOMEWHERE

Theosophy and the Occult Roots of Abstract Art

This essay appeared as an introduction to the 2020 reissue of the 1905 Theosophical work, Thought Forms, *published by Sacred Bones. I consider this publication of* Thought Forms *groundbreaking not only because of its signature quality but also because the reissue and its supplemental material definitively establish the clairvoyant-based work as the ignition point of abstract art in the early twentieth century.*

It is sometimes difficult to appreciate the impact that the late-nineteenth century (and ongoing) occult movement called Theosophy had on global culture—spiritually, politically, and artistically.

Thought Forms emerged in 1905 from what might be considered the second generation of the Theosophical Society's leaders, Annie Besant and Charles Webster Leadbeater.* Although not possessed of the arousing title and thunderous impact of earlier Theosophical works like *The Secret Doctrine* (1888) by cofounder Madame H. P. Blavatsky, the illustrated book may, in its concision and intrepidness, prove the most

---

*There is bibliographical confusion about the work's publication date, which is often listed as 1901. Historical records indicate that the 1901 date was introduced by error into a later printing and was subsequently repeated. The earliest traceable publication is 1905.

widely read, lasting, and directly influential volume to emerge from the revolution that Theosophy ignited. By many estimates, *Thought Forms* marks the germination of abstract art.

To speak of revolutions can seem exaggerated. But there is no other term for what this cluster of esoteric seekers accomplished, and how that appears in the endurance of *Thought Forms.*

▲

The Theosophical Society emerged in New York City in 1875, where it was founded by a small circle of seekers—who months earlier had briefly called themselves "The Miracle Club"—and was led by the Russian world traveler Blavatsky and Henry Steel Olcott, a retired staff colonel from the Civil War who had made some of the earliest arrests in the Lincoln assassination. The society's aim was to explore the esoteric truths of all religions. Blavatsky and Olcott were first united in their fascination with Spiritualism, or talking to the dead, but less as an end to itself and more as a doorway to Blavatsky's real aim: opening the West to Eastern spirituality and revealing a primeval occult philosophy that underscored all faiths.

Within a brief time, Blavatsky attracted widespread press coverage and influential acolytes (including Thomas Edison)—only for her and Olcott to depart New York City for India in 1878, relocating to a nation then as unfamiliar to most Westerners as the surface of Mars. Nearly a century before the Beatles' trek to Rishikesh—and decades before the literary sojourns of W. Somerset Maugham and the Eastern imaginings of books and movies like *Lost Horizon*—Blavatsky and Olcott laid the template for the Westerner seeking wisdom in the East.

Blavatsky and Olcott's travels made a lasting impact. Olcott ignited Buddhist revivals in nations pressed under the joint machinery of colonialism and missionary campaigns. His passing is marked as a national holiday today in Sri Lanka. The pair also helped spark the Indian independence revolution completed by Gandhi. In 1885, Theosophists founded the Indian National Congress, the movement's policy-making body. Blavatsky's successor, English reformer Annie Besant, the coauthor of *Thought Forms,* was elected its first woman president in 1917.

It was Besant herself who bestowed upon Gandhi the title by which he became world famous: *Mahatma,* a Hindu term for "Great Soul," and the same term by which Theosophy called its own reputedly hidden Masters, advanced adepts said to clandestinely direct the group's activities.*

When Besant and her collaborator Leadbeater, an iron-willed and sometimes ruthless British seeker and author, collaborated on *Thought Forms,* Theosophy was riding a wave of cultural significance. Allies, students, and members included poets W. B. Yeats and George William Russell (Æ), composer Igor Stravinsky, American reformer and vice-president Henry A. Wallace, and artists Piet Mondrian, Nicholas Roerich, Agnes Pelton, and Hilma af Klint, whose own work has recently undergone revelatory reassessment in light of its Theosophical influences. This almost hard-to-believe (yet still fragmentary) roster returns us to the significance of *Thought Forms.*

▲

Even a glance through the plates in *Thought Forms* reveals the nascence of psychedelia, spiritual expressionism, and abstract art itself. *Thought Forms* was a widely acknowledged influence on pioneering abstractionist Wassily Kandinsky (1866–1944), a member of the Theosophical Society who owned his own copy. Hence, to call the book visionary, as with calling the authors' backgrounds revolutionary, is not hyperbole. What was the inspiration for such unprecedented visuals?

I mentioned earlier that Theosophy considered itself an occult movement—by occult I mean belief in extra-physical forces whose effects are felt on and through us. The term is rooted in the Latin *occultus,* for *unseen* or *hidden,* popularized during the Renaissance to

---

*There are various claims around who bestowed on Gandhi the title *mahatma,* with credit sometimes going to poet Rabindranath Tagore. I am relying on scholar of religion Arthur H. Nethercot's biography, *The Last Four Lives of Annie Besant* (University of Chicago Press, 1963).

refer to primeval and vanished religious traditions, which Blavatsky said emerged from a still older and unifying occult philosophy. This fueled the Theosophical Society's radical ecumenism, which briefly attracted a young Gandhi to Blavatsky's orbit.

As alluded, Blavatsky further said that she and Olcott were guided by Far Eastern Masters who could materialize at will (Olcott said one appeared to him in their apartment in New York's theater district), communicate clairvoyantly, and even generate "phenomenally precipitated" letters, which guided the couple. Besant and Leadbeater, for their part, said that the images in *Thought Forms* emerged from their own second-sight trance states in which the authors viewed auras, vortices, etheric matter, astral projections, energy forms, and other expressions from the unseen world. They conveyed these to visual artists who translated them into paintings.

Make what you will of the backstory, but I have always found a mystery in the construction of these visual works, which historical study and conversations with painters has never settled for me: how do you communicate an inner vision with such exactness to an artist so as to produce works of such unprecedented departure and vividness? The authors made scant reference to their methods.

The most detailed explanation of their process appeared nine years earlier. In 1896, Besant described the efforts that burgeoned into this book in an article in the Theosophical journal *Lucifer:*

Two clairvoyant Theosophists [Besant and Leadbeater] observed the forms caused by definite thoughts thrown out by one of them, and also watched the forms projected by other persons under the influence of various emotions. They described these as fully and accurately as they could to an artist who sat with them, and he made some sketches and mixed colours, till some approximation of the objects was made.

Besant also highlighted three causative factors: "1. Quality of thought determines colour. 2. Nature of thought determines form. 3. Definiteness of thought determines clearness of outline."*

▲

I leave it to others to trace out the full impact of *Thought Forms*. That requires a work of its own, and I believe this reissue takes significant steps in that direction. But I will conclude by asking whether the claimed origins of Theosophy, with its hidden Masters and inner visions, are anything other than theater. I once raised this question with a friend, a highly regarded scholar of religion who wanted to keep public distance from the topics I study, namely occult religious movements.

He reminded me that, in addition to what I have highlighted here, Besant and Leadbeater, four years following *Thought Forms,* "discovered" a fourteen-year-old Jiddu Krishnamurti (1895–1986) playing on a beach in South India. They proclaimed the adolescent an avatar—a future world leader of spiritual thought. Krishnamurti, then a poor and frail teen, did, in fact, quickly emerge as one of the most remarkable and unclassifiable voices of twentieth-century spirituality.

"They must've had something . . . " my friend's voice trailed off. Was Leadbeater "guided"? Was Blavatsky and Olcott's fateful journey to India phenomenally directed? Are the images in this book born of extrasensory perception?

The response to such questions probably rests on the extant beliefs of whoever is considering them. But this much is clear: what appears in *Thought Forms,* like other works by these not-so-long-ago seekers, reflects a shattering of boundaries and an unknown methodology, the effects of which are still being felt in our culture today.

---

*I am indebted to Richard Smoley for these references.

22

THE MAGIC STAFF

The Strange History of the Law of Attraction

My personal favorite of my books is One Simple Idea: How Positive Thinking Reshaped Modern Life. *This historical work reveals the lives and struggles of the pioneers of positive-mind metaphysics, many of whom influenced me. These happy warriors had "one simple idea"—to think positively—and it remade our culture. This essay explores the little-understood origin of the Law of Attraction and how this now-ubiquitous spiritual concept morphed over time. Due to space and flow, I cut this passage from the original opening chapter of that book, and I am glad to have it memorialized here, as it clarifies important aspects of New Age history and notes a few of the surprising figures—including Edgar Allan Poe and an ancestor to the Bush presidential family—who crisscrossed with it.*

I must add a tragic note in connection with my references to the Hudson Valley, New York, town of Poughkeepsie. This place with a magickal past (and present) was the scene of a hate crime on a winter night in early 2021, when a masked arsonist burned down a historic home owned by a member of the Church of Satan; its two occupants narrowly escaped alive. You may recall what I mentioned earlier about how near we are to a return of the Satanic Panic. Hate can harm the independent thinker but never deter the development of ideas.

America in the 1840s was awash in liberal spiritual and social ideas—particularly the principle that the everyday person could forge his own relationship and communication with the Divine. Many Americans saw the young nation as a place provided by God—an "American Israel"—where a new people was entitled to a new covenant.

Ralph Waldo Emerson signaled the tenor of the times in 1841 when he published his first series of essays, which extolled the power of ideas to shape a person's life. "The ancestor of every action is a thought," he wrote in "Spiritual Laws." The Transcendentalist philosopher saw the touch of divine power in an active, sensitive mind.

By 1845, the mystical writings of eighteenth-century Swedish mystic Emanuel Swedenborg became widely available in English for the first time. In a precursor to the work of American mediums, the Swedish seer wrote that he could enter trance states in which his astral body traveled to other realms, planets, and dimensions, including different levels of the afterlife.

Mysteries appeared in humble quarters. In March of 1848, a pair of teenage sisters outside Rochester, New York, told their Methodist parents that the rapping sounds heard throughout the family cabin were actually "spirit raps"—communiqués from the afterworld. Scientists and ministers, journalists and judges, descended on the cabin to evaluate, and often affirm, the Fox sisters' claims. Newspapers spread word of the "Rochester rappings," and soon people from Maine to Ohio organized into séance circles. By the middle of the next decade, about 10 percent of Americans participated in the movement called Spiritualism.

All these currents culminated in the life of a young man who newspapers (somewhat teasingly) called the "Poughkeepsie Seer," after his Hudson Valley, New York, hometown. His real name was Andrew Jackson Davis, so called for the populist hero Andrew Jackson. Davis united the threads of mediumship, Spiritualism, and social progress in a manner that converged with mental-healing experiments and gave rise to the American belief in the practical potentials of the positive mind.

He went on to give the positive-thinking movement its most enduring phrase and concept: Law of Attraction.

POUGHKEEPSIE MYSTERIES

Davis's beginnings hardly suggested a public career. In 1843, he was a seventeen-year-old cobbler's apprentice in the Hudson Valley. His father's alcoholism left the family near the poverty line, with Andrew, his mother, and older sister forced to work odd jobs to survive. He had no more than five months of classroom education. The bearded teen was considered polite and likeable but showed little sign of rising beyond the circumstances of his household. Davis's life took a strange turn, however, when he met J. S. Grimes, an area Mesmerist (what is today called a hypnotist) who visited Poughkeepsie that fall to deliver a series of lectures and demonstrations.

An instructor at Castleton Medical College in Vermont, Grimes was a well-established figure on the New England Mesmerist scene. When he appeared in Davis's Hudson Valley town, Grimes proceeded, as had become common among traveling Mesmerists, to "magnetize"— or entrance—volunteers from the audience. Davis volunteered, but Grimes failed to put him under. The failure may have been due to Davis's instant dislike of Grimes, whom he called "somewhat egotistic." (Although Davis cultivated an image as an uneducated farm boy, he used surprisingly cosmopolitan expressions.) But in the failed episode, Davis's destiny had been sealed.

A few days later, a local tailor dropped by the shoemaking shop where Davis worked. The tailor, William Levingston, himself moonlighted as an amateur Mesmerist. "During a recital of many magnetic marvels he had himself performed, both at home and abroad," Davis recalled, "he addressed himself to me and said: 'Have you ever been mesmerized?' In reply, I informed him of the unsuccessful experiment upon me by Mr. Grimes. Then he said: 'Come to my house to-night. I'll try you, if you don't object.'"*

---

*The Magic Staff: An Autobiography of Andrew Jackson Davis, 1857.

Under Levingston's control, Davis fell into a remarkably deep trance—he felt an incredible, and somewhat frightening, physical sensation of traveling out of his body and standing on a darkened shore, waiting, it seemed, for some kind of message. Davis began nightly sittings under Levingston's hand. The teen claimed that from a magnetized state he could journey in his astral body to unseen dimensions, he said he could read books without opening the cover, and, like other American and French mediums, he reported the ability to gaze into the bodies of the sick, diagnosing diseases and ailments. Davis also described out-of-body travels to other planets and heavenly realms—accounts that echoed the experiences of Swedenborg.

After a particularly deep trance-session on a winter evening in 1844, Davis had difficulty returning to ordinary consciousness. He stumbled back to the room where he was staying at the home of his tailor friend. In his third-floor bedroom, Davis fell into a deep sleep. He recalled being awakened by a voice—it was his dead mother, urging him to go outside. He rushed downstairs and out onto Main Street where he encountered a vision of a flock of unruly sheep and a shepherd who seemed to need his help. The vision vanished in a "rosy light" and Davis, his mind illumined and his body light, embarked on a psychical "flight through space," which took him across the frozen landscape of the Catskill Mountains. Whether his journey was astral or physical was not altogether clear, although it may have been both as he vanished until the following day.

His journey culminated inside the stone walls of a small country graveyard deep in the woods. There he said he met the spirit of Swedenborg himself. The Swedish healer told the boy, "By thee a new light will appear." Davis also received a "Magic Staff," which at first seemed physical but he later deemed mental in nature. Afterward, an astral message revealed to him the true meaning of its magic: "Behold! Here is Thy Magic Staff: UNDER ALL CIRCUMSTANCES KEEP AN EVEN MIND. Take it, Try it, Walk with it. Believe on it. FOR EVER." The staff was not an object but a principle. Davis later called his autobiography *The Magic Staff.*

The next day, Davis reappeared at the home of his tailor friend and told of the "new directions" their work must take. The youth said he would continue to diagnose the sick but would no longer perform clairvoyant feats for local "wonder-seekers." In the months ahead, Davis spoke of a "new mountain . . . looming in the distance," summoning him to his true mission in life. The young seer began delivering metaphysical lectures from a trance state. Davis assumed the form of an American Swedenborg, using his "mental illumination" to explore cosmic visions and the mechanics of creation.

By spring of 1845, Davis quit working with the tailor Levingston. "He can't carry me any higher in clairvoyance," Davis complained. That fall, Davis departed Poughkeepsie for Manhattan and began working with a new pair of helpers. S. S. Lyon, a doctor of herbal remedies from Bridgeport, Connecticut, became Davis's new Mesmerist control. William Fishbough, a Universalist minister from New Haven, became his "honored scribe," recording the seer's dispatches from the spirit world.*

Together, the three began a series of daily sittings. They had little money and bounced among a string of furnished rooms in lower Manhattan. Yet a drive and energy fueled their sessions, which could last for hours. The herbalist Lyon would place Davis into a trance in his "sleeping chair," while the minister Fishbough took dictation. Davis described visits to heaven, to other dimensions and planets, and, finally, to the heart of universal creation itself.

On January 13, 1846, Fishbough published a letter in the *New York Tribune*, outlining Davis's philosophy—in particular, the powers of a universal "Positive Mind":

---

*Davis's long life—the seer lived until January 1910—was marked by a willingness to discard old partners and helpmates in favor of new ones. In 1885, after thirty years of marriage and public collaboration with suffragist Mary Fenn Love, Davis divorced her, saying his spirit guardians told him that the couple's "'central temperaments' do not harmonize." Davis remarried (his third time), and left Mary to raise four grandchildren placed in her care by her deceased daughter. Mary died of cancer the following year in West Orange, New Jersey.

At the back of all the visible operations of nature, however, there is a hidden cause, to which all mechanical and organic causes are but secondary and subordinate; and the admission of this undeniable fact should open our minds to conviction of well-attested phenomena, especially as connected with the mysterious economy of mind . . . that matter was originally formed from a spiritual essence, and that in its progress of refinement, from the earth to the plant, from the plant to the animal, from the animal to man, it will finally form spirit individualized—and that this is endlessly progressive in knowledge and refinement, continually approaching nearer and nearer to the great eternal *Positive Mind*—the Foundation and Controller of all existence.

Although Davis's visions were partly drawn from the ideas of Swedenborg (a repeat criticism of his work) the correspondence did sketch out an excitingly fresh mental metaphysics. Davis stopped just short of calling the human mind a channel of the great "Positive Mind" of creation, or endowing man with the ability to harness this force for creative purposes. It would fall to another generation of seekers to close the circle that Davis had begun. Nonetheless, the Poughkeepsie Seer, having not yet published his first book, laid out the earliest language of the positive-thinking movement.

THE SEER IN SEASON

By 1847, Davis and his collaborators were ready to share their visions with the world. The men assembled Davis's 157 trance lectures into a metaphysical opus, *The Principles of Nature, Her Divine Revelations and a Voice to Mankind*. It was a massive, sprawling book that retold the story of creation: "The ever-controlling influence and active energies of the Divine Positive Mind brought all effects into being, as parts of one vast whole."

While thickly worded and torturously long, *The Principles of Nature* sold a remarkable 900 copies in its first week of release. Davis's references to the "Great Positive Mind," or "Great Positive Power," established the idea, at least for enthusiastic Americans, that all of creation was a mental act, emanating from a higher intelligence and concretizing all forms of reality.

Not everyone was impressed with Davis's cosmology. Edgar Allan Poe, then a struggling journalist and short-story writer, sat in on some of Davis's New York trance sittings. Poe came to regard Davis with a mixture of intrigue and contempt. In 1849, Poe used one of his last short stories, *Mellonta Tauta,* to poke fun at Davis by mangling his high-sounding name as "Martin Van Mavis (sometimes called the 'Tougkeepsie Seer')."* At the same time, Poe contributed to the popularity of Mesmerism by using themes from Davis's trance sittings in one of his most popular stories, *The Facts in the Case of M. Valdemar.* It told of a Mesmerist who keeps an ill man from slipping into death by holding him in a magnetic trance. Poe completed the story in New York the year he met Davis.

For his part, Davis also harbored mixed feelings toward Poe. In a January 1846 journal entry, Davis described seeing Poe's personal aura in the form of a gloomy landscape of dark hills that always hung around the writer's head—"a kind of blooming valley, surrounded by a high wall of craggy mountains." Davis's powers of perception, whatever their source, were psychologically astute when focused on Poe:

> So high appear these mountains that the sun can scarcely shine over their summits during any portion of the twenty-four hours. There is, too, something unnatural in his voice, and something dispossessing in his manners . . . as he walked in through the hall, and again when he left, at the conclusion of his call, I saw a perfect *shadow* of himself in the air in front of him, as though the sun was constantly shining behind and casting shadows before him, causing the singular appearance of one walking into a dark fog produced by himself.†

---

*Poe's satirical remark appears in an epigraph that often gets omitted from anthologized versions of the story. Poe is referencing President Martin Van Buren, who in 1837 succeeded Davis's namesake, Andrew Jackson.

†*Events in the Life of a Seer* by Andrew Jackson Davis, 1868.

Poe ultimately had no patience for Davis's vision of the "Divine Positive Mind." He dismissed the medium in May 1849 in one of his last published works, "50 Suggestions"—a set of maxims satirizing the spiritual trends and experiments of the era. Of Davis, Poe concluded, "There surely can*not* be 'more things in Heaven and Earth than are dreamt of' (oh, Andrew Jackson Davis !) 'in *your* philosophy.'"

Yet Davis was not without significant defenders. Among them was a Rev. George Bush—a first cousin, four and five times removed, to Presidents George H. W. and George W. Bush. While long forgotten, the Rev. Bush was a respected religious scholar and speaker who shared podiums with Ralph Waldo Emerson. Bush stirred enormous controversy in 1845 when he left the Presbyterian pulpit to become a minister in the Church of the New Jerusalem, a congregation based on the mystical ideas of Swedenborg. Bush was one of the Swedenborgian faith's most prominent converts—and a stalwart defender of Davis.

Bush had personally witnessed some of Davis's New York trance sittings. Davis's journals actually show Poe and Bush visiting together on January 19, 1846. The Bible scholar believed that Davis's statements reflected a genuine and mysterious form of genius. Bush said that the entranced Davis expounded on matters of ancient geology and archaeology, and employed the Hebrew language, in a manner impossible for an unschooled cobbler's apprentice.

"Indeed," Bush wrote, "if he has acquired all the information he gives forth in these Lectures, not in the two years since he left the shoemaker's bench, but in his whole life, with the most assiduous study, no prodigy of intellect of which the world has ever heard would be for a moment compared with him."[*]

Davis struck a special chord with Americans. He claimed that the mind could be awakened to a "superior condition;" and through the example of his humble background, Davis reinforced the ideal that any ordinary person could attain this higher state. The connection

---

[*]*Mesmer and Swedenborg* by George Bush, 1857.

between the awakened human mind and the creative powers of the "Great Positive Mind" was a key-turn away.

GIVER OF THE LAW

In the mid-nineteenth century, Davis coined a concept that has far outlasted his name. It was the Law of Attraction. But he imbued the term with a different meaning from the one later attached to it.

Never one for brevity, Davis in 1855 produced a six-volume treatise on metaphysical laws, *The Great Harmonia*. In volume four, he defined the Law of Attraction not as a principle of cause-and-effect thinking, nor as a method for using the mind to attract wealth, but, rather, as a cosmic law governing the cycles and maintenance of life. "The atoms in human souls," Davis wrote, "are attracted together from the living elements of soil and atmosphere; and, when these atoms complete the organization or individuality, they then manifest the same law of Attraction in every personal relation, inward and outward, through all the countless avenues of existence!" He called this law "the fundamental principle of all Life, which is Attraction."

In Davis's original rendering, the Law of Attraction was a gravitational force of affinities, one that was ever-present in all cosmic and human affairs. The law dictated where a person's soul would dwell in the afterlife based on the traits he had displayed on earth. It explained human attraction (or its absence). The Law of Attraction governed the types of spirits that would be drawn to séances based on the character and intention of the people seated around the table.

Davis did allow that the Law of Attraction governed certain material and earthly goals: "A mysterious wand, termed the 'Law of Attraction,' guides the traveller." He probably would have agreed with Joseph Campbell's maxim "follow your bliss," and seen the mythologist's expression as a sound interpretation of the Law of Attraction. But it was not until positive-thinking impresarios revised Davis's ideas that the Law of Attraction connoted a direct bond between thought and object.

The remaking of Davis's law began in 1892, in the final volume of journalist and spiritual explorer Prentice Mulford's book *Your Forces, And How to Use Them*. Mulford, who died the previous year, had written: "Such a friend will come to you through the inevitable law of attraction if you desire him or her . . . " In 1897, Ralph Waldo Trine used the term as a mental law in his bestselling *In Tune with the Infinite,* as did Helen Wilmans, who invoked the Law of Attraction in her 1899 book, *The Conquest of Poverty.*

In June of that year, New Thought leader Charles Brodie Patterson showcased the phrase in his influential article titled "The Law of Attraction," published in his journal, *Mind.* Patterson celebrated the Law of Attraction as a metaphysical super-law that dictated that everything around us is an outpicturing of what our thoughts dwell on. "Upon the recognition of this law depend health and happiness," Patterson wrote, "because neither can ensue unless in our thought we give out both." This became the point where the Law of Attraction assumed the form in which it is known today, becoming a catchphrase of *The Secret,* the Hicks-Abraham readings, and much of the New Age culture.

It is not that Davis wouldn't have recognized today's use of the Law of Attraction, so much as its current iteration as a mental law of cause and effect reflects a narrower and more proscribed concept than what the Hudson Valley medium had in mind. Does that mean that today's version of the Law of Attraction is wrong or corrupted? Not necessarily. Religion throughout human history is the story of borrowing, rephrasing, and revising ideas from other cultures and belief systems. This has been true from the biblical age up through our own. It has been famously remarked that laws are like sausages: one should never see them being made. The same might be said of religions.

23

THE PREFACE THE CHINESE GOVERNMENT BANNED

I was excited in 2014 when a Chinese publisher licensed rights to issue a Mandarin-language edition of my One Simple Idea. *I worked happily over numerous Skype sessions with the Shanghai-based translator, attempting, sometimes fitfully, to make Western spiritual ideas (and Western interpretations of Eastern ideas) understandable within modern Chinese culture—which, under Communist Party rule, is officially atheistic. It was not always easy to reframe extra-physical concepts to readers in a society where all things spiritual are considered verboten or even seditious. The publisher asked me to write a preface introducing New Thought to Chinese readers. Just before publication, however, government censors cut about a third of the book, including my explanation of American metaphysical tradition. Here is what my Chinese readers never got to read. On a cautiously hopeful note, in 2020 a Saudi publisher licensed rights to my short book* Awakened Mind. *It represented, to my knowledge, the first publication of a New Thought work in Arabic.*

Humanity has faced many urgent questions over the past century: What is the best way to structure a society? What economic system is the most humane and effective? Is ecological meltdown avoidable?

One of our most pressing questions, however, is deeply personal—it can be answered only by inner experience: Does what we think determine the course of our lives? *Are thoughts causative?*

The belief that *thoughts are destiny* is the core principle of what I call the positive-thinking movement, a modern psychological and spiritual belief system that has shaped the cultures of self-help and business motivation, and has deeply influenced Western politics, medicine, and business.

Although this book is primarily a work of history—of how a "simple idea" revolutionized today's world—each chapter and character portrait offers a practical method, which the reader can test in his life. My deepest hope is that you will apply—and challenge—some of these ideas to determine whether, or under what conditions, they work. Usefulness is the ultimate test of philosophy.

The civilizations of China and other Eastern nations are much older than most Western cultures; hence, some of the modern insights in this book may seem to have antecedents in Eastern philosophies, such as Taoism, Hinduism, Confucianism, and Buddhism. And there are, indeed, confluences between ancient wisdom and modern psychology and metaphysics.

When American readers say, "positive thinking" and Chinese readers say, "universal principles," they are expressing very similar ideas. Most American seekers believe that affirmative thought places a person into the flow of natural laws and forces, allowing one's projects and plans to unfold with harmony and vigor.

But most of the American pioneers of positive thinking were unschooled in cultures beyond the small towns and cities where they lived. Most of them were self-educated. They read the Bible, some psychological and medical texts, perhaps a smattering of religious theory and theology, and little else. They were not scholars, but independent explorers and adventurers. The architects of mental metaphysics tested their ideas primarily through personal experiments.

In writing this book, I came to feel a deep affection for these intrepid thinkers. Many were born in the nineteenth century—an era that bridged traditional religious belief and modern psychology. The early positive thinkers believed that religious insight and psychology could be bound together to produce a workable spiritual system of personal achievement, sometimes called "New Thought," and known to later generations through books such as *The Power of Positive Thinking* and *The Secret*.

The key principle of the movement has remained the same over time: your thoughts and emotive states, whether by psychological or metaphysical means (or both), determine the quality of your life, from health to wealth.

Such claims are sharply divisive. Millions embrace the notion that our thoughts possess some power of attraction, a belief stoked in self-help books, motivational seminars, and by media personalities, such as Tony Robbins and Oprah Winfrey. Critics damn this notion as a childish fantasy, which distracts us from the real economic and social forces at work in our lives.

But in some important instances modern medicine and science have validated or given partial credence to the claim that *thoughts are causative.* The insights of the early positive thinkers prefigured some of today's most talked about scientific theories and advances. The fields of placebo studies, neuroplasticity, behavioral science, and—most controversially— interpretations of quantum physics, have deepened and expanded our questions and conceptions of the mind's possibilities

Arguments about positive thinking will not be settled anytime soon—or perhaps ever. As I began by saying, the ultimate value of these ideas must be determined in the experience of the individual.

Chinese and English-speaking people obviously inhabit very different cultures, but I am convinced of an enormous commonality among individuals who are searching for ways to fulfill their highest potential. People who passionately seek out practical ideas—ethical, metaphysical, motivational, or any combination—are almost always able to sit down together and experience an immediate bond, and a shared stake in comparing philosophies, methods, and discoveries.

As you read this book, I want you to feel that you are having an exchange with a friend. Although I may not know your name or personal circumstances, I share the questions and sense of inner striving that may have brought you to this book. I hope its ideas draw us together in understanding—and stimulate you to explore your own self-potential.

Finally, I encourage you to approach the ideas of mental metaphysics in the spirit of one of my personal heroes, martial artist Bruce Lee, who wrote in *Tao of Jeet Kune Do*: "Take what is useful and develop from there."

AFTERWORD

HOW IT FEELS TO BE BLACKLISTED

In the summer of 2019, a New Age spiritual organization with which I had enjoyed years of fruitful collaboration as a speaker and writer (I wrote and contributed a book to them as a fundraiser) expelled me from its programs and erased my work from its websites and media. In this short piece, which appeared at Medium *on June 28, 2019, I reflect on the parameters of the alternative spiritual scene and the nature of the independent search.*

Opposition to expression comes from surprising places. On the other side of the spectrum (or is it?), an anthropology professor who is a critic of New Age wrote this about me on Facebook in 2018: "Mitch Horowitz has almost single-handedly insured [sic] that a long list of obscure and New Thought literature will be in print for a generation or two. I don't think anyone has done more to make the term 'occult' one of the grand ironies of the 21st century. Personally, I think he has done humanity great harm. There are good reasons why this literature was suppressed." Good reasons for literary suppression. This comes from a tenured faculty member at a state university.

The simple truth about free expression is: threats to it are varied, and unless free inquiry is thoughtfully and critically practiced, it is reduced to a slogan.

My spiritual search is controversial. There is no easy way to explain this—actually there is an easy way to explain but not to be heard—but I explore a highly personal version of what I consider Satanism.

By that I do not mean evil, violence, maleficence, or anything that has gotten historically and religiously misapplied to that term.

Rather, I see the Satanic as the Romantic poets did: as the force of rebellion, radical self-expression, artistic freedom, usurpation, and revolution. I believe the snake in the garden was a trickster-emancipator without whom humanity would not be itself. The price for that human creativity can be friction—but without it we would not be sentient beings.

As you can see, I am open and forthright about my search. This is because I believe in transparency and in a search without barrier or compulsion.

But there is a price. And I accept it.

A New Age organization with which I have had years of productive collaboration, and for which I have raised money, recently hosted me for a conference. I was told that some members were uncomfortable with my search and its connotations but that management nonetheless supported me, which I appreciated. I delivered two talks, entirely unrelated to this topic, which received standing ovations. But do not look for them on YouTube.

After one talk, an audience member tensely confronted me. I replied, much as I have here, and further explained that I have a code of nonviolence—by which I do not mean desistance from legitimate self-defense, but rather doing nothing to disrupt another's search for highest potential. I added that I also believe in "cosmic reciprocity," or what might be called karma, and I do not take a go-it-alone or hedonistic approach to life. More applause.

The next day numerous people, including the organization's director, congratulated me. All seemed well.

Then I arrived home.

Two days after arriving I got an email stating that more people had complained, and in light of an unrelated lecture I delivered in New York City on Satanism, I was being cut loose—expelled. They immediately scrubbed me from their website, YouTube page, and catalogue. Gone. Like that.

How did it feel? I was not angry. I felt they were acting from fear. I admit I was worried about further repercussions—but not worried enough to deny the same freedom of search for myself that I defend for others.

I will lose some income, and I have lost some people I considered friends.

But when I think of figures I wrote about in *Occult America*—from mystic Johannes Kelpius to Shaker founder Mother Ann Lee to Vice President Henry A. Wallace—I am reminded of people who made far greater sacrifices, and suffered calumny, for the integrity of their search.

Expulsions are a funny thing. Historically speaking, the people who commit them are usually next in line. And when that occurs, I will speak up for their rights to search, to seek, and to consensually experiment. It does not matter to me if it is a one-way street. The search has no lanes other than ahead.

ACKNOWLEDGMENTS

I am grateful to many friends and collaborators who over the years encouraged me in these pieces, including Carl Abrahamsson, Josh T. Romero, Laura Kwerel, Harv Bishop, Greg Salyer, Kelly Carmena, Jeffrey J. Kripal, Paul M. Barrett, Richard Smoley, April DeConick, Stephanie Georgiades, Bob Roth, Tod Lippy, Lucy Lord Campagna, Dean Radin, and Gilles Dana. Special thanks to my editor Jon Graham at Inner Traditions for his enthusiasm, editor Albo Sudekum for her excellent work, Will Solomon for restoring my faith in copy editing, Erica Robinson for her dedication, and to publicist Manzanita Carpenter Sanz for her continual support. Jacqueline Castel, to whom this book is lovingly dedicated, was a decisive source of encouragement in my assembling this collection and a critical eye in its final shaping.

INDEX

ABOUT THE AUTHOR

Mitch Horowitz is a historian of alternative spirituality and one of today's most literate voices of esoterica, mysticism, and the occult.

Mitch illuminates outsider history, explains its relevance to contemporary life, and reveals the longstanding quest to bring empowerment and agency to the human condition.

He is widely credited with returning the term "New Age" to respectable use and is among the few occult writers whose work touches the bases of academic scholarship, national journalism, and subculture cred.

Mitch is a writer-in-residence at the New York Public Library, lecturer-in-residence at the Philosophical Research Society in Los Angeles, and the PEN Award–winning author of books, including *Occult America, One Simple Idea: How Positive Thinking Reshaped Modern Life, The Miracle Club,* and *Daydream Believer.*

He has discussed alternative spirituality on CBS Sunday Morning, Dateline NBC, Vox/Netflix's Explained, VICE News, Kesha and the Creepies, and AMC Shudder's Cursed Films, an official selection of SXSW. Mitch hosted and produced a feature documentary about the occult classic *The Kybalion,* directed by Emmy-nominee Ronni Thomas, and shot on location in Egypt. The movie premiered as the #3 top documentary on iTunes.

Mitch has written on everything from the war on witches to the chequered career of professional skeptic James Randi for the *New York Times, Boing Boing,* the *Wall Street Journal,* the *Washington Post, Time, Politico,* and a wide range of zines and scholarly journals. He narrates audio books including *Alcoholics Anonymous* and *Raven: The Untold Story of the Rev. Jim Jones and His People* (the author of which hand-picked him as the voice of Jones).

Mitch's books have appeared in Arabic, Chinese, Italian, Spanish, Korean, French, and Portuguese.

Mitch worked for many years in publishing, including as a vice-president at Penguin Random House where he was editor in chief of Tarcher/Penguin, an imprint dedicated to metaphysical topics.

His book *Awakened Mind* is one of the first works of New Thought translated and published in Arabic. Mitch received the Walden Award for Interfaith/Intercultural Understanding. The Chinese government has censored his work.

Visit him at MitchHorowitz.com, on Twitter @MitchHorowitz, and on Instagram @MitchHorowitz23.